T0319903

# Risk Management in Trading

# Risk Management in Trading

*Techniques to Drive Profitability of Hedge Funds and Trading Desks*

DAVIS W. EDWARDS

WILEY

Published by John Wiley & Sons, Inc., Hoboken, New Jersey.
Published simultaneously in Canada.

For general information on our other products and services or for technical support, please
contact our Customer Care Department within the United States at (800) 762-2974, outside
the United States at (317) 572-3993 or fax (317) 572-4002.

Wiley publishes in a variety of print and electronic formats and by print-on-demand. Some
material included with standard print versions of this book may not be included in e-books or
in print-on-demand. If this book refers to media such as a CD or DVD that is not included in
the version you purchased, you may download this material at http://booksupport.wiley.com.
For more information about Wiley products, visit www.wiley.com.

*Library of Congress Cataloging-in-Publication Data:*

Edwards, Davis W.
  Risk management in trading : techniques to drive profitability of hedge funds and trading
desks / Davis Edwards.
    pages cm. — (Wiley finance)
  Includes index.
  ISBN 978-1-118-76858-7 (hardback) — ISBN 978-1-118-77285-0 (ePDF) —
ISBN 978-1-118-77284-3 (ePub) 1. Risk management. 2. Investment banking.
3. Hedge funds. I. Title.
  HD61.E374 2014
  332.64′524—dc23

                                                                              2014005542

Printed in the United States of America

10  9  8  7  6  5  4  3  2  1

*This book is dedicated my wife, Angela, and my children, Spencer and Brianna.*

*I would also like to thank everyone who acted as a pre-reader to the book. All of the mistakes are mine, and I am fortunate that they caught as many as they could.*

Angela Edwards

Colin Edwards

Barbara Sapienza

Dan Gustafson

Clint Carlin

John Vickers

Andrew Dunn

Ken Parrish

William Fellows

Matt Davis

Haseeb Khawaja

Andrew Coleman

Alexander Abraham

Varun Chavali

Kirat Dhillon

Iordanis Karagiannidis

# Contents

# Preface

I started learning about trading strategies and managing trading risk while working on statistical arbitrage trading desks at two investment banks—first at JP Morgan and later Bear Stearns. The core of the job was converting some type of analysis into an action. In other words, I had to use data to make a decision and think through the effects of those decisions. Over time, that most risk management is focused on analysis rather than making decisions. In most risk management texts, there is very little discussion on what decisions are made as the result of analysis.

My first exposure to risk management came when I worked as a programmer on JP Morgan's proprietary trading desk in the early 1990s. Just before I'd taken that job, I'd left my job at a computer game company and needed a short-term job to pay the bills. At the time, I intended it to be temporary and lasting long enough for me to raise enough capital to start my own company. My life would have taken a different turn had I ever managed to get that IPO completed. Instead, I was sucked into the world of trading and risk management. I started off as a junior programmer focused on implementing a new approach to managing risk on a trading desk called "value at risk".

The goal of that first job was to give the CEO of JP Morgan, Douglas (Sandy) Warner III, a summary that told him "how much money does the firm have on the table" within 15 minutes after the close of trading. This report was to be short—something that could be conveyed in a minute. It should be something that could be compared to the previous day's report to indicate whether risk was rising or falling. But, mostly it had to concisely give information to business leaders to make trading decisions.

When I was later managing a trading desk at Bear Stearns, and even later as a consultant, the intuition behind that first report—a concise summary designed to help managers make specific decisions—is contrasted against the analysis that I often observe being used—lengthy analysis not linked to any action steps. In one extreme case, I reviewed a daily risk management report that was more than 200 pages long. The last 150 pages of the report were filled with #N/A results instead of numbers. The report had failed 17 months previously, and despite being distributed to more than 100 readers, no one had caught the fact that the report wasn't running properly. Clearly, no one was using the report as an input into their daily decision making process.

A goal of this book is to help improve the use of risk management by linking risk analysis to a set of actions that a trader might take based on that analysis. There are a wide range of activities that can cause trading losses or diminished opportunity for profit. Describing those risks is often very complicated. However, there are only a couple of trading decisions related to risk management that can actually be made. As a result, one common way to manage risk more effectively is to think about the decisions that can be made from the analysis.

The four main categories of risk management decisions are:

- **Avoidance.** The best way for traders to avoid losses is to make better trading decisions. This includes elimination of risk and/or withdrawal from activities that might lead to that risk.
- **Control.** Traders can reduce risks through the use of organizational safeguards to reduce the likelihood of problems. One common way to do this is to calculate profits and losses on a daily basis (daily mark to market) and to limit the size of trading positions.
- **Transfer.** Transferring risk involves offloading risk to a third party (or a different group in the organization) by trading, purchasing insurance, outsourcing, or contract modification. It is done when a trader can't avoid the source of the risk and wants to limit the size of the risk.
- **Acceptance.** Acceptance involves taking on risks and establishing a budget that will cover potential losses.

This book focuses on techniques that professional traders use to assist in making decisions. The first three chapters establish the building blocks that are used in the rest of the text. The first chapter introduces trading and two major types of professional traders (*hedge funds* and *proprietary trading desks*). The second chapter discusses the major financial markets, and the third describes some of the terminology used by professional traders. The final six chapters of the book describe decisions that are made by traders.

Risk avoidance and acceptance are discussed in Chapter 4: Backtesting and Trade Forensics. Avoiding risk is a strategic decision that involves determining the markets where a trader has the biggest advantage relative to other traders. It is difficult to do all things well, and successful traders often have to choose some opportunities to avoid. Specializing allows traders to concentrate on the opportunities that are the most promising.

Techniques to control risk are discussed in Chapters 5, 6, 8, and 9: Mark to Market; Value at Risk; Options, Greeks, and Non-Linear Risks;

and Credit Value Adjustments. In a nutshell, the primary way to control risks is to set limits on how much risk will be allowed and then develop ways to quantify those risks on a daily basis. Adopting a consistent framework for risk allows different types of risks to be compared to each other.

Transferring risk is primarily discussed in Chapters 7 and 9: Hedging and Credit Value Adjustments. For a cost, traders can selectively pay to remove risks from their trading portfolios. However, since there is a cost associated with removing risk, this can remove the possibility for profits too.

There are a couple of themes that run throughout the book. First, risk management can be risky. It is always worthwhile to think through the implications of a risk management policy before committing to a course of action. Massive trading losses can come from trades intended to manage risks as easily as they come from speculative trading. Even worse, trades for risk management purposes are much less likely to be scrutinized or second-guessed by management.

A second theme running through the book is that details are important. Risk management simplifies details to make decisions easier. However, this simplification can lead to problems since critical details are in danger of being lost. There isn't always a set of rules to indicate how much abstraction is best. There is no substitute for somebody who knows what is actually going on being involved in decisions.

Finally, risk isn't always bad. Risk is largely a description of an investment's size and not a measure of whether an investment is good or bad. Assuming an identical investment mix, a large retirement account is riskier than a small retirement account. This is because the large account can lose more money on any given day than the small account. As a practical example, this means that billionaires can completely eliminate financial risk by giving away all of their money. That doesn't make giving away money a good business decision.

Effective risk management is as much an art as it is a science. I hope you find that the practical focus of the chapters helps bridge the gap between theoretical risk management and successful trading.

Davis W. Edwards
Houston, 2014

## CHAPTER 1

# Trading and Hedge Funds

This chapter introduces how trading organizations, such as hedge funds or the proprietary trading desks of investment banks, apply risk management concepts to operate their businesses. Risk is uncertainty or a potential for loss. Risk isn't necessarily bad. Risky activities often provide higher profits than safe investments. Techniques developed to manage risk are used by trading desks to drive profitability by balancing risk and reward. Some of these techniques include choosing the most profitable investments, allocating a limited amount of money between multiple investments, eliminating risks through hedging, and assigning size limits to various investment strategies.

There are a limited number of decisions that can be made by trading desks to manage risk. Profitability starts when traders do a good job identifying investment opportunities. After that point, common decisions are: how to allocate capital between investment opportunities, limiting how much money is allocated to any single investment, and reducing the size of investments by liquidating or placing protective trades.

## OVERVIEW OF BOOK

This book describes how risk management techniques are used by professional traders to reduce risk and maximize profits. The focus of the book is how traders working at hedge funds or on investment bank proprietary trading desks use risk management techniques to improve their profitability and keep themselves in business. However, these techniques can be applied to almost any trading or investment group.

This book focuses on six major activities that are part of managing trading businesses.

1. **Backtesting and Trade Forensics.** Backtesting is a disciplined approach to testing trading ideas before making bets with actual money. Trade forensics

1

is a post-mortem analysis that identifies how well a trade is tracking pre-trade predictions and if markets have changed since the trade was initiated.

2. **Calculating Profits and Losses.** Once a trade has been made, traders have to calculate the daily profits and losses. For some financial instruments, this is as simple as checking the last traded price from an exchange feed. For other investments, calculating the fair value of the trade is challenging.

3. **Setting Position Limits.** The size of investments that traders can make are typically limited by the volatility of their expected daily profits and losses. In other words, risk can be a way to measure size. As a result, the goal of hedge fund traders is to maximize the profits relative to a fixed amount of risk.

4. **Hedging.** Hedging is a trading strategy designed to limit profits and losses in one investment by taking an offsetting position in another asset. For example, a hedge fund might want to lock in profits associated with a physical asset like an oil well that they can't sell right away. They can agree to sell oil at a fixed price and remove the risk of price fluctuations.

5. **Managing Option Risk.** Certain types of financial instruments, particularly options, present much more complicated risk management challenges for traders. Risk managers have developed a variety of techniques to model this risk and fit options risk with other position limits.

6. **Managing Credit Risk.** Trading can't be done in isolation. Every time someone wants to buy an asset, someone else needs to sell. Not all trades settle right away—trading often involves obligations that are taken on in the future. As a result, traders depend on their trading partners meeting their trading obligations, and are exposed to the risk that their trading partners will default on their obligations.

## TRADING DESKS

Professional traders often work on teams called *trading desks*. A trading desk is a group whose members are traditionally seated side-by-side at a series of long desks (usually filled with computer equipment) that is responsible for buying and selling financial products for an organization. Trading desks will typically specialize in one or two types of financial products. Some trading desks will specialize in stocks, others in bonds, and so on.

Many types of companies will maintain trading desks. Some of these desks will focus on supporting the company's other lines of business—buying fuel for a trucking company or financial products on behalf of investors, for example. However, a couple types of trading desks are operated as their own line of business. The most prominent of these are *mutual funds*, *hedge funds*, and *proprietary trading desks* at banks.

Some organizations whose focus is on trading for profit are:

- **Mutual Funds.** Mutual funds are a pooled-investment fund where the leadership of the fund manages investments on behalf of investors. These funds are restricted from many investment strategies deemed too speculative or risky for uninformed investors.
- **Proprietary Trading Desks.** A trading desk found in many investment banks that operates like an internal hedge fund to invest the firm's capital.
- **Hedge Funds.** Hedge funds are pooled investment funds similar to mutual funds. They differ in that they do not cater to the general public—only to accredited investors. Many hedge funds seek to profit in all kinds of markets by using leverage (in other words, borrowing to increase investment exposure as well as risk), short-selling, and using other speculative investment practices that mutual funds are restricted from using.

One of the largest differences between hedge funds and proprietary trading desks compared to mutual funds or individual investors is that they will often make trades designed to make profits when prices decline. This is called *shorting* the market and allows profitability in both rising and falling markets. Shorting is not exclusive to hedge funds and trading desks—it can be done by individual investors. For example, shorting is commonly practiced in various commodity markets.

Shorting involves agreeing to sell something that the trader does not currently own. For example, a soybean farmer might agree to sell his crop (which hasn't been grown yet) for a fixed price per bushel when the crop is harvested. If prices fall after that point, the sales contract will acquire value to the farmer. If the contract allows him to sell 10,000 bushels of soybeans at $20 per bushel and prices fall to $10 per bushel, the contract is worth $10 per bushel (or $100,000) to the farmer. The contract is an asset to the farmer, and if a trading market exists for those contracts, could be sold to another trader.

## HEDGE FUNDS

Hedge funds are a prototypical trading organization. They have few restrictions on their activities and typically have no source of income other than their skill at trading. In this book, hedge funds are used as an example of firms that use risk management techniques to help them compete more effectively.

**KEY CONCEPT: LEVERAGE AND SHORTING**

Two activities differentiate professional trading groups from most other types of investors. First, professional traders often finance trading positions through borrowed money. Second, professional traders have the ability to make trades that benefit from both rising and falling markets.

■ *Leverage* is any activity (like borrowing money) that increases the size of the investment without increasing the capital that needs to be contributed by investors. This is sometimes called *gearing*.
■ *Shorting* is entering into a trade that makes money when prices decline.

Hedge funds are private partnerships that invest in the financial markets. Like mutual funds, hedge funds pool money from investors and invest the money in an effort to make a profit. Their organizational structure varies from other investment structures because the investors in the fund are typically limited partners rather than clients. This allows hedge funds an extremely high level of flexibility in their operations and allows them to trade in markets deemed too risky for typical investors.

Hedge funds require that their investors meet certain qualifications before they are allowed to invest in the fund. By catering only to qualified investors, hedge funds can avoid many limitations designed to protect the average investor. The reasoning behind government rules to protect investors is that not all investors are sufficiently qualified to understand the risks associated with exotic or risky investments. In other words, the government limits investors from focusing only on an investment's profit potential without regard for the associated risks.

Hedge funds offer investors, traders, and hedge fund managers the possibility of making a lot of money. However, the hedge fund industry is also a competitive and stressful environment where the most successful traders win big and unsuccessful ones go broke. Hedge funds use risk management to successfully run a complex and risky business.

Hedge funds are usually arranged as limited partnerships. A limited partnership is composed of two tiers of investors. The first tier of investors, called the *general partners*, has management authority and is personally liable for any debts incurred by the firm. These general partners take on the most risk, but have a tremendous ability to make money. The second tier of

**KEY CONCEPT: ACCREDITED INVESTOR**

An investor with substantial assets or sufficient financial expertise that they can voluntarily exempt themselves from rules designed to protect the average investor.

investors, the *limited partners*, have no management authority and are only liable up to the amount of their investments.

Hedge funds often charge very high investment fees. For example, a standard annual fee for hedge funds is to charge 1 to 2 percent of the limited partners' investments in addition to 20 percent of net profits every year. For example, if an investor were to make a million-dollar investment, the annual fees might be $20,000 (2 percent of the investment). In addition, if the hedge fund were to make a 10 percent return ($100,000 profit), the hedge fund would keep another $20,000, and the investor would make a $60,000 profit.

Organizationally, a hedge fund will be managed by one or more general partners (the *hedge fund managers*) who manage a staff of employees (the traders, risk managers, information technology team, and so on). The fixed management fee will typically cover the salaries and fixed expenses of the hedge fund. The variable fees will be paid in bonuses to the general partners and the traders. For example, in a fund with a 20 percent of net profit payout, the payout might be split 50/50 between the general partner and the trader (an employee) who managed each strategy.

## HEDGE FUNDS TODAY

Hedge funds have very few operating restrictions. They can make investments that benefit from both rising and falling markets. In addition, hedge funds can use various strategies and financial products to increase their *financial leverage*. Leverage is a term that describes the ability of a trader to make larger bets—increasing both the potential for profit and loss—for the same amount of initial investment.

Hedge funds have this flexibility because the investors in hedge funds have decided to opt out of some regulations designed to protect investors. The mechanism for opting out of these regulations is to become designated as an *accredited investor*. In the United States, the Securities Act of 1933, Regulation D, describes the conditions that allow investors to qualify as accredited investors.

Some of the requirements pertaining to individuals who may be considered accredited investors:

1. *A director, executive officer, or general partner of the company selling the securities*
2. *A natural person who has individual net worth, or joint net worth with the person's spouse, that exceeds $1 million at the time of the purchase, excluding the value of the primary residence of such person*
3. *A natural person with income exceeding $200,000 in each of the two most recent years, or joint income with a spouse exceeding $300,000 for those years and a reasonable expectation of the same income level in the current year*
4. *A trust with assets in excess of $5 million, not formed to acquire the securities offered, whose purchases a sophisticated person makes*

**Source: U.S. Securities Act of 1933, Regulation D**

Hedge funds are often in the news since they can have an immense impact on financial markets. Since the first hedge fund was started by Alfred Winslow Jones in 1949, hedge funds have experienced exponential growth. By 2013, the assets managed by hedge funds was estimated to be approximately $2 trillion. This large size, combined with hedge funds' heavy use of leverage and use of rapid-fire trading strategies, makes hedge funds some of the most active traders in many financial markets.

## STRATEGIES

Trading desks and hedge funds commonly specialize in a specific market or trading style. They don't try to be the best at everything. Instead, they try to pick and choose situations where they have an advantage. As a result, hedge funds will often have a standard approach to investing. Then, groups of traders will be organized into trading desks that are further specialized. Finally, the trading desk itself will be broken into *strategies*. A strategy is typically a systematic approach to trading managed by one or more traders who will focus on a very narrow style of trading. Traders often manage several strategies and their pay will be personally linked to the success of their strategies. (See Figure 1.1, Trading Desk Strategies.)

Both trading desks and hedge funds can vary substantially in composition. Some are based on a single strategy, while others may be focused on a market sector (like healthcare or energy) or geography (like a Brazil-focused

**FIGURE 1.1** Trading Desk Strategies

fund). Some of the more common types of hedge fund styles are Global Macro, Relative Value, and Event-driven styles.

### Global Macro

Global Macro strategies make *big-picture* bets based on the economy as a whole. For these strategies, investment decisions are commonly based on interest rates, Gross Domestic Product, unemployment rates, or similar economic data. When executed, trades are commonly made in stock indices, government bonds, and currency markets.

Global Macro trades are often directional—they speculate on the rise or fall of the overall market. For example, a hedge fund might buy broad based market indices when the market is expected to rise. It would sell or short these same indices when the market is expected to fall. By taking advantage of markets that allow short selling, these strategies can make profits in both rising and falling markets.

Many global macro strategies are based on an analysis of economic trends. In particular, traders study when trends are likely to persist and when they are likely to reverse. Through modeling, or intuition, the traders will rebalance their trading portfolios in an attempt to properly time the market.

### Relative Value

Relative Value strategies make bets based on spreads between assets. Typically, these are long/short strategies where traders simultaneously buy one asset while shorting another. *Shorting* is making a trade that benefits the trader when the price of an asset falls. This can be done by borrowing an asset from another trader and selling it (called *short selling*) or by entering into a derivative contract (like an agreement to sell an asset expected to be owned in the future at a fixed price).

Relative value strategies are often *market neutral*. By taking offsetting positions in related assets, the impact of the broader market move is mostly eliminated. For example, a trader might identify two bank stocks. By buying one stock and short selling the other, the trader will benefit if the long stock position (the stock that has been purchased) outperforms the short position (the stock that has been sold short). However, if the entire market goes up or down, both assets should change in value with offsetting profit or loss.

### Event-Driven

Event-driven strategies analyze the tendencies of market participants around the time of certain events. In many cases, events like an upcoming economic announcement will make traders change their normal trading habits. This can create an inconsistency in how the market values assets immediately before and after the event.

A large number of event-driven strategies focus on corporate actions like mergers, acquisitions, and spin offs. For example, if two companies are merging, the value of the two companies' stocks and bonds will be linked. If prices did not move to reflect the new information, there would be a trading opportunity. Alternately, a previously announced takeover might be rumored to be falling apart. In that case, the trader might bet that the prices will become decoupled.

## FUND OF FUNDS

One of the major factors behind the growth of the hedge fund industry is the development of *funds of funds*. A fund of funds will allocate investors' money into a variety of different hedge funds. These funds simplify the job of investing in hedge funds since the fund-of-funds manager has the responsibility for monitoring hedge funds and allocating capital to them. This can make diversification easier and allow investors to invest in more than one hedge fund.

For this service, a fund of funds will typically charge its own fees. This creates a double fee structure where the fund-of-funds costs are charged in addition to the fees paid to the underlying hedge funds. For example, a fund of funds might charge an additional 1 percent of assets and 10 percent of net profits on top of the hedge fund's fees. These fees can easily cut into the benefits of holding a fund of funds.

Whether a hedge fund relies on fund of funds to acquire capital will have a big effect on the structure of the hedge fund. Funds of funds will typically want to handle their own diversification. As a result, they will typically want to invest in single strategy hedge funds. Funds of funds will also want to regularly modify the investments that are made in each hedge fund. This can be problematic for hedge funds, since they have to balance inconsistent funding with the needs to pay ongoing expenses like salaries and office space.

## RISK MANAGEMENT

Risk measures uncertainty and potential for loss. Although this sounds like a bad thing, there is a strong relationship between risk and reward. In other words, risky activities typically offer a high potential for profit. Because of that, risk is largely a measure of an investment's size rather than a way to measure whether an investment is good or bad. For example, given the choice between investing $50,000 in the market and keeping cash, many people would choose the investment because of the higher profit potential.

Risk management is a systematic, logical approach to limiting or mitigating risk. It is called "management" because its purpose is not focused strictly on eliminating risk. In most cases, eliminating risk will eliminate the possibility for profit. At its core, trading risk management has two focuses. The first aspect of trading risk management is concerned with putting in place processes to minimize or prevent unwanted risks. The second focus is is to help decision makers better understand the tradeoffs between risk and reward.

Risk management is complicated by the fact that each group in an organization may understand risk differently. Even using common terminology, each stakeholder in the risk management process may have their own preconceptions and spin about what type of data is being provided by risk management analysis. This problem is exacerbated by the busy schedule of many senior decision makers. Quite often, decision makers don't want to understand risk management—they just want someone else to take care of it for them. This creates a danger that analysis prepared for one purpose will be used for other purposes without anyone taking the time to ensure that the data is used properly.

Some of the common uses for risk management:

- **Decision making tools.** In a trading organization like a hedge fund or trading desk, risk management is often used to help make decisions. For example, a trading desk might have a choice of investing in two strategies and wants to maximize their profits for a given level of risk.

- **Regulatory Compliance.** In heavily regulated industries such as banking, risk management is often used to demonstrate compliance with regulations. An example of risk management being used for compliance is the calculation of the regulatory capital that banks need to keep on hand to meet government requirements.
- **Worst-Case Scenarios.** Senior managers at many firms often want to limit the amount of damage that could be caused by riskier parts of their businesses. As a result, there is a substantial interest in calculating worst-case scenarios for investments.
- **Process and Controls.** Risk management is often used to contribute to processes that limit the size of trader investments, make sure that trades are working as expected, and that each trade is allowed under the firm's policies.

## RISK AND TRADING DECISIONS

For many hedge funds, risk management isn't just a theoretical exercise. There are a variety of practical applications to risk management that are used to make sound trading decisions in a very competitive industry. These processes have developed over time, because hedge fund managers—for all the potential profits that might be possible—have very little margin for error.

### Backtesting and Trade Forensics

Professional traders such as hedge funds and investment banks' proprietary trading desks often follow a disciplined approach of testing investment strategies before placing any money at risk. The typical approach is to start with historical tests in a process called *backtesting*. Once that is finished, the historical tests are followed up with live simulations called *paper trading*. Then, once real money is at risk, the strategy is constantly monitored using tools called *trading forensics*.

### Calculating Profits and Losses

Financial investments have to be valued every day. Unlike other assets, where the profit isn't known until the asset is resold, financial investments get *marked-to-market* every day. Typically, this process calculates the fair value of the assets based on recent transactions. This creates a substantial risk to traders in markets without heavy trading volume. Many protective measures, like risk limits and forced liquidations, are triggered by price movements. This creates risks because prices can be set by a small transaction that does not provide the opportunity for all of the traders affected by the transaction the opportunity to transact at that price.

## Hedging

Many trading companies want to lock in profits or protect an investment that can't be easily liquidated. Hedging is the term that describes an investment strategy designed to limit profits and losses in another investment. Hedging is a way for traders to pay money to transfer the possible risks (and rewards) of holding an asset to another investor. For example, an airline might limit its exposure to uncertain jet fuel prices by entering into a long-term purchase agreement.

## Setting Position Limits

A fundamental way to control risks is to limit the size of investments. This is relatively easy when trading is limited to a single asset. However, a coherent approach to position limits that combines different types of assets in a highly leveraged environment becomes much more difficult. To handle this complexity, hedge funds and trading desks use risk management techniques to compare the sizes of various assets and liabilities consistently across asset types.

## Managing Option Risk

Certain types of financial instruments, particularly options, present much more complicated risk management challenges for traders. As a result, the terminology associated with valuing and managing option risk is now inseparable from options trading. Formulas like the Black-Scholes formula have been developed to value options and calculus techniques are used to fit options into a value-at-risk framework.

## Managing Credit Risk

Trading is not done in isolation. Every time someone wants to buy an asset, someone else needs to sell for a transaction to occur. Not all trades settle right away—trading often involves obligations that are taken on in the future. As a result, traders depend on their trading partners meeting their trading obligations, and are exposed to the risk that their trading partners will default on their obligations.

## TRADING

Hedge funds use the money given to them by their investors, called *capital*, to make investments. Commonly, the hedge fund will actively manage these investments, buying and selling assets as needed to improve profitability and reduce risk. The term *trading* is used to describe the activity of buying and selling financial assets.

The difference between a professional investor who works at a hedge fund and an individual investor is often a matter of scale and seriousness. Successful hedge funds take trading seriously. As much as possible, they eliminate emotion and follow a disciplined, analytical approach to making trades. A key part of disciplined trading is to consider both potential profits and the uncertainty associated with those profits.

*Risk management* is a specialized portion of active management that focuses on monitoring and controlling risks that might affect an organization. For a hedge fund, this commonly means the risks associated with trading. However, on a broader level, risk management techniques can be applied to anything that might cause a loss or a diminished opportunity for gain.

## MAKING A TRADE

Individual investors will have to handle all aspects of trading by themselves. However, many hedge funds are large enough that they can support specialists in every aspect of the trading process. In these hedge funds, there will be a wide variety of people involved in making trades and managing the risk of those trades. Commonly these groups are divided into a couple of major categories: front office, middle office, back office, and various support groups. (See Table 1.1, Groups Involved with Trading.)

### Front Office

In a trading organization, the front office consists of various teams whose goal is to make trades on behalf of the organization. The front office is also referred

**TABLE 1.1**  Groups Involved with Trading

| Front Office | Support and Control | Back Office |
| --- | --- | --- |
| Sales | Middle Office | Reconciliation (Clearing) |
| Deal Structuring | Risk Management | Margining |
| Scheduling | Financial Control | Documentation |
| Trading | | |

to as the *commercial* group. This team is responsible for identifying trading opportunities, making trades, and managing any ongoing investments.

- **Sales and Origination.** The sales team is responsible for identifying potential trading partners and clients who need trading assistance. In cases where clients are likely to have complex needs, the sales team may be called the *origination team*.
- **Deal Structuring.** In many cases, determining a price for an asset requires substantial mathematical analysis. The deal-structuring team on a trading desk will be responsible for calculating fair prices and valuing complex (*structured*) transactions. These are typically quantitative, math-heavy groups found in front offices that trade derivatives or other complex products.
- **Scheduling.** Trading physical assets like commodities often involves a substantial amount of operational complexity. When trading desks trade products that are complicated to deliver (or accept delivery on), a dedicated team focuses on making sure that process goes smoothly. Scheduling teams need to understand minute details of the markets for which they are responsible.
- **Trading.** The trading desk is responsible for executing transactions and the market-focused follow up of monitoring and managing existing positions. In some firms, there are a variety of trading desks specializing in different areas. Different trading teams will usually have descriptive names like *foreign exchange trading* or *natural gas trading*. If the trading is done on behalf of the firm, this may be called *proprietary trading* to distinguish the trading desk from one supporting clients.

### Support and Control

The trading desk is supported by several teams that provide operational controls over trading activity. Even though these groups generally sit close to the trading desk, they typically report to a different management team—one that is not directly in the trading chain of command.

- **Middle Office.** The middle office is responsible for ensuring the trading desk works smoothly. The middle office ensures that trades are properly entered into tracking systems, that existing positions are valued on a daily basis, and that all of the paperwork is completed properly.
- **Trading Desk Risk Management.** Risk managers assigned to trading desks ensure that traders are not taking on too much risk and keep management informed of ongoing risks associated with the current trading positions.

■ **Financial Control.** The financial control team is responsible for accounting and profit and loss (P&L) reporting. The trades done by the trading desk ultimately need to be reflected in the firm's books and records and reported to the limited partners (shareholders if it is a public corporation) and the government. The financial control team is responsible for putting together those reports.

### Processing (Back Office)

The back office provides post-trade processing, settlement, and clearing functions to the trading desk. These functions are commonly performed in a location that is remote from the trading desk.

■ **Reconciliation (Clearing).** The reconciliation team ensures that the counterparty's back office agrees on the terms of every trade. If the two parties to the trade can't mutually agree on the terms, this team might need to pull phone records (trader's phone lines are typically recorded), instant messages, or emails where the traders agreed to the terms of the trade.

■ **Margining.** Trading desks often require trading partners to post collateral when owed a large amount of money. The margin group is responsible for posting and receiving collateral. A request for additional collateral is called a *margin call*. This can usually be done by either trading organization.

■ **Documentation.** The documentation team is responsible for finalizing all the paperwork necessary for trading. Just like the paperwork on any other legal agreement, a substantial amount of work goes into ensuring paperwork is correct for trades.

## TRADES

A trade is a special type of transaction where the asset being traded can be resold at approximately the same price that it was purchased. This makes a trade different from many other transactions. For example, buying stock in a company is a trade. The stock can be resold at a later date. The price of the stock may have gone up or down, but it remains valuable. However, buying a cheeseburger is not a trade since the cheeseburger probably cannot be resold.

Another key element that allows assets (or liabilities) to be traded is the ability to substitute identical products for one another. For example, it is very difficult to set up trading based on unique works of art. The negotiation between buyer and seller is too specific, and the worth of the piece too subjective, for prices to be fully generalized. However, it is possible to trade interchangeable products and use those transactions to determine a fair price. The ability to substitute equivalent products is called *fungibility*. For example, shares of common stock in a company are interchangeable. It is possible to buy shares of the same stock from two different people and the shares will be identical in all respects.

Like any type of transaction, trading requires two parties—typically a buyer and a seller. From the perspective of a trader (or a firm employing a trader), the other party in the transaction is called the *counterparty*. Typically, the price at which the asset (or liability) is transferred is based on voluntary negotiation between the two parties.

There are three major transaction types:

- **Buy.** *Buying* is associated with paying money to acquire an asset.
- **Sell.** *Selling* is associated with receiving money as compensation for transferring an asset to the buyer.
- **Short Sell.** *Short selling* is the practice of agreeing to sell something that isn't currently owned but is expected to be owned in the future.

Buying and selling are sometimes confusing terms when cash is not being exchanged. It is possible to swap non-cash assets for each other. In those cases, another descriptive term might be substituted for the terms buyer and seller to clarify the obligations of each party in the transaction. In this book, the terminology of *buyer* and *seller* will be used since it is the most commonly used terminology.

Because it involves both a buyer and a seller, trading is impossible in isolation. Trading is a group activity. Some markets, like exchanges, obscure the buyer/seller relationship. However, even in those markets, buyers and sellers are matched up and work together to create prices. Markets where buyers and seller can easily find one another are called *liquid* markets. Markets where it is difficult for a buyer and a seller to meet are called *illiquid* markets. Regardless of how much an asset might be worth to the right buyer, unless that buyer is willing to buy it right then, there is no way to convert an asset into cash. This is called *liquidity risk*.

Another complexity to trading is that, in many cases, it is not necessary to own an asset to sell it. This has its own term—the practice of selling assets that are not currently owned is called *short selling* or *shorting*. For example, a farmer can arrange to sell corn to a buyer through a forward contract before the corn is grown. After agreeing to the sale, the farmer could decide to grow soybeans. He is not required to grow corn. The farmer's obligation is to acquire corn before the delivery and not necessarily to grow it himself.

## KEY CONCEPT: REQUIREMENTS FOR TRADING

Trading requires:

- A buyer or a seller willing to take the other side of the transaction
- The ability to both buy and sell without a substantial loss of value. A substantial loss of value might be defined as 10 percent.
- The ability to define standard products which can be interchanged with one another (these are called *fungible* products)

Other markets also allow short selling. In the stock market, short selling is made possible by borrowing shares and agreeing to repay them at some point in the future.

If done for purely speculative purposes, short selling is a way of betting that prices will decline over time. However, short selling can be used for a variety of other purposes. For example, a broker might short a stock to allow a customer to make an immediate transaction. The broker would then have to purchase in a later transaction. This can help small investors who want a one-stop solution for trading.

## MARKETS

Trades can occur in a variety of venues. While this can be as simple as finding a trading partner and signing a contract, the customized nature of many contracts prevents them from being traded (transferred to another trader for a cash payment). As a result, it is common for traders to use resources that can help them find trading partners and sign standardized trading contracts. (See Table 1.2, Types of Trading Venues.)

## KEY CONCEPT: REGULATIONS AROUND SHORT SELLING

Many countries and markets have restrictions on short selling. In those markets, specific actions, those designated as "short selling," might have regulatory and compliance implications. Depending on how the regulations are written, there may be little relationship between "short selling" as a trading concept and "short selling" as a regulatory concept.

**TABLE 1.2**   Types of Trading Venues

| Bilateral | Broker | Dealer | Exchange |
| --- | --- | --- | --- |
| Traders directly find one another. | Traders are introduced to each other through use of a broker. | Traders transact directly with a dealer | Traders are matched up on an exchange. The exchange simultaneously transacts with both traders. |

Some common types of trading venues:

**Bilateral Trading.** The trader is responsible for finding a trading partner and signing a contract directly with that partner. Commodity markets where a limited number of producers and consumers interact regularly are often bilateral markets.

**Broker.** A broker introduces customers to one another for bilateral trading. In some cases, the broker has the ability to trade on behalf of the customer. This is a common way for traders with limited trading connections to get access to trading markets. Brokers typically get paid a commission for arranging trades.

**Dealer.** A dealer executes customer trades against the dealer's own account. In other words, the dealer is the counterparty for a trade. In many cases, the dealer is a broker/dealer, with the capabilities of both a broker and a dealer. Like the broker market, traders with limited trading connections often use broker/dealers to get access to trading markets. Dealers will make a profit by offering slightly different prices to buyers and sellers—a *bid price* that indicates where they are willing to buy and an *ask price* where they are willing to sell.

**Exchange.** An exchange is a centralized location for trading standardized products. It is necessary to be a member of an exchange to trade on it. The exchange interposes itself between buyers and sellers and requires its members to post a refundable good faith deposit, called *margin*, when they transact. This margin payment will be held as collateral to ensure buyers and sellers meet their trading obligations.

## MARKET AND LIMIT ORDERS

When traders are working with brokers and exchanges, they typically have to provide instructions for how they would like to trade. This is different from a bilateral contract (like a forward) where terms can be individually negotiated. Brokers and exchanges allow a limited number of instructions, and the terminology for those instructions is reasonably standardized.

### Market Orders

In many cases, traders want a fast execution at the prevailing market price. These are called *market orders*. Market orders are executed by the broker or exchange as soon as possible. These trades should receive the best price available at the time of execution. A market order specifies only the name of the security and the action to be taken (either buy or sell).

- Market orders are the most common type of order.
- Market orders are executed as soon as possible.

### Limit Orders (Limit Buy, Limit Sell)

In other cases, traders might want to accept a trade only under certain conditions. In these cases, traders can use a *limit order* to specify the price at which a customer is willing to transact. For example, a buy limit order will specify the highest price that the trader is willing to pay. A sell limit order will specify the lowest price that a trader is willing to accept.

- Limit orders do not guarantee an execution.
- If they are not executed, limit orders will typically remain active for the remainder of the trading day. However, this can be changed—traders can specify different instructions or cancel limit orders.
- Limit orders have a time priority—the first trader to place a limit order at a specific price receives the first execution.
- A *bid price* is the price at which a trader is willing to buy an asset while using a limit order.
- An *ask price* (also called an *offer price*) is the price at which a trader is willing to sell an asset while using a limit order.

### Stop Orders (Stop Buy, Stop Sell)

Traders can submit orders that are initially inactive but become active under specific conditions. One type of activated order is a *stop order*. Stop orders convert into market orders if the market reaches or goes through a certain price level (the *stop price*). *Buy Stop* orders are placed above the current market price and become market buy orders if the price reaches the stop price. *Sell Stop* orders are placed below the current market price and will become market sell orders if the price reaches the stop price.

- Stop orders are most commonly used to limit losses to existing positions from large price moves. This is called a stop-loss. For example, a trader might enter a stop-loss order to liquidate a stock investment if prices drop more than 10 percent.
- Stop orders can also be used to enter positions if the market hits a certain level. For example, a trader following a technical analysis strategy may wish to trigger a buy order if the market rises above some resistance level.

### Stop Limit Orders

If traders need to give more complex instructions, they can create *stop limit* orders. Stop limit orders combine features of both stop and limit orders. These will work similarly to stop orders, except that a limit order will be created rather than a market order.

## ORDER LIFESPAN

Another factor in submitting transactions is how long the order will stay active before it is executed or cancelled. These instructions primarily apply to limit orders since market orders are filled immediately. By default, limit orders are good only on the day that they were submitted and the instructions go into effect when the broker or exchange receives the order. However, other instructions are possible.

### Day Orders

The most common lifespan for a limit order is the remainder of the trading day on which it was submitted. This is typically the default lifespan for orders if no special instructions are provided.

### Good till Canceled (GTC)

Traders can submit orders that are good indefinitely (unless they are canceled). GTC orders, also called *open orders*, remain in effect until they are canceled.

### Fill-or-Kill (FOK)

In some cases, traders want an immediate execution but want to place a limit on the maximum price they pay (or minimum price they receive) for an execution. Fill or Kill orders are immediately executed to the extent possible and then canceled. In many cases, these orders will not be fully executed.

### At-Open, At-Close

Most orders become active as soon as they are submitted. However, sometimes traders want to match the opening or closing price rather than get an immediate execution. For example, a derivative contract might depend on the market close price on the expiration date. To limit the risk associated with a mismatch between the contract and the trading price, the trader might wish to transact as near to the closing transaction as possible.

Open and close orders are typically executed on a best-effort basis. It is also common for exchanges to require these orders to be submitted early. For example, an exchange might stop accepting market-on-close orders 15 minutes prior to the close. If a large number of orders come in right at the open or closing time, the market on open/close orders might only be guaranteed to be executed at a price within the range of prices being traded during the open or close—not necessarily at the official open or close price.

## TRADING POSITIONS

For a trading desk, a differentiation is made between *trades* and *positions*. A *trade* is a transaction, a *position* is the net exposure that results from one or more trades. For example, if a trader executes two trades, each purchasing 300 metric tonnes of aluminum, the result is a 600 metric tonne position. The terminology that describes positions is different from the terminology used to describe trades.

The terms buy and sell can get confusing because contracts can be traded in the same way as assets. For example, it is possible to buy a contract that obligates the owner of the contract to sell an asset. The transaction that led to the position (buying a contract) is less important than the end result (the trader now has an obligation to sell an asset). To reduce confusion, traders use the terms *long* and *short* to describe positions:

- A *long position* profits when the price of the asset increases and loses money when prices drop.
- A *short position* profits when the price of the asset declines and loses money when prices rise.
- A *flat position* neither gains nor loses money when prices change.

When risk management or the head of a trading group examines trading positions, the terms long and short typically refer to the underlying asset exposure rather than the individual contracts. This allows the exposure from multiple contracts to be combined together (netted) and reported as a single number.

## PRICES

There are many different prices that exist in the financial markets. The simplest definition of price is the amount of money that someone would pay to acquire an asset. However, prices also have a time component. Not only do prices change every day, traders can agree to deliver assets at some point in the future.

Some common types of prices:

- **Spot Prices.** The spot price is the price at which an asset can be bought or sold *on the spot* (for immediate delivery).
- **Forward Prices.** A forward price is the price at which two traders have agreed to transact at some point in the future. A forward price will need to be described by two dates—the valuation date (the date when the price was transacted) and the delivery date (when the product needs to be delivered).
- **Quotes.** A quote is the price where limit order traders are willing to buy or sell some quantity of an asset. Quotes are often characterized as a bid/ask spread and consist of two numbers—the highest price that a trader is willing to buy and the lowest price that a trader is willing to sell. Since quotes don't actually result in a transaction, these are often not recorded.

## MANAGING TRADING RISK

Coinciding with the rapid growth of hedge funds, the last quarter of the twentieth century provided a renaissance to the fields of trading and risk management. New financial markets and products exploded onto the financial consciousness of investors, computers allowed individual investors to directly access market data, and large financial firms pioneered the use of methodologies to categorize and contain risk. New legislation soon followed creating requirements and rules with which companies had to comply.

Traders have managed risk for many years. However, the business of risk management was largely created by banks in the early 1990s. From the time of the Great Depression in the 1930s until the late 1990s, banks in the United States were divided into commercial banks and investment banks by the Glass-Steagall Act (the U.S. Banking Act of 1933). This act prevented financial institutions that take deposits from customers (commercial banks) from engaging in many financial activities involving financial markets.

Under the Glass-Steagall Act, deposit-taking institutions were prevented from:

- Buying or selling securities for customers
- Investing in securities on their own behalf
- Underwriting or distributing securities
- Owning or affiliating with companies involved in securities activities
- Sharing employees with securities firms.

During the Glass-Steagall era, U.S. banks were split into two categories—commercial banks that took customer deposits and investment banks that handled securities. Over time, both types of banks found ways to expand into the other side of banking by taking advantage of loopholes and ambiguity in several of the Glass-Steagall clauses. These loopholes allowed commercial banks to create subsidiaries that handled securities trading. Coinciding with the growth of the derivatives market in the mid-1970s, U.S. commercial banks started creating subsidiaries to enter securities markets in a limited manner.

Demonstration of sound risk management practices convinced banking regulators to allow the use of these loopholes. Over time, these exemptions grew. By the time the Glass-Steagall Act was finally repealed in 1999, it was mostly a symbolic action—large financial conglomerates handling both commercial and investment banking already existed.

The risk management concepts pioneered by banks were soon adopted by hedge funds. This helped hedge funds improve their profitability and attract more investors. The concepts applied by large financial institutions for managing trading and investment risk are now applied by most trading organizations.

## KEY CONCEPT: SECURITIES

*Securities* are tradable financial instruments like stocks, bonds, and derivatives.

## KEY CONCEPT: MODERN RISK MANAGEMENT

Modern risk management was developed by commercial and investment banks. The banking industry is still subject to extensive regulations focusing on controlling risk. As a result, risk management is closely associated with the regulations affecting large financial institutions. Even so, a variety of other companies make extensive use of risk management concepts. These include hedge funds, trading desks, and companies subject to commodity price movements like airlines and natural gas drillers.

## WHAT IS RISK?

Risk, broadly defined on an organizational level, is a potential for loss or the diminished opportunity for gain. It isn't always bad since higher risk is closely associated with higher profit potential.

Terminology to describe risks falls into two broad categories. Some risks, like a trading partner going bankrupt, involve a limited number of possible outcomes. These risks are called *discrete risks*. Other risks involve a continuous range of possible outcomes. These types of risk are called *continuous risks*. Risk management uses slightly different terminology for each type of risk.

The two broad categories of terminology to describe risk are:

- **Discrete Risks.** These risks will either happen or not happen. *Discrete risks* are commonly described in terms of their probability and magnitude. For example, a discrete risk might be a described as a 5 percent chance of losing $2 million.
- **Continuous Risks.** Some risks involve a range of potential outcomes. *Continuous risks* are described using the same terminology used to describe statistical distributions. For example, statistics might be used to define both an average outcome and the expected variance in outcomes. (See Figure 1.2, Discrete Risks, and Figure 1.3, Continuous Risks.)

Risks are further described based on the source of the risk. The two most important risks facing hedge funds are commonly related to price movements (*market risk*) or the ability of counterparties to meet their obligations (*credit risk*). However, it is important to recognize that any organization is actually exposed to many sources of risk. Some of the more common risks faced by trading desks are listed below. (See Table 1.3, Types of Risk.)

## Discrete Risks
Described by a probability and expected magnitude.

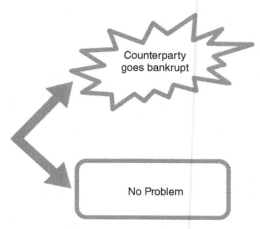

**FIGURE 1.2**   Discrete Risks

## Continuous Risks
Described by average or expected result and variation.

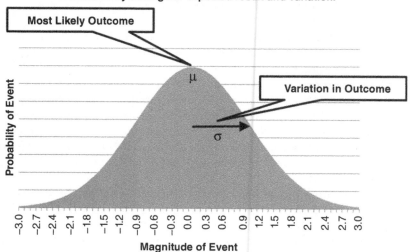

**FIGURE 1.3**   Continuous Risks

**TABLE 1.3** Types of Risk

| Risk | Definition |
| --- | --- |
| Market Risk | Market risk is the loss of money or resources due to adverse price moves. |
| Credit Risk | Credit risk is the loss of money or resources due to a trading partner not repaying a debt or a loan. |
| Litigation Risk | Litigation risk is the risk of loss due to lawsuits or arbitration proceedings. |
| Compliance Risk | Compliance risk is the risk of losses due to regulatory actions, fines, or sanctions. |
| Reputational Risk | Reputational risk is the risk of lost revenue or a decline in shareholder value due to damage to a firm's reputation. |
| Strategic Risk | Strategic risk is the potential outcome of a strategic decision. For example, what happens to a firm's future prospects if a strategy is successful? It is the risk that a strategy is well executed but still doesn't result in the desired outcome. |
| Operational Risk | An operational risk is a loss occurring from a failure to execute some process. For example, failing to schedule the proper size dock space for an oil tanker can result in the failure to deliver oil to a client. |

## KEY CONCEPT: MARKET AND CREDIT RISK

Risk is a potential for loss or the diminished opportunity for gain. The Traders are responsible for managing a wide variety of risks. Of those, the two most important risks to traders are typically *market risk* and *credit risk*:

- **Market Risk.** Losses resulting from changes in prices.
- **Credit Risk.** Losses resulting from bankruptcy of trading partners.

Traders, and risk managers associated with trading desks, are the groups closest to these two risks. While other risks, like reputational risk, are still important to traders, a trading desk is the front line group focused on monetary risks. Of course, this focus can go too far. Many trading desks have been criticized for focusing on market and credit risk to the exclusion of other risks.

## RISK AND REWARD

From a trading perspective, there is a strong relationship between risk and reward. Generally speaking, high-risk activities typically have a greater opportunity for profit than lower-risk activities. As a result, it often makes sense to monitor and manage risks rather than eliminate or avoid risky activities. For example, complex jobs that require specialized skills and precise execution tend to have higher profit margins than jobs that can be done easily.

The business of trading for profit, called speculation, might be defined as "assuming substantial investment risk to obtain a commensurate profit". This is very different than gambling, which might be defined "playing a game where the results depend on luck rather than player skill". Risk management can help identify situations that have a better than average risk/return relationship. This can improve the profitability of a hedge fund and differentiate a hedge fund from its peers.

While risk management is often mathematical, it still requires good judgment to be effective. An often-repeated maxim at hedge funds is that the best way to avoid trading losses is to make smart trading decisions. While risk management might reduce the uncertainty of the final result, it will do little to improve profitability if the initial investment was fundamentally flawed.

It is also a mistake to look at uncertainty separate from returns. In efficient markets, risk and reward are closely related. As a result, reducing risk typically means reducing the size of an investment rather than making a better investment. It is also easy to replace a profitable, but uncertain, strategy with one that is certain to lose money.

It is much harder to find a strategy that makes a profit without taking risk. In fact, this is so rare that it has its own name—*arbitrage*. A strategy that gives the potential for making a profit without any risk is called an arbitrage opportunity. Arbitrage opportunities are quite rare. In fact, the concept of a *fair price* in financial modeling is based on the assumption that arbitrage doesn't exist. A fair price is defined as a price at which neither the buyer nor the seller can make a risk-free profit.

Terminology associated with arbitrage:

- **Arbitrage.** A risk-free opportunity for profit
- **Fair Price.** A price that allows neither side a risk-free profit (often called an *arbitrage opportunity*).

For example, a trader might believe that the price of oil is rising to $500 per barrel in the next six months. However, if the trader can buy that oil today for $100 per barrel and pay $10 per barrel for risk-free storage of oil, the fair price of oil delivered in six months is $110 per barrel. Any other price would

## KEY CONCEPT: ARBITRAGE

*Arbitrage* is a risk-free opportunity for profit. It doesn't have to be a guaranteed profit—a 50/50 chance of winning money would be considered arbitrage if it didn't cost any money.

allow some trader to make a risk-free profit (buying oil today, storing it, and reselling it in the future). If the trader can find someone to pay him $500 per barrel, rather than $110 per barrel, he will have found an arbitrage opportunity.

## MONITORING RISK

Risk management work is split between monitoring risk and taking steps to actively manage risk. In this work, identifying and monitoring comes before managing. Trying to manage a risk without understanding it is a recipe for disaster. As a result, the starting point for managing risk typically involves predicting what types of risks might face an organization and monitoring those risks.

### Identifying and Classifying Risk

The first step to monitoring risks is to establish a set of risks that might affect the organization. Typically, the responsibility to identify risks is shared across a wide number of business units. This involves an examination of items that have caused previous losses and brainstorming about what might cause losses in the future. Many types of risk are well known (market risk, credit risk, and so on). Using pre-defined risk categories can provide a structure for brainstorming about risk and make sure some risks aren't being ignored.

### Measuring and Quantifying Risk

Once risks are identified, it is necessary to estimate the relative importance of each risk. Typically, this is done by establishing a common framework for comparing risks (like their direct or indirect monetary impact upon the organization). This step typically involves mathematical modeling and discussion on how to get the right amount of information to decision makers. Either too much or too little information is bad. For example, producing a 10,000 page report on a daily basis might be comprehensive, but it would be almost impossible for any business leader to use it in making daily decisions.

## Risk Monitoring

After risks are identified and the framework for tracking the risks has been established, ongoing daily processes are used to keep the information up to date. Typically, there is a team dedicated to tracking the most important identified risks to an organization. This team is often supplemented by a broader group on a regular basis (several times a year) to identify newly developing or previously unidentified risks.

## Compliance and Reporting

Many firms, especially financial institutions like banks and hedge funds, need to comply with government regulations concerning risk. Typically firms need to establish controls to prevent certain types of risks from occurring and monitor those controls to make sure they are effective. In addition, firms need to report their risk activities to shareholders and senior managers on a regular basis.

## MANAGING RISK

To be effective, risk management can't just monitor risks. To use risk management effectively, decisions have to be made about how to handle risks. Making those decisions is often a collective effort of a large number of teams. In most firms, at the front lines of risk management is a dedicated risk management function headed by a senior manager called the *Chief Risk Officer*. In addition to that group, commercially focused teams (like the trading desk) are often heavily involved in day-to-day risk management. Then, there are a broader set of stakeholders like the chief executive officer (CEO), the chief financial officer (CFO), and heads of each business line that have the ultimate responsibility for decisions that will affect the corporation.

Typically, risk management decisions are tiered so that smaller decisions are made at the trading desk and decisions with more serious implications get made by senior managers. The different types of decisions that can be made to manage risk are generally fairly limited. Techniques to manage the risk fall into one of four major categories. (See Table 1.4, Risk Management Techniques.)

## Risk Avoidance

Avoidance is the practice of avoiding activities that could carry specific risks. For example, a company might decide not to do business in a certain area of the world due to concerns over regional conflict or risk that the foreign

**TABLE 1.4**   Risk Management Techniques

| Technique | Description |
| --- | --- |
| Avoidance | The elimination of risk and/or the withdrawal from activities that might lead to that risk. |
| Control | Reduction of the risks through organizational safeguards and other techniques to reduce the likelihood of problems. |
| Transfer | The offloading of risk to a third party (or different group in the organization) by purchasing insurance, outsourcing, or contract modification. |
| Acceptance | Taking on risks and setting aside a budget that will cover potential losses and adverse events. |

government will seize assets. Typically, in these situations, a company is giving up potential profit opportunities to focus on other activities where the risks can be more easily controlled.

## Risk Reduction

Diversification, the use of collateral, and checklists to prevent operational errors are all techniques that trading desks use to reduce risks. In many cases, risk reduction takes the form of optimization—maximizing the return that could be earned for a given level of risk.

## Risk Transfer

Risks can often be transferred to another market participant or between risk categories. This typically involves a cost or a tradeoff of some type. For example, credit risk might be mitigated by either purchasing protection (called Credit Default Swaps) from a third party or by requiring that additional collateral be posted for trading. If additional collateral is chosen as the mitigation, money might be saved, but the trading partner might ask for collateral too. This could lead to a new risk exacerbating cash flow problems when prices change.

## Risk Acceptance

Risk acceptance involves accepting the possibility for loss. For example, a trading company may set aside reserves to cover non-payment of monies that are owed the company by its trading partners. Alternately, a trading desk might limit a trader to having no more than a $1 million cumulative loss in a strategy.

## TEST YOUR KNOWLEDGE

1. What is market risk?
   - **A.** The risk that causes the reputation of the firm to be adversely affected.
   - **B.** The risk that activities internal to an organization (like properly scheduling a commodity delivery) will cause a loss.
   - **C.** The risk that a trading partner will default on its obligations.
   - **D.** The risk of losses arising from adverse price movements.
2. Choose the best answer. Can you buy a contract to sell an asset?
   - **A.** Yes. However, the purchase and sale offset, so there won't be any purpose in making this trade.
   - **B.** No. It is not possible to purchase a contract to sell an asset.
   - **C.** Yes. A contract is a piece of paper, which can have value, and be bought and sold like any other asset.
   - **D.** No. Financial contracts cannot be transferred.
3. If an investor is long a gasoline/crude oil spread, what will happen?
   - **A.** The investor will benefit if the spread gets larger.
   - **B.** The investor will benefit if the spread gets smaller.
   - **C.** The investor will benefit if gasoline and crude oil both rise in price equally.
   - **D.** The investor will benefit if both gasoline and crude oil drop in price equally.
4. Which group is typically responsible for the filing of financial statements?
   - **A.** Risk Management
   - **B.** Trading Desk
   - **C.** Financial Control
   - **D.** Middle Office
5. Hedge funds are typically organized in what type of structure?
   - **A.** Corporation
   - **B.** Limited Liability Company (LLC)
   - **C.** Limited Partnership
   - **D.** Sole Proprietorship
6. Who can invest in hedge funds?
   - **A.** Anyone.
   - **B.** Only accredited investors or officers of the hedge fund.
   - **C.** Only citizens of the United States.
   - **D.** Only employees of the hedge fund.
7. What kind of investments are made by a global macro hedge fund?
   - **A.** Directional bets on major economic events.
   - **B.** Spread positions in closely related assets.

C. Positions in stocks of companies undergoing corporate actions like mergers or restructuring.

D. Investments in other hedge funds.

8. Which answer correctly defines a *short sale* in the financial markets?

A. A sale that has to be executed quickly, that is "on short notice."

B. A sale made under distressed conditions.

C. An asset sale at a price that falls short of repaying the loan that was originally used to purchase the asset.

D. A sale of a borrowed asset.

9. Lynne is a trader at a hedge fund. She has a flat position in gold. What happens to the position if the price of gold rises?

A. The position makes money.

B. Nothing.

C. The position loses money.

D. Insufficient information.

10. What kinds of fees are typically charged by hedge funds?

A. Hedge funds will charge investors a percentage of net assets invested.

B. Hedge funds will charge investors a percentage of any net profits.

C. Hedge funds will charge investors a fixed fee regardless of the size of their assets.

D. Hedge funds will charge investors both a percentage of net assets and a percentage of net profits.

## CHAPTER 2

# Financial Markets

This chapter introduces many commonly traded financial products like stocks, bonds, futures, and options. These products are broadly grouped into real assets, financial assets, and derivatives. Then, these broad product types are further broken down to describe some unique features of the individual products that make up that general category.

## FINANCIAL INSTRUMENTS

Traders, whether individual traders or institutional traders like hedge funds, are in the business of buying and selling special types of contracts, called *financial instruments*. *Financial instrument* is a general term that refers to any type of tradable financial contract. Another term for financial instrument is *security*, as in *securities markets*. Originally, securities referred to instruments that provided an ownership right like stocks and bonds. However, in many jurisdictions, the term *security* now includes financial instruments that derive their value from commodities and from other financial instruments (*derivatives*).

The three main types of financial instruments are *real assets, financial assets*, and *derivatives*. Real assets include physical commodities (like gold, oil, corn, or cattle), real estate, and legislatively created rights (like carbon emissions rights). Financial assets are primarily composed of contracts that give an ownership interest in a company (stocks), borrowing (bonds), or currencies. Derivatives are financial contracts that derive their value from other financial instruments. For example, a derivative might be an agreement to buy a physical commodity at some point in the future (a futures contract) or a contract that gives its owner the right, but not the obligation, to purchase stock in a company (a stock option). (See Table 2.1, Financial Instruments.)

A necessary prerequisite for trading a financial instrument is *assignability*. Assignability means the ability to transfer the asset (or liability) from one party to someone else.

**TABLE 2.1**   Financial Instruments

| Category | Financial Instruments | Created by |
|----------|----------------------|------------|
| Real Assets | Physical commodities | Mining, oil drilling, farming |
|  | Real estate | Builders |
|  | Emissions rights | Governments |
|  | Patents | Inventors |
| Financial Assets | Stocks | Corporations |
|  | Bonds | Borrowers |
|  | Currencies | Governments |
| Derivatives | Futures | Sellers |
|  | Forwards | Sellers |
|  | Swaps | Sellers |
|  | Options | Sellers |

To be tradable, assets also need to be interchangeable with similar assets. The term *fungibility* describes the ability to substitute, replace, or interchange one asset for another similar asset. For example, shares of a company stock are interchangeable regardless of how they are acquired—shares purchased through an initial public offering are the same as shares purchased on an exchange. This simplifies trading because it is easier to establish a price for a common type of product.

If assets are not interchangeable, there will typically be some subjective value assigned to the asset. For example, a unique piece of framed art might be sellable. However, the value of the art and the timeliness of arranging a sale might be difficult to estimate. Some other examples of non-fungible assets are property and intellectual property such as patents.

To be a financial instrument, assets need to be *tradable*. Tradable means that it is possible to both buy and sell the financial instrument without giving up a substantial amount of the asset's value. For example, it is generally possible to buy a cheeseburger (a standardized commodity) anywhere in the world. However, it is very difficult to buy cheeseburgers and then resell them.

In determining tradability, it is necessary to consider both the time needed to set up a transaction and the price that can be obtained. Tradable assets can be converted into cash in a reasonably quick amount of time without taking a substantial loss. Typically, the term tradable encompasses a range of trading ability. As a result, terminology has developed to describe how easy it is to turn an asset into cash (or pay money to remove a liability). This term is called *liquidity*.

- **Liquid Market.** A liquid market allows an asset to be easily converted into cash, or a liability to be removed by paying cash, without a

## KEY CONCEPT: REQUIREMENTS FOR FINANCIAL INSTRUMENTS

*Financial instruments need to be tradable*

There are many types of assets that are not financial instruments. To be a financial instrument, an asset (or liability) needs to be tradable. In other words, it needs to be assignable (possible for someone else to own) and there needs to be an ability to both buy and sell the asset (or liability) without incurring large losses on the transaction.

Some common features of financial instruments:

- **Assignable.** The asset has to be transferable to someone else and there needs to be other traders willing to buy and sell.
- **Fungible.** The asset typically must be interchangeable with similar assets.
- **Cost Effective.** Buying and immediately reselling the product can't involve a substantial loss in value. A difference of more than 10 percent between purchase and sale prices indicates a market where active trading is difficult.

significant loss of money. Typically, liquid markets have low transaction costs, low volatility, and it is easy to execute a trade at a favorable price.

- **Illiquid Market.** An illiquid market does not allow easy trading. Typically, an illiquid market requires the trader to spend a substantial amount of time finding a trading partner or to take an unfavorable price.

## REAL ASSETS

Real assets include both tangible and intangible assets. Tangible assets are physical assets like physical commodities, buildings, equipment, and land. Intangible assets don't have physical form but still have value. Some examples of intangible real assets are inventions, works of art, and advertising trademarks.

Some of the most commonly traded real assets are petroleum products, metals, and agricultural commodities. These assets are typically highly fungible products with well-known quality standards that define a particular *grade* of commodity. These products often require a high degree of sophistication when trading due to the need to store and transport physical products.

The market for trading physical products is a type of *spot market*. In a spot market, physical commodities are exchanged for cash *on the spot*. It should be noted that due to the complexity of storing and delivering physical products, most commodity trading is actually done in the derivatives markets (discussed below), where contracts are used to arrange transferring the item at a later point in time. This substantially simplifies trading since storage and transportation can be worked out prior to delivery.

Compared to most financial instruments, commodities have several unique features. First, commodities have to be at the right place at the right time. A warehouse of cotton located in Egypt isn't useful if you have agreed to sell it to a factory in the United States. Different locations might also have different regulations (like taxes) applied to the commodity as well as having different levels of supply and demand. Second, the units of trading are very important for commodities. For example, crude oil can be traded in units of volume (barrels) or weight (metric tonnes). If a trader is quoting a price for a commodity, understanding the units in which the price is being quoted is important. Third, most commodities have to meet specific standards for purity and quality. These are typically set by industry groups and describe the *grade* of the commodity.

Some features of commodities that are different from other financial instruments:

- **Location.** Commodities have a physical location. This is important since commodities are often expensive to transport and different locations can have variations in supply and demand that lead to different prices.
- **Units.** Commodities can trade in different units. For example, oil can trade in units of volume (barrels or gallons) or weight (metric tonnes). Different types of crude oil have different densities. As a result, one type might have 7.2 barrels per metric tonne and a second type of crude oil might have 6.9 barrels per metric tonne.
- **Grade.** Most commodities will need to meet certain quality specifications to be tradable. The grade of a commodity describes which quality standard is met by the commodity.

### KEY CONCEPT: REAL ASSETS

Many real assets are not tradable because there may not be enough market participants ready to buy or sell those assets on short notice. This can lead to illiquid markets with high transaction costs. When real assets are not tradable, prices may be based on other market mechanisms like auctions or prices set by retailers selling products to consumers.

## FINANCIAL ASSETS

Financial assets represent ownership of real assets or cash flows created by real assets. Financial assets differ from real assets because financial assets are created by issuers. For example, a corporation could create a financial asset by issuing either stock or bonds. This will create a liability on the balance sheet of the issuer and an asset on the balance sheet of the purchaser.

The terms *primary market* and *secondary market* are used to describe the trading of financial assets. The primary market for financial assets involves the issuance of the financial assets and the initial sale to investors. An *initial public offering* is the issuance of new shares of stock. The secondary market for financial assets involves the subsequent trading of already-issued assets. For example, buying shares of a stock on an exchange, like the New York Stock Exchange, is a secondary market transaction.

The two markets for financial assets are:

- **Primary Market.** A marketplace for issuing new financial assets such as a bond offering or an initial public offering for a stock.
- **Secondary Market.** A marketplace for trading existing financial assets such as a stock exchange

While companies can directly issue assets to buyers, the process of issuing assets is commonly facilitated by an *underwriter*. An underwriter is a financial institution, or a group of financial institutions organized into a *syndicate*, which helps find buyers for an issuance. Typically, the underwriters of an issue will agree to purchase the financial assets if buyers cannot be found. This is called a *firm offering*. In other cases, the underwriter will act only as a broker, without guaranteeing a sale, in a *best-efforts offering*. There are few limits on how many financial assets can be issued as long as there are a sufficient number of buyers.

## DERIVATIVES

A derivative contract is a financial contract whose value is based on the value of some other asset. The asset that determines that value of the derivative is called an *underlying asset*. Some common examples of derivatives are futures, forwards, swaps, and option contracts. However, derivatives don't necessarily need to be stand-alone contracts. Derivatives can also exist embedded inside larger contracts.

Some factors common to most derivatives include:

- The underlying asset is tradable or readily convertible to cash
- Created by transactions that transfer wealth between buyer and seller

- Have a limited lifespan
- Depend on future prices of the underlying asset
- A fixed quantity of the underlying asset is traded

To be considered a derivative, the underlying asset has to be tradable. A trader needs to be able to both buy and sell this asset for cash at approximately the same price in a reasonable amount of time. In other words, the underlying asset has to be *readily convertible into cash* for the contract to be considered a derivative. In the case of an embedded derivative, the exposure created by that portion of the contract designated as a derivative needs to have the ability to be settled in cash or offset through trading.

Another feature of derivatives is that they require both a buyer and a seller. Derivatives are created by the process of a buyer and a seller agreeing to a transaction. As a result, there are always an equal number of people holding positions on either side of the market. In other words, there is *zero net supply* of derivatives. For example, if prices go up in a stock market, every stockholder can benefit. However, with a derivative, because there is always the same number of buyers and sellers, wealth is only transferred between the buyer and seller.

In almost all cases, derivatives are contracts that have a limited lifespan. In other words, they expire after a certain amount of time (on the *expiration date* or *expiry*). On the expiration date, the transacting parties need to fulfill their obligations to one another. This might involve a physical transfer of the underlying asset or settlement in cash.

The value of the obligations that have to be fulfilled to settle a derivative typically depends on price movements that occur between the initiation of the transaction and the expiration date. One implication of this is that many derivatives don't cost any money to transact. Another implication is that derivative transactions typically do not include payments for already existing value or past events. Their value typically depends only on things that might occur in the future.

Next, derivatives usually specify the quantity of the underlying asset (the *notional*) or dollar amount of the exposure (the *notional value*). Movements in the price of the underlying asset along with the fixed notional determine the magnitude of the obligations that need to be settled between the buyer and seller. For example, the change in a derivative's value might be calculated by multiplying the price change in the underlying by the notional (a volume) to calculate a change in value.

Finally, derivatives require some way to settle the obligations of the buyer and seller. Depending on the needs of the buyer and seller, some derivatives might require the delivery of a physical product (barrels of oil, bushels of corn, tons of steel). Other derivatives might allow the obligations to be settled in cash. From a risk perspective, net settlement in cash is typically much less risky than exchange of a physical commodity for cash.

Derivatives may be settled in several different ways:

- **Physical Settlement.** A physical settlement involves a delivery of a physical asset (like live cattle, gold, or oil) that is exchanged for cash. For example, a trader might have to pay $50 million to receive 500,000 barrels of oil. Physical settlement involves substantial operational risk due to the need to transfer ownership of physical assets. As with other financial instruments, there is a risk/reward relationship— many profitable trading opportunities only exist in the physical settled market.
- **Financial (Cash) Settlement.** A financial settlement involves an exchange of cash flows, typically on a net basis. Financial settlement reduces many of the operational risks associated with physical delivery. In addition, the size of the settlement is much smaller. For example, a trader might agree to receive the difference between $50 million in cash and the value of 500,000 barrels of oil.

## KEY CONCEPT: TYPES OF DERIVATIVES

There are many types of derivatives:

**Interest Rate Swap Contracts.** A swap is an exchange of two sets of cash flows. Swaps are typically cash settled. In the bond markets, fixed rate and floating rate cash flows are often swapped. In the commodity markets, the term swap commonly refers to financially settled commodity contracts. Because swaps are an exchange of cash, the terms buyer and seller commonly are often replaced with more descriptive terms.

**Forward Contracts.** In a forward contract, the buyer agrees to purchase a physically delivered asset from the seller at a fixed price (the *strike price*). Delivery is arranged at a specific point in the future. These contracts typically specify the *grade*, or quality, of the asset to be delivered, the location for delivery, and the price that will be paid by the buyer. Forwards typically involve no up-front payments to either party. The value of a forward at expiration is based on the difference between the strike price and the value of the physical asset at the delivery date.

**Futures Contracts.** Futures contracts are exchange-traded versions of forward contracts. The primary difference between a forward and

*(Continued)*

**KEY CONCEPT: (*Continued*)**

a future is *daily margining*. Daily margining works by resetting the strike price of the contract and requiring a cash settlement each day. This is similar to selling and rebuying the contract every day. Buying or selling futures typically requires a good faith deposit, called *margin*, which is returned when the trade is exited.

**Option Contracts.** An option buyer has the right to take some action, but is not required to take that action if it is unprofitable. Options are a way to transfer risk from a buyer to a seller. The option seller has all the risk in these contracts. A substantial amount of mathematical finance is dedicated to the problem of calculating how much money (usually quite a bit) needs to be paid to the option seller to have them take this risk. The two main types of rights are the right to buy at a fixed price (a *call* option) and the right to sell at a fixed price (a *put* option). Options are also often characterized by when the option buyer can make a decision to take delivery. A *European option* can only be exercised at expiry while *American options* can be exercised at any time.

**Embedded Derivatives.** Contracts that are not considered derivatives may contain clauses that are considered derivatives for accounting purposes. These embedded derivatives might act like forwards, options, or any other type of derivative. For example, a contract between two firms might specify that a minimum quantity of a standardized product is purchased at a certain price.

**Credit Default Swaps (CDS).** Credit default swaps are derivatives whose value is based on corporate bonds issued by some corporation. In the event that the issuer of the bond defaults, the CDS issuer will take possession of the corporate bond and give a payoff to the CDS buyer. In compensation for taking on this risk, the CDS seller will receive a series of payments from the CDS buyer. The issuer of the bond (the *reference entity* or *reference obligor*) is not a party to the transaction.

## COMMODITY SPOT MARKET

Physical commodities are a type of real asset. For many commodities, there is an active trading market for commodities that can be exchanged for cash on the spot. This is called a *commodity spot market*. This market typically requires traders to be able to be able to handle physical deliveries. This increases the risk of these markets and provides a barrier to casual investment.

The most commonly traded real assets are fuel, electricity, raw materials, and agricultural products. Typically, the quantity of spot commodities available for trading is limited by the need to mine, grow, or refine the commodity as well as the need to have it in a location where a buyer is located. As a result, a mismatch between supply and demand can cause a glut or surplus in the market. Combined with the fact that commodities are often difficult to store and transport, this can cause commodity prices to be very volatile. Consumers drive prices up during shortages as they compete for the limited available quantity. During surplus periods, just the opposite happens—prices can go close to zero once no one can use any more.

Due to the complexity of storage and transport, the price of physical commodities is often heavily influenced by their location. Typically, spot commodities are priced off a benchmark (commonly a futures price rather than a spot market price) with adjustments for location and quality of the commodity. The difference between the benchmark price and the price of the physical commodity at some other location is called the *basis price*. (See Figure 2.1, Natural Gas Basis.)

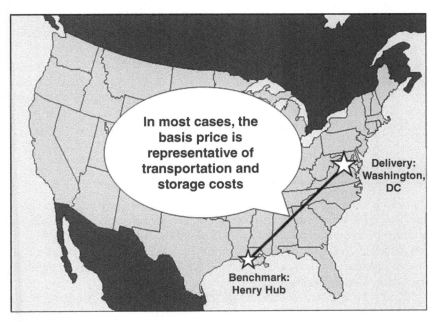

In most cases, the basis price is representative of transportation and storage costs

Delivery:
Washington, DC

Benchmark:
Henry Hub

**FIGURE 2.1** Natural Gas Basis

---

### BASIS

The term basis has other meanings in the financial markets. In the commodity markets, basis refers to a difference in price due to a difference in location. In a more general sense, basis refers to a difference in price relative to a benchmark or index.

---

In addition to location, the composition of commodities is very important. Commodities need to meet certain quality standards published by governments or industry trade associations. If they don't meet the standards, the price of the commodity will be adjusted for the difference. By meeting those quality standards, the traders have an objective measure to test if the responsibilities of each party have been met. (See Figure 2.2, U.S. Standards for Wheat.)

There are a wide variety of traded commodities. Some of the most common commodities are energy commodities, metals, and agricultural commodities.

- **Fuels.** Crude oil and the products refined from crude oil (products like gasoline, diesel, and jet fuel) form one of the largest commodity markets. Other fuels include natural gas (methane), propane, and butane.
- **Electricity.** Electricity
- **Precious Metals.** Gold, silver, platinum, and palladium
- **Ferrous Metals.** Iron and steel
- **Non-Ferrous Metals.** Aluminum, copper, lead, tin, and zinc are major non-ferrous metals.
- **Agricultural Products.** Corn, wheat, sugar, soybeans

### EQUITIES (STOCKS)

Equities (also called stocks) are a type of financial asset issued by *corporations* that give an ownership share of the corporation. A corporation is a specific type of legal entity with assets, liabilities, and power distinct from its investors. This is a limited liability structure where the owners of the company, called *shareholders*, are not personally liable for any debts or liabilities incurred by the corporation.

During an initial public offering, investors give corporations money in exchange for an ownership share in the company. As part owners, stockholders are entitled to regular payments from the company (*dividends*) and

| Grading Factors | Grades U.S. Nos. | | | | |
|---|---|---|---|---|---|
| | 1 | 2 | 3 | 4 | 5 |
| Minimum pound limits of: | | | | | |
| Test weight per bushel | | | | | |
|   Hard Red Spring wheat or White Club wheat | 58.0 | 57.0 | 55.0 | 53.0 | 50.0 |
|   All other classes and subclasses | 60.0 | 58.0 | 56.0 | 54.0 | 51.0 |
| Maximum percent limits of: | | | | | |
| Defects: | | | | | |
|   Damaged kernels | | | | | |
|     Heat (part of total) | 0.2 | 0.2 | 0.5 | 1.0 | 3.0 |
|     Total | 2.0 | 4.0 | 7.0 | 10.0 | 15.0 |
|   Foreign material | 0.4 | 0.7 | 1.3 | 3.0 | 5.0 |
|   Shrunken and broken kernels | 3.0 | 5.0 | 8.0 | 12.0 | 20.0 |
|     Total[1] | 3.0 | 5.0 | 8.0 | 12.0 | 20.0 |
|   Wheat of other classes:[2] | | | | | |
|   Contrasting classes | 1.0 | 2.0 | 3.0 | 10.0 | 10.0 |
|     Total[3] | 3.0 | 5.0 | 10.0 | 10.0 | 10.0 |
|   Stones | 0.1 | 0.1 | 0.1 | 0.1 | 0.1 |
| Maximum count limits of: | | | | | |
| Other Material in one kilogram: | | | | | |
|   Animal filth | 1 | 1 | 1 | 1 | 1 |
|   Castor beans | 1 | 1 | 1 | 1 | 1 |
|   Crotalaria seeds | 2 | 2 | 2 | 2 | 2 |
|   Glass | 0 | 0 | 0 | 0 | 0 |
|   Stones | 3 | 3 | 3 | 3 | 3 |
|   Unknown foreign substances | 3 | 3 | 3 | 3 | 3 |
|     Total[4] | 4 | 4 | 4 | 4 | 4 |
|   Insect-damaged kernels in 100 grams | 31 | 31 | 31 | 31 | 31 |

U.S. Sample grade is Wheat that:
(a) Does not meet the requirements for U.S. Nos. 1, 2, 3, 4, or 5; or
(b) Has a musty, sour, or commercially objectionable foreign odor (except smut or garlic odor) or
(c) Is heating or of distinctly low quality.

1/ Includes damaged kernels (total), foreign material, shrunken and broken kernels.
2/ Unclassed wheat of any grade may contain not more than 10.0 percent of wheat of other classes.
3/ Includes contrasting classes.
4/ Includes any combination of animal filth, castor beans, crotalaria seeds, glass, stones, or unknown foreign substance.

**FIGURE 2.2** U.S. Standards for Wheat

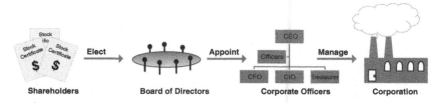

**FIGURE 2.3**   A Corporation

benefit when the value of the company increases. Shareholders also help determine the management of the company. Typically, shareholders elect a *board of directors* that appoints the corporate officers who manage the daily operations of the company. (See Figure 2.3, A Corporation.)

The ownership of a corporation is typically divided into portions, called *shares*, where each share represents an equal level of ownership in the corporation. For example, if a company issues 100,000 shares, a shareholder who owns 10,000 shares would own 10 percent of the company. Owning shares gives shareholders more votes to elect the board of directors.

The board of directors acts on behalf of the shareholders to oversee the company. The board is responsible for corporate actions like changing the dividend payment and appointing the senior officers of the firm. These senior officers commonly include a chief executive officer (CEO) and various lieutenants like the chief financial officer (CFO), chief investment officer (CIO), chief risk officer (CRO), treasurer, and corporate secretary.

## KEY CONCEPT: EQUITIES

Equities provide an ownership interest in a company. There are a variety of types:

**Common Stock.** Common stock is the most common type of equity investment. Each share of common stock represents an ownership share in a company. Investors that own common stock are called *shareholders*. Shareholders indirectly control corporations by electing the board of directors. The board of directors is then responsible for appointing the senior managers of the corporation (like the chief executive officer or CEO) who perform the day-to-day management of the firm and its employees.

**Preferred Stock.** Preferred stock is a form of stock with a higher guaranteed dividend but less ability to benefit from appreciation in corporate assets. It is not a better version of common stock. Preferred stock pays dividends at specified intervals and gives preference over common stock in case of a bankruptcy. Typically, preferred stock dividends must be paid before dividends are paid to common shareholders. It is often possible to convert preferred stock into common stock to benefit from capital appreciation. However, preferred stock generally does not have voting rights.

**American Depository Receipts (ADRs).** ADRs hold shares of a foreign company in a trust for buyers in the United States. Each ADR holds stock in a single foreign company. ADRs simplify the process of buying shares in foreign companies because they avoid international settlement problems. Outside the United States, the term Global Depository Receipt or a country specific name might be used.

**Exchange Traded Funds (ETFs).** Exchange traded funds are investment funds which hold a basket of stock investments. Some especially popular ETFs mirror broad market indexes like the S&P 500 or the Dow Jones Industrial Average.

**Real Estate Investment Trusts (REITs).** REITs are investment funds which own real estate. These funds allow investors to trade real estate.

## BONDS (FIXED INCOME, DEBT)

Debt instruments (bonds) are financial assets that are created when investors loan money to a corporation, nation, or other legal entity. These instruments allow investors to loan money to companies and receive interest payments in return. Debt instruments are often called *fixed income* investments because the borrower is required to make fixed payments at regular intervals that are determined when the bond is issued. The owner of the bond is the lender (*creditor*) and the issuer of the bond is the borrower (*debtor*).

Bonds typically have a limited lifespan. At some point, the bond will expire (*mature*) and the bondholder will be repaid a large lump sum (called the *principal, par value,* or *face value*). Prior to that point, the bondholder will receive regular payments (called *coupon payments*). These bonds are commonly described by their *coupon rate*—the annual amount of coupon payments divided by the par value.

For example, if the ABC Company decides to raise money by issuing bonds, it might decide to issue bonds with a $1000 par value with a $50 coupon payment paid every six months. Bonds are commonly issued at their par value. As a result, the initial bondholders would need to pay $1000 to

## KEY CONCEPT: BOND PRICES

Most bonds are issued with a $1000 par value. Bond prices are commonly quoted relative to par value. For example a bond price of 99.5 might indicate that a $1000 bond is trading at $995 (or a $5 discount to its par value).

**Examples: Corporate Bonds**

- 100  Selling at par ($1000, 100 percent of par value)
- 102  Selling at a premium ($1020, 102 percent of par value)
- 98.5  Selling at a discount ($985, 98.5 percent of par value)

**Example: Government Bonds**
Government bonds are often traded in 32nds.

- 100:16  Selling at a premium, 100 16/32nds is 100.50 ($1005)
- 95:8  Selling at a discount, 95 8/32nds is 95.25 ($952.50)

Bond pricing is further complicated based on the timing of when bonds pay coupon payments. The owner of the bond on a record date, called the *ex-interest* date, will receive that coupon. However, bond prices are adjusted to pro-rate the payment based on trading date. On the ex-interest date, the value of the bond will drop by the amount of the coupon payment. To smooth out prices and make them easier to compare over time, bonds are commonly quoted at a *clean price* that excludes the accumulated value from the upcoming payment. The accumulated interest will need to be added to the clean price to determine the actual cash price (the *dirty price*) paid by the buyer.

Some definitions needed for bond pricing:

- Ex-Interest Date. The date on which a purchaser is no longer entitled to a coupon payment.
- Clean Price. The price of the bond that excludes any accrued value from the upcoming coupon payment.
- Dirty Price. The actual cash price paid by the buyer. This is calculated by adding any accrued interest to the clean price.

purchase each bond. Additionally, the coupon rate on the bond is 10 percent. This is called the *nominal yield* and can be calculated by dividing the coupon payments for the year ($100 = two $50 payments) divided by the par value. (See Equation 2.1, Nominal Yield.)

$$Nominal\ Yield = \frac{Annual\ Interest\ Payment}{Par\ Value} \qquad (2.1)$$

Bonds are priced as a percentage of their face value. For example, if a bond is trading at 95, the current price is 95 percent of the face value. For example, if a $1000 par value 10 percent bond is trading at 95, it can be purchased for $950 from another trader. The bond will continue to pay the same coupon rate for the life of the bond. The current yield is calculated as a percent of its trading price. (See Equation 2.2, Current Yield).

$$Current\ Yield = \frac{Annual\ Interest\ Payment}{Trading\ Price} \qquad (2.2)$$

To compare two bonds, it is necessary to consider both the current price of the bond (relative to its face value) and the size of the coupon payments. A bond with no coupon payments might still be quite valuable. For example, a zero coupon bond which is trading at 50 percent of its par value will still have a substantial payoff if the issuer doesn't default before maturity. To compare bonds with different prices and coupon payments, bond traders will use a calculation called *yield to maturity*. (See Equation 2.3, Yield to Maturity.)

The yield to maturity calculation can be approximated as:

$$YTM = \frac{C + \dfrac{F - P}{n}}{\dfrac{F + P}{2}} \qquad (2.3)$$

where

C  **Coupon.** The annual coupon payment

F  **Face Value.** The face value (par value) of the bond

P  **Price.** The current price of the bond

n  **Years to Maturity.** The number of years to maturity

## KEY CONCEPT: BASIS POINTS

When the yield to maturity of two bonds is being compared, the difference is often less than a whole percentage point. To make the units whole numbers, differences in interest rates are commonly quoted in a smaller unit called *basis points*, abbreviated *bps*. A basis point is 1/100th of a percent—one part per ten thousand.

Once a company issues bonds, they can be traded to other investors. This does not change the contractual terms of the bond. In other words, trading a bond to someone else does not change the *par value* or the *coupon payment* associated with a bond. Trades can occur at any price. This can be a major source of risk for bonds that are not held to maturity.

Another major risk factor associated with bonds is the credit quality of the issuer. Borrowers only get compensated if the lender repays the loan. As a result, companies that are at a high risk for bankruptcy typically need to pay bondholders higher interest rates to increase the demand for their bonds. As the credit quality of the issuer changes over time, the resale value of bonds will go up and down as well.

A third risk factor that is associated with bonds is interest rates. An *interest rate* is the prevailing rate which borrowers need to pay lenders for the use of the lender's money. The interest rate on a bond is measured by its yield to maturity. Bonds of similar credit quality will typically have similar yields to maturity. Higher interest rates (higher coupon rates on newly issued bonds) make existing bonds with lower coupon rates less attractive. As a result, the lower coupon rate bonds will drop in value. The opposite occurs when interest rates fall—existing bonds tend to become more valuable.

Bond prices and interest rates tend to move in opposite directions. If interest rates go up, that means coupon rates on newly issued bonds are going up. That makes existing bonds with lower coupon rates less attractive to investors and their prices to fall. As a result, prices of existing bonds tend to move in the opposite changes in interest rates. (See Figure 2.4, Bond Prices and Interest Rates.)

## CURRENCIES (FOREIGN EXCHANGE)

Currencies are financial assets issued by governments. Each government determines which currency will be accepted as legal tender within its boundaries. Currencies are traded in the foreign exchange (FX) market.

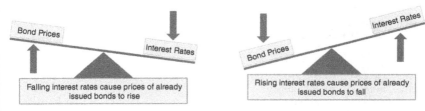

**FIGURE 2.4** Bond Prices and Interest Rates

## KEY CONCEPT: TYPES OF DEBT SECURITIES

The terms *fixed income securities*, *bonds*, and *debt investments* are all largely synonymous. These assets give the debt holder (the lender) a creditor position in the borrower.

These instruments often have specific terms associated with them:

**Debenture.** A debenture is an unsecured corporate bond. It is backed by the full faith and credit of the issuer. If the issuer doesn't pay the bond, a default will be triggered that ultimately leads to bankruptcy proceedings unless a settlement is achieved. In the event of a bankruptcy, there is a priority order that determines when creditors get paid. Bondholders are fairly high on the list and paid after taxes and unpaid employee wages.

**Collateralized Bonds.** Borrowers can sell bonds that are backed by a specific asset that is pledged to repay the bond. If the collateral loses value, the bond is still backed by the full faith and credit of the issuer. Because of the collateral backing the loan, collateralized bonds have less risk (and probably a lower coupon payment) than debentures.

**Treasury Bills, Notes, and Bonds.** Debt securities issued by the U.S. government have different names based on maturity. Treasury bills have terms of less than one year. Treasury notes typically have terms of 2, 3, 5, and 10 years. Treasury bonds have a maturity of 30 years. These are generally considered very safe investments and have a correspondingly low interest rate. These all work similarly and are typically referred to by the name *Treasuries*.

**Zero Coupon Bonds.** As their name implies, zero coupon bonds do not have a coupon payment. Instead, they are issued at a discount to their par value.

**Asset-Backed Securities (ABS).** An asset-backed security is a type of collateralized bond that has an asset or pool of assets pledged to

*(Continued)*

## KEY CONCEPT: (*Continued*)

help repay the bond. The asset backing the loan might be a physical asset (like manufacturing equipment) or an expected stream of income (like taxes or rental income).

**Mortgage-Backed Securities (MBS).** A mortgage-backed security is a special type of asset-backed security that is secured by a pool of real estate mortgages. Unlike many other bonds, borrowers have the ability to repay their mortgages at any time. As a result, MBS lenders face pre-payment risk—borrowers repaying their loans early (refinancing) if interest rates fall. This pays the lenders back their money early, which then has to be reinvested in other investments (likely at a less attractive yield to maturity due to the lower interest rates).

**Collateralized Mortgage Obligations (CMOs).** A CMO is a special type of mortgage-backed security that separates the cash flows from a pool of mortgages into categories called *tranches*. The first tranche will have the highest priority for receiving cash flows. Other tranches will have progressively lower priority. In the case that one of the borrowers defaults on their obligations, the lowest tranches are the last to get paid. As a result of this structure, the first tranche is an extremely safe investment (usually with a correspondingly low interest rate paid to the lender) and the last tranches are extremely risky (with correspondingly high interest rates).

A government can control how much of its currency is in circulation, both by printing more money and by open market activities like borrowing or lending money. Of the two approaches, borrowing money (or repaying loans) is the primary way that governments control how much money is available. When a government (or any other market participant) borrows money, the amount of tradable assets in that country increases. For example, if a country issues bonds (borrows money), it can spend the money. In addition, the bond buyer obtains a valuable asset (the bond) that can be resold or used as collateral.

FX trades are quoted as currency pairs with each currency indicated by a three-letter identifier—like USD for U.S. dollars, EUR for Euros, or RMB for Chinese Renminbi. The first currency listed is the *base currency*. There is one unit of the base currency for a variable quantity of the second currency. For example, 1.3369 EUR/USD means that one Euro equals $1.3369 dollars. FX trades are typically quoted to four decimal points. A one point move (a .0001 move) is called a *pip*.

> ## KEY CONCEPT: CURRENCY CODES
>
> In 1973, the International Organization for Standards (the ISO) adopted a standard methodology using three-letter identifiers to represent each currency. This replaced simple names (like Indian Rupee) and symbols (like $ for U.S. dollars or € for Euros) in most trading applications.

Because of sovereignty issues involving two currencies, where no country wants another regulating trading in their currency, there is very little regulation in the FX market. The FX spot market is a decentralized market dominated by large international banks. This is sometimes called an *interbank market*. FX trades occur around the clock every day of the week except for a couple of weekend hours.

## FORWARDS AND COMMODITY SWAPS

Forward contracts (forwards) are financial contracts between two parties to buy or sell a specific amount of a commodity for a fixed price (the *strike price*) in the future. The contracts specify the asset that needs to be delivered, the quality specifications the asset needs to meet (the *grade*), and when delivery needs to be made (the *delivery date*). These contracts are negotiated directly between the buyer and seller. If the contract is settled in cash rather than by physical delivery, the trade is called a *commodity swap* rather than a forward.

Most forwards contracts conform to standards set by the International Swap Dealers Association (ISDA). As a result, they typically list the same type of terms and refer back to the ISDA master agreement that sets out standard business practices. This gives a common framework so that forwards can be more easily transferred between traders. (See Figure 2.5, A Commodity Swap Contract.)

From a paperwork perspective, trading within an ISDA framework means that forwards and commodity swaps are not stand-alone contracts. Usually, forward trades are treated as an amendment to a *master trading agreement* signed between the two trading parties. The entire trading agreement, the master agreement, is often quite lengthy—it can be several hundred pages long. However, each additional trade is usually written up

The Terms of the particular transaction to which this confirmation relates are as follows:

| | |
|---|---|
| **Transaction** | Commodity Swap |
| **Trade Date** | 9 September 2013 |
| **Commodity** | Brent Crude |
| **Quantity** | Total 3, 600,000 BBLs |
| | Period: See below |
| **Term** | 01 January 2013 to 31 Dec 2013 |
| **We pay you:** | Fixed price of $102.50 per barrel USD |
| **You pay us:** | Brent Crude |
| | Contract setting price of last three trading days each month (see Schedule A) |
| **Payment** | Exactly 5 business days after the end of the relevant determination period. |

**Schedule A**

| Pricing Month | Quantity(BBLs) |
|---|---|
| January 2013 | 310,000 |
| February 2013 | 280,000 |
| March 2013 | 310,000 |
| April 2013 | 300,000 |
| May 2013 | 310,000 |
| June 2013 | 300,000 |
| July 2013 | 310,000 |
| August 2013 | 310,000 |
| September 2013 | 300,000 |
| October 2013 | 310,000 |
| November 2013 | 300,000 |
| December 2013 | 310,000 |

**FIGURE 2.5**   A Commodity Swap Contract

in a one-page summary called a *trade confirm*. Using a master agreement simplifies trading.

Another advantage of using a master agreement is that this forces all trades between two trading parties to be considered a single transaction. The term for this is *master netting*. Master netting reduces credit risk by allowing purchases to offset sales between two counterparties. Without netting, a bankruptcy court would freeze the outgoing payments of the bankrupt entity but leave the amounts owed to the company intact. In the case of a forward contract to exchange cash for a commodity, this would be disastrous. It would result in a counterparty having to deliver a commodity for which they would not be paid (or paying for a commodity which they would not receive).

Forward contracts don't require any money up front. Forwards are typically traded at fair value. The fixed price in the transaction, the *strike price*, is usually set so that it is equal to the forward price of the commodity. As a result, a forward trade will typically be an exchange of two equally valued items and have zero net value at time of trading. After the trade is made, the forward price of the asset will change over time. This will change the value of the forward since it is no longer an exchange of equally valued items. (See Equation 2.4, Forward/Commodity Swap Value.)

$$Value = Volume * (F - X) \tag{2.4}$$

where

| | | |
|---|---|---|
| Volume | **Volume.** The number of units that have been traded. This needs to be in the same units as the price | |
| F | **Forward price.** The forward price of the underlying asset on the valuation date | |
| X | **Strike price.** The price which the buyer will pay the seller at delivery. The strike price will usually be equal to the forward price at the time of trading | |

## FUTURES

A futures contract is a standardized financial contract to buy or sell an asset at some point in the future, similar to a forward. Futures are a type of financial derivative. The difference between a future and a forward is that a third party (the *futures exchange*) will interpose itself between the buyer and seller. Instead of transacting with each other, the buyer and seller will each enter into contracts with the exchange. Since the buyer and seller don't sign contracts with each other, trading futures is anonymous. All the buyer and seller know is that someone was willing to take the opposite side of the exposure. (See Figure 2.6, Forwards versus Futures.)

The futures exchange will protect itself in several ways. First, the exchange will require both traders to post a refundable deposit, called *initial margin*, whenever a trade is executed on the exchange. Next, the exchange will calculate a daily closing price and will pass through any gains and losses on the contract to the traders. One of the traders will have to deposit money, called *daily margin*, to the exchange to cover the daily price movement while the other trader will have that money credited to their account.

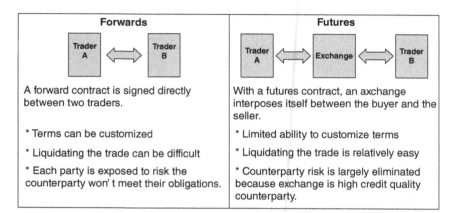

**FIGURE 2.6** Forwards versus Futures

## INTEREST RATE SWAPS

An interest rate swap is a financial derivative that allows traders to exchange a series of fixed and floating rate cash flows. In the most common type of interest rate swap, one trader will pay the other a fixed cash flow, while the

### KEY CONCEPT: FUTURES, FORWARDS, AND COMMODITY SWAPS

Futures, forwards, and commodity swaps are the most common ways for traders to access the commodity markets. These contracts allow buyers and sellers to arrange transactions on commodities at a specific time and place in the future.

- **Futures.** Futures are standardized contracts traded on an exchange. Commodity futures involve physical delivery, although most futures are liquidated through trading rather than actually delivered physically.
- **Forwards.** Forwards are bilateral contracts that are directly negotiated between a buyer and a seller. They can be more customized than futures although, in practice, most of the terms are fairly standardized.
- **Commodity Swaps.** Commodity swaps are financially settled versions of futures. These trades involve net cash settlement rather than delivery of a physical commodity.

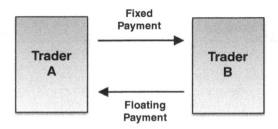

**FIGURE 2.7**   Interest Rate Swap

other trader will pay a payment based on a floating interest rate. The fixed rate and the formula to calculate the floating rate will be determined when the trade is signed. (See Figure 2.7, Interest Rate Swap.)

Companies will enter these agreements to modify their exposure to interest rates. For example, a bank may have issued mortgages that pay the bank a fixed interest rate. Since the bank pays a floating rate on its savings accounts, it might want to exchange those fixed-rate payments for floating-rate payments. This will help it match its income (from the mortgages) to its expenditures (payments to savings accounts). If it can find a counterparty that is interested in receiving a fixed rate on its investments, they can agree to exchange cash flows.

Interest rate swaps are traded directly between two traders (*bilaterally*) or facilitated by a bank (*over the counter*). Trades can be individually negotiated and, as a result, there can be a wide variety of interest rate swaps. Some common variations of interest rates swaps allow fixed/float payments to be denominated in two separate currencies, two floating rates to be exchanged, or fixed rates in two different currencies to be exchanged.

## OPTIONS

Options are a type of derivative that is particularly important to risk management and financial mathematics. Options are contracts that give one party (the buyer) the right to make a decision. The buyer pays the seller for that right. Essentially, with an option transaction, the seller takes on all of the risk of the transaction for a fixed amount of money, called the *option premium*. Because the option seller gets paid for taking on the risk, option pricing is important to risk management.

The option buyer purchases the right to make a decision. In some cases, this is the right to buy an asset for a fixed price (a *call option*). In other cases, this is the right to sell an asset for a fixed price (a *put option*). The date on

---

### KEY CONCEPT: OPTIONS

Buying an option gives the buyer the right to make a decision. To compensate someone for selling an option, the option seller gets paid a premium when the option is signed. A substantial amount of financial mathematics is dedicated to ensuring that the seller is paid a sufficient amount of money to be compensated for taking on the risk of that decision.

---

which the buyer has to make the decision is called the *exercise date*. The process of making the decision is called an *execution*.

Some common terms associated with options are:

- **Option Buyer (Long Option Position)**. The party who has the right to make a decision.
- **Option Seller (Short Option Position)**. The party who gets paid the premium and is obligated to abide by the decision of the option buyer.
- **Option Premium**. The payment from the option buyer paid to the option seller in exchange for certain rights.
- **Strike Price**. The price at which the option owner can decide to buy or sell.
- **Exercise**. A decision by the owner to use the rights granted to him by the option contract.
- **Expiration Date**. The last date that the owner of the option can decide to exercise his rights.
- **Underlying Asset**. The asset that must be delivered or purchased by the seller if the option is exercised.

There are two basic types of options—the right to buy the underlying asset at a fixed price (a *call* option) and the right to sell the underlying asset at a fixed price (a *put* option). As a result, the option buyer, who has a long option position, might have a long position in the underlying (for a call) or a short position in the underlying (for a put).

The two major types of options are:

- **Call**. A call option gives the owner the **right to buy** the underlying asset at the strike price. The owner of a call option benefits if the price of the underlying appreciates in value. In other words, the owner of a call is *long* the underlying.

■ **Put.** A put option gives the owner the **right to sell** the underlying asset at the strike price. The owner of a put option benefits if the price of the underlying falls in value. In other words, the owner of a put option is *short* the underlying.

At the end of the option's life, the value of the option depends on how much the asset's price varies from the strike price. Options are not always profitable to exercise. When an option would be profitable to execute under current conditions, it is called *in-the-money*. When an option would be unprofitable to exercise at current prices, it is called *out-of-the-money*. The break-even point is called *at-the-money*. (See Equation 2.5, Option Payoffs.)

$$C = Max(0, S - X)$$
$$P = Max(0, X - S)$$

(2.5)

where

| | | |
|---|---|---|
| C or P | **Option Payoff.** The value of the option for a Call or a Put, respectively | |
| S | **Asset Price.** The price of the underlying asset | |
| X | **Strike Price.** The agreed upon price at which the option buyer can buy (for a call option) or sell (for a put option) | |

Because they involve a decision, options do not have a linear payoff. There is a discontinuity where the buyer can decide not to exercise the option and limit his or her losses. As a result, the profit or loss from holding an option is often explained through the use of payoff diagrams. These diagrams illustrate that options have no value at certain points and a value at other points.

On option payoff diagrams, the payoff is shown on the y-axis and the price of the underlying is shown on the x-axis. This payoff is the value that will be obtained for various prices of the underlying asset. The graphs can be shown with the premium (the total payoff) or without the premium (the payoff at expiration). (See Figure 2.8, Option Payoff Diagrams.)

These graphs are additive. For example, it's possible to replicate a forward by buying a call and selling a put with the same strike price. (See Figure 2.9, Put-/Call Parity and Equation 2.6, Put-Call Parity.) This links the value of the calls and puts with one another.

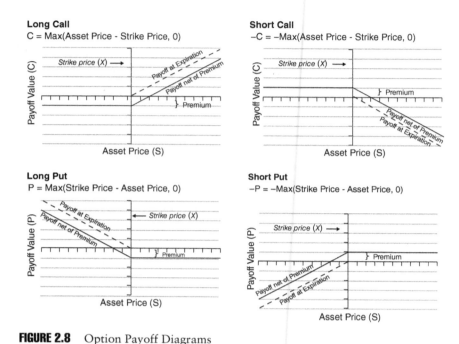

**FIGURE 2.8**   Option Payoff Diagrams

Put-call parity, like any other type of financial math, requires that calculations have all values brought to the same point in time. Usually this means that any future values need to be present valued.

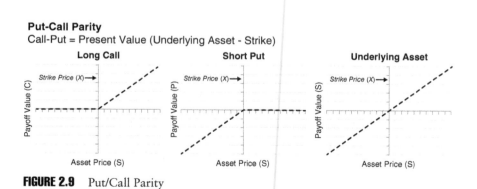

**FIGURE 2.9**   Put/Call Parity

$$C - P = S - Xe^{-rt} \qquad \textit{Option on Common Stock}$$
$$C - P = (S - X)e^{-rt} \qquad \textit{Option on Futures} \qquad (2.6)$$

Where

| | | |
|---|---|---|
| C or P | **Option Payoff.** The value of the option for a Call or a Put, respectively |
| S | **Asset Price.** The price of the underlying asset |
| X | **Strike Price.** The agreed upon price at which the option buyer can buy (for a call option) or sell (for a put option) |
| r | **Interest Rate.** The annual interest rate |
| t | **Time to Maturity.** When using annual interest rates, $t = 1.0$ means the option expires in one year |

## TEST YOUR KNOWLEDGE

1. What is the difference between a broker and a dealer?
   A. A broker is a person, while a dealer is a firm.
   B. A broker deals with individual investors (retail market), while a dealer trades with institutions (wholesale market).
   C. A broker is limited to introducing traders and executes trades on behalf of others, while a dealer can make trades on its own behalf.
   D. There is no difference.
2. What is not an example of a derivative?
   A. Shares of common stock.
   B. A call option on a bond.
   C. A forward contract to sell crude oil.
   D. A fixed/float interest rate swap.
3. Tom owns a portfolio of bonds. If interest rates rise, what will happen?
   A. Tom will make money.
   B. Tom will lose money.
   C. Tom's risk will increase.
   D. Tom's risk will decrease.
4. If a financial asset is described as *fungible*, what does that mean?
   A. The position has been sold short and is in danger of being recalled by its original owner. This will force the short seller to rebuy it immediately.
   B. The trader who owns the asset is being investigated by a regulatory agency.

      **C.** The asset is distressed and there are no buyers for it.

      **D.** The asset is interchangeable with like assets.

5. What is an underlying asset?

      **A.** A benchmark asset which is widely used by market participants to track fundamental changes in the economy.

      **B.** An asset that is less profitable than another asset.

      **C.** An asset whose value determines that value of another, derivative, asset.

      **D.** An asset that provides an ownership interest in a corporation.

6. If a hedge fund wishes to take an ownership position in a corporation, what kind of asset should it purchase?

      **A.** Common Stock

      **B.** Interest Rate Swap

      **C.** Commodity Swap

      **D.** Real Assets

7. What kind of position does the owner of a put option have in the underlying asset?

      **A.** Long position

      **B.** Flat position

      **C.** Short position

      **D.** Insufficient information is provided to answer the question.

8. A bond is an example of what type of security?

      **A.** Real Asset

      **B.** Financial Asset

      **C.** Derivative

      **D.** Insufficient information is provided to answer the question.

9. What is a liquid market?

      **A.** A physical commodity market where crude oil is traded.

      **B.** A market where there are a large number of buyers and sellers willing to transact.

      **C.** An inter-bank market for transacting interest rate swaps.

      **D.** A derivatives market where traders can buy both put and call options.

10. What is an example of a primary market for financial assets?

      **A.** Brokers

      **B.** Inter-bank trading desks

      **C.** Stock Exchanges

      **D.** A market where new assets are issued to investors

## CHAPTER 3

# Financial Mathematics

**R**isk managers and traders use mathematics to concisely describe trading strategies and the risks involved with trading. This notation can be overwhelming at points. Learning to read financial notation is much like learning a foreign language. The complexity of learning the language of finance is compounded by the fact that financial mathematics incorporates terminology from many branches of mathematics including algebra, probability, statistics, and calculus. This chapter provides a brief survey of these disciplines and their associated terminology.

## OVERVIEW

Since the late 1970s, trading has become heavily dependent upon mathematics to describe and analyze investment opportunities. To meet this need, hedge funds and other financial firms have heavily recruited mathematicians, engineers, and scientists for trading positions. These transplanted employees continued to advance the mathematics used by the financial industry. This has helped propel the hedge fund industry into the twenty-first century. Unfortunately, this trend has also brought an extensive amount of financial jargon into trading. Learning to read financial notation is much like learning a foreign language.

This section introduces mathematical concepts and terminology used by traders and risk managers. Financial mathematics uses terminology pulled from many financial disciplines. Some of the branches of mathematics that contribute terminology to trading and risk management are:

- **Algebra.** Algebra is a branch of mathematics that substitutes symbols like English or Greek letters for unknown or changing numbers. Financial mathematics makes heavy use of these symbols, called variables, to model complex problems and present relationships between variables (functions).

- **Probability.** Probability is the mathematical study of how likely or un-likely events are to occur. Many of the concepts used in finance (like the possible price of an asset in the future) are uncertain and need to be described in probabilistic terms.
- **Statistics.** Statistics is a branch of mathematics concerned with the col-lection and analysis of data. Statistics is often used to describe what will happen on the average and the variation that could be expected around that average result.
- **Calculus.** Calculus is the mathematical study of how functions are af-fected by small changes in inputs. Finance uses calculus to predict how much one quantity (like the value of an asset) might change when an-other quantity (like the value of another asset) changes.

## VARIABLES AND FUNCTIONS

In finance, variables are often used to describe financial concepts like prices, volatility, and correlation. A variable is a symbol used to stand for an unknown or changing number. There are several types of variables. For example, a vari-able that depends on some other variable is called a *dependent variable*. A variable that exists on its own is an *independent variable*. A common type of relationship between variables used in finance is called a *function*. A function is a special type of dependent variable that has a single output value for each combination of input values. (See Equation 3.1, An Example of a Function.)

A function is a dependent variable that calculates a unique result based on the values of several independent variables. For example,

$$f(x) = x^2 + 6 \qquad\qquad (3.1)$$

The dependent variable, abbreviated $f(x)$, depends on the value of the dependent variable x. There will be only one value of $f(x)$ for each value of x. A function can also be abbreviated by a letter or symbol that is equivalent to $f(x)$. For example, the variable y or the symbol $\theta$ might be used instead of $f(x)$:

$$y = x^2 + 6$$

or

$$\theta = x^2 + 6$$

The abbreviation for a function, like $f(x)$, indicates that the function, ab-breviated f in this example, depends on the value of an independent variable x. Some functions represent mathematical relationships. Other functions

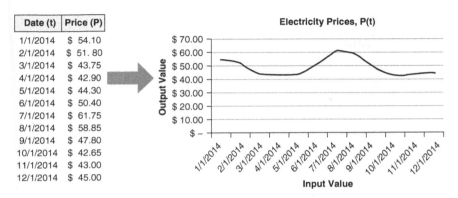

| Date (t) | Price (P) |
|----------|-----------|
| 1/1/2014 | $ 54.10 |
| 2/1/2014 | $ 51. 80 |
| 3/1/2014 | $ 43.75 |
| 4/1/2014 | $ 42.90 |
| 5/1/2014 | $ 44.30 |
| 6/1/2014 | $ 50.40 |
| 7/1/2014 | $ 61.75 |
| 8/1/2014 | $ 58.85 |
| 9/1/2014 | $ 47.80 |
| 10/1/2014 | $ 42.65 |
| 11/1/2014 | $ 43.00 |
| 12/1/2014 | $ 45.00 |

**FIGURE 3.1**    Prices as a Function

indicate a sequence of points located over uniformly spaced intervals of time (a *time series*). With a time series, the input variable might be time and the output value a price that existed at that point in time. For example, the function P(t) might indicate a price P associated with a specific point in time t. (See Figure 3.1, Prices as a Function.)

There are several ways to make mathematical notation more concise. First, it is possible to remove the parentheses containing the independent variables from the names of dependent variables. In this way, a price at time t might be represented as either "P(t)" or just "P." Second, subscripts may be appended to any variable name to indicate additional information about the variable. There is no convention for this. For example, if there were two assets being examined, $P_1(t)$ might refer to the price of the first asset and $P_2(t)$ the price of the second asset. This can be combined with removing parenthesis, or words can be used in addition to numerical subscripts. For example $P_{stock}$ and $P_{bond}$ might be used to represent the price of a stock and the price of a bond.

An important attribute of a function is that the data forms a continuous series and the dependent series has a single value for every independent variable. In the case of a time series, there will be one (and only one) price at each specific moment in time t.

## RANDOM NUMBERS

Another use of variables is to represent a random quantity. Randomness, in finance, is typically described using notation from probability. Probability is the branch of mathematics that studies how likely or unlikely something is to occur. The probability that an event will occur is represented as a value

## KEY CONCEPT: STOCHASTIC PROCESSES

Stochastic is a term that describes a type of random process that evolves over time. In a stochastic process, prices might be modeled as a series whose next value depends on the current value plus a random component. This is slightly different than a completely random process (like the series of numbers obtained by rolling a pair of dice).

between a 0 percent chance of occurrence (something will not occur) and a 100 percent chance of occurrence (something will definitely occur).

In finance, the term *stochastic* is often used as a synonym for random. Stochastic describes a type of random sequence that evolves over time. In this type of sequence, the value of the next item in the sequence depends on the value of the previous item plus or minus a random value. In finance, stochastic processes are particularly important. This is because prices are often modeled as stochastic processes, and prices are a fundamental input into trading decisions.

Common examples of random numbers are the results of throwing dice or flipping a coin. Each roll of the dice or flip of a coin generates a *realization* of a defined process. The probability of the coin landing on either a head or a tail is 50 percent and the probability of any single number on a regular, six-sided die is 1/6 (assuming a fair dice roll and fair coin flip). However, in a die roll, only one of the numbers will actually be observed.

Both a coin flip and a die roll are examples of *discrete* random numbers, since there are a limited number of outcomes associated with each *realization*. Random numbers are described as *continuous* if there are an infinite number of possible values. This does not mean that any value is possible. With a continuous distribution, the range of values might still be bounded. For example, if a school measured the height of children in a particular class, there might be a range of observations clustered around a typical height. No two heights would be exactly the same—one child might be 48.012 inches tall, while another is 47.991 inches tall. However, there would be no possibility of a 20-foot-tall second grader. (See Figure 3.2, Discrete and Continuous Distributions.)

The most common way to describe a continuous distribution is with a *probability density function,* abbreviated *PDF.* A probability density function describes the relative likelihood that a realization will result in a particular number. It is similar to a bar chart or similar histogram that has a very large number of columns. In this type of function, the possible results will be indicated on the x-axis and the likelihood that the result will be observed is located on the y-axis. The area between two points (represented as

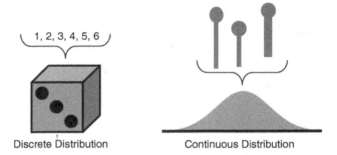

Discrete Distribution          Continuous Distribution

**FIGURE 3.2** Discrete and Continuous Distributions

a percentage of the total area underneath the curve) indicates how likely it is that a realization will end up between those two points. (See Figure 3.3, Probability Density Function.)

A *cumulative distribution function*, abbreviated *CDF*, is an alternative way of presenting the same data. A cumulative density function gives information about the percentage of samples that have values equal to or less than a particular value. The y-axis goes between 0 and 100 percent. With a cumulative density function, subtracting the y-axis values between two points will give the percentage of samples in that area. Although they are not quite as intuitive, being easier to use makes cumulative distributions a popular choice for spreadsheet-based analysis. (See Figure 3.4, Cumulative Density Function.)

Traders will use these probability density functions and cumulative density functions for a variety of applications. A common use for these functions

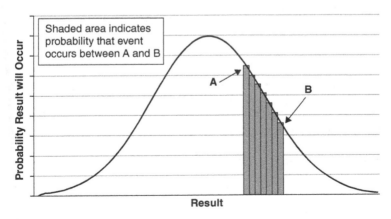

**FIGURE 3.3** Probability Density Function

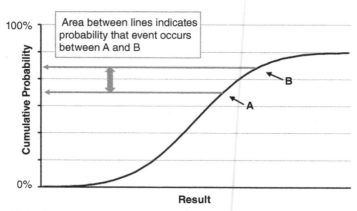

**FIGURE 3.4**   Cumulative Density Function

is to represent the potential profits or losses in a trading strategy. Many common distributions are pre-defined on spreadsheets. Traders and risk managers will need to be able to convert between PDF and CDF representations, depending on which calculation they need to perform.

## STATISTICS

Statistics are pieces of information that concisely describe random numbers or other types of data. The characteristics of probability distributions are often described using statistics. For example, someone might find it useful to describe the height of male fifth graders in a school district by the height of the typical student or by describing the height of the shortest and tallest students. This gives users of the data a simple description of a complex data set and removes excess detail.

Summarizing a probability distribution with a couple of data points makes analysis easier. For example, it is much easier to identify a trend associated with average height of students over a 20-year period. However, summarizing the data also removes details about individual data points. This requires a judgment as to which data is important and which data can be safely ignored.

There are three main goals of statistical analysis:

- **Summarizing** key items in a distribution or a population
- Establishing how much **confidence** one should have in that summary
- Identifying **relationships** between separate data series

To be analyzed, data typically has to be summarized in some manner. In addition to making the quantity of data more manageable, summarization allows different quantities (like measurements from two different years) to be compared to one another. The technique of consolidating data into a couple of key points is called *data reduction*. Some common statistics describe commonly occurring results (called a *central tendency*) or the amount that the results are dispersed around the central point.

To reduce the chance that an incorrect summary is made, a second focus in statistics is to estimate the accuracy of calculations. This is typically represented as a *margin of error*, or *confidence interval*, associated with each statistic. For example, the average price of new cars might be $35,000 +/- $15,000. This describes both the average cost of a car and a commonly observed band around the central point. To be completely accurate, the statistic would give the confidence observations of the estimate. This would look something like "*95* percent of car prices are within +/- $15,000 of the mean."

Finally, statistics are used to describe the similarity and difference between two distributions. This is done by examining pairs of variables to see if they vary in a similar manner. There needs to be some relationship between the two variables for this to work. For example, if the height and weight of a population is measured, the heights will form one distribution and the weights a second distribution. Each person in the population will have a height and a weight. In this case, the height and weight associated with each person forms a pair.

Statistics has contributed a wide variety of abbreviations to the financial markets. (See Equation 3.2, Common Mathematical Abbreviations.)

## Common Mathematical Abbreviations

$x, \delta, y$    **Variables**. Letters and Greek characters are commonly used to represent variables. In finance, variables commonly represent time series

$x_n$    **Subscripted Variables**. When examining a time series, a subscript commonly indicates an element of a time series. For example, $x_n$ indicates the nth member of a time series

$\bar{x}$    **Average**. A bar over a letter indicates the average of a series of   (3.2) numbers. The variable (x in this case) indicates which series

$\sum_{i=1}^{100} x_i$    **Sum**. The capital Greek letter Sigma is used to represent a sum. In this example, this is a sum of the first 100 elements of the x series. The value below the Sigma is the starting point of the sum (i = 1) and the value above the Sigma indicates the ending point of the series (100)

## MEAN, MEDIAN, AND MODE

*Mean, median,* and *mode* are statistics that describe the most commonly occurring part of a probability distribution. In other words, they describe a typical result that might be obtained by sampling a large population. These statistics describe the *central tendency* of the distribution.

The **mode** of a distribution is a statistic that identifies which value occurs most often. For example, a distribution might contain the names {Tom, Bill, John, Heather, Bill, Frank, and Sally}. The name that occurs most frequently is Bill. As a result, the name Bill is the *mode* of the distribution. In practice, *mode* is difficult to calculate and not used very often. Calculating the mode of a distribution requires searching the entire distribution for the value that comes up most frequently. Additionally, there can be more than one *mode* for a distribution. For example, on six-sided dice, the numbers 1 to 6 are equally likely to occur. As a result, all of the numbers are *modes.*

The **median** of a distribution is a statistic that summarizes the middle element in the distribution. It is the value that separates the greatest half of samples from the least half. For examples, in a distribution of 7 numbers, {1, 2, 3, 4, 5, 6, 7}, the middle of the distribution is 4. There are three numbers less than 4 and three numbers greater. In the case of an even number of samples, the mid-point between the two middle numbers is used as the median. Like the mode of a series, the median of a large series can be difficult to calculate—it requires sorting the series. This is easy with a small set of numbers, but sorting a very large quantity of numbers can take a while even with a very fast computer.

The **mean** (arithmetic mean) is the final and most important measure of central tendency. The mean is a statistic that describes the average value. The biggest benefit of the *arithmetic mean* is that sorting the series is not required. It can be calculated by adding up each value and dividing by the number of values. (See Equation 3.3, Arithmetic Mean.)

$$\bar{x} = \frac{1}{n} \sum_{i=1}^{n} x_i \tag{3.3}$$

where

$\bar{x}$     **Mean of x.** The line over x indicates that it is the average

n     **Number of items.** The number of items in the data series

$\sum_{i=1}^{n} x_i$     **Sum.** The capital Greek letter Sigma indicates a summation. In this case, it is the sum of the elements in the series named "x"

**Centrally Distributed**

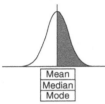

| Mean |
|---|
| Median |
| Mode |

**Bi-Modally Distributed**

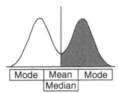

| Mode | Mean | Mode |
|---|---|---|
| | Median | |

**Skewed**

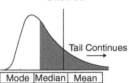

Tail Continues →

| Mode | Median | Mean |
|---|---|---|

When a distribution is distributed around a central point, the mean, median, and mode will be similar numbers.

In a bi-model distribution, the most common values are not located in the middle of the distribution. In this case, the mode(s) may be very different than the mean or median.

In a skewed distribution, the mean, median, and mode are arranged in a line. The mean is particularly impacted by outlying values on one side of the distribution.

**FIGURE 3.5** Mean, Median, and Mode

The effectiveness of each of these statistics at describing a typical member of a distribution varies substantially between distributions. In some cases, the mean, median, and mode of a series are all very close to one another. However, in other cases, they can differ greatly from one another. When a distribution is symmetrically clustered around a central value, all three measures will generally be close to one another. However, when distributions are not clustered around a single value (a bi-modal distribution) or skewed to one side, the differences between these statistics are more pronounced. (See Figure 3.5, Mean, Median, and Mode.)

## VARIANCE AND VOLATILITY

In addition to finding the central tendency of a distribution, financial mathematics often uses statistics to describe the dispersion of values within a distribution. It is possible to have two sets of data with the same average behavior that are very different from one another. For example, even though two bell curves have the same mean, median, and mode, they can be substantially different than one another. (See Figure 3.6, Dispersion.) In this example, one distribution has a much wider range of results than the other distribution.

The two statistics most commonly used to measure dispersion are *variance* and *standard deviation*. Both of these statistics are calculated by examining the difference between each sample and the mean of the distribution. Standard deviation is typically abbreviated with the lower case Greek letter sigma ($\sigma$). *Volatility* is a synonym for standard deviation. Variance is commonly abbreviated as sigma squared ($\sigma^2$). (See Equation 3.4, Variance and Standard Deviation.)

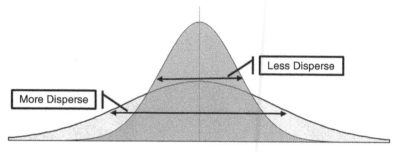

**FIGURE 3.6** Dispersion

**Variance and Standard Deviation**

$$\text{Variance} = \sigma^2 = \frac{\sum (x_i - \bar{x})^2}{n}$$

$$\text{Standard deviation} = \sigma = \sqrt{\text{Variance}} = \sqrt{\frac{\sum (x_i - x)^2}{n}}$$

(3.4)

Where

$\sigma^2$    **Variance.** The variance is the mean square error (MSE) of the series. It is the mean of the difference between each observation and the average observation

$\sigma$    **Standard Deviation.** Standard deviation is the square root of variance

n    **Number of items.** The number of items in the data series

In finance, variance and volatility are often used to describe the uncertainty associated with profits and losses that might occur in the future. Even though the future is unknown, certain events are more likely than others. Being able to estimate the size of potential trading losses is an important factor to determining the size of a trading strategy. For example, if a trader expects that a trading strategy has a high probability of loss large enough to drive the trader into bankruptcy, either the strategy will need to be avoided or reduced in size.

## SKEW AND KURTOSIS

Two other statistics that are commonly used to describe probability distributions are *skew* and *kurtosis*. These are generally less important than measures of central tendency (like the average value) and uncertainty (like

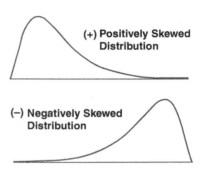

**Skew.** Skew measures the *asymmetry* of the distribution.
- A normal distribution has zero skew.
- Prices and many other financial distributions are often skewed to the right. For example, prices can go infinitely high but usually can go no lower than zero.

**(+) Positively Skewed Distribution**

**(−) Negatively Skewed Distribution**

**FIGURE 3.7**   Skew

volatility). However, these are in the set of terms expected to be known by traders and risk managers.

The skew of a distribution describes its asymmetry. If a series has zero skew, it will be symmetrically distributed around its central point. If it is skewed right (a *positive skew*), the values on the right of the distribution will extend further than the values on the left. Similarly, if a distribution is skewed left (a *negative skew*), the left tail will be longer than the right.

In finance, skewed distributions are often used to describe prices. Prices generally will not be negative. However, they can rise arbitrarily high. As a result, when the distribution of prices in the future is graphed, the graph will be skewed to the right. (See Figure 3.7, Skew.)

Kurtosis is a measure of whether the data set is peaked or flat. A data set with a high kurtosis (a *leptokurtic* distribution) will have a distinct peak near the mean, will decline rapidly, and have wide tails. A data set with a low kurtosis (a *platykurtic* distribution) will have a flattened peak.

In finance, kurtosis is used to examine how likely a distribution is to have results far from the average result. Finance tends to approximate a variety of distributions with a normal distribution (which will be described later in the chapter). This is a reasonable approximation for many purposes. However, a major problem with using a normal distribution is that extreme results are often more commonly observed compared to what is predicted using a normal distribution.

Traders primarily need to know how to interpret the kurtosis calculation. The most common calculation involving kurtosis is to compare the kurtosis of an observed data series to the kurtosis of a normal distribution. This has led to the term *excess kurtosis*. Excess kurtosis is the kurtosis of the observed series minus the kurtosis of a normal distribution. A normal distribution has a kurtosis of three. (See Figure 3.8, Kurtosis.)

**Kurtosis.** Kurtosis measures the *peakedness* of the distribution.

- A normal Distribution has kurtosis of 3.
- *Excess kurtosis* is the kurtosis of a series minus the kurtosis of a normal distribution. (Excess kurtosis = kurtosis-3).
- Higher kurtosis indicates a more sharply peaked distribution.
- Kurtosis affects the relative frequency of extreme events relative to events near the center of the distribution.

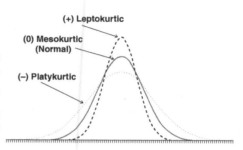

**FIGURE 3.8**    Kurtosis

# RANDOM WALKS (STOCHASTIC PROCESSES)

A random walk is a special type of random process that describes the path taken by a series of random steps. In finance, random walk processes are commonly used to model how prices or interest rates might move in the future. In finance, most models are usually limited to a single dimension (like an interest rate rising and falling) rather than a more general case (like a model of a gas particle, which can move in three dimensions).

Mathematically, a random process is usually described as the current value being equal to the previous value plus some random change in value. The change in value is commonly represented by the capital Greek letter Delta, $\Delta$. (See Equation 3.5, A Simple Random Process.)

Simulating price of some asset, abbreviated P:

$$P_t = P_{t-1} + \Delta P \tag{3.5}$$

where

$P_t$    **Price at time t.** The current value or current price

$P_{t-1}$    **Price at time t-1.** The previous value or previous price

$\Delta P$    **Change in Price.** This is commonly called "Delta P". Typically the change in price is described as a random variable like a coin flip (+/– a fixed value) or a statistical distribution (like a normal distribution)

An alternate way of looking at a random series is that the current value is the sum of all of the changes in value. (See Equation 3.6, A Simple Random Process, continued.)

Simulating price of some asset, abbreviated P, but with a change in notation:

$$P_n = \sum_{t=1}^{n} \Delta P_t \qquad (3.6)$$

where

| | |
|---|---|
| $P_n$ | Price at time n |
| $\Delta P_t$ | The price change between time t and time t − 1 |
| $\sum_{t=1}^{n} \Delta P_t$ | The sum of price changes between time t =1 (indicated below the sigma) to time n (indicated above the sigma) |

A common type of random process is called *Brownian motion*. Brownian motion may also be called the *Wiener process*. In this process, the percent change in price (ΔP) is a random number described by a normal distribution. The end result of this process is equal to the sum of normally distributed movements.

Brownian motion is commonly used to model how something might disperse over time. In finance, it is most commonly used to model price movements. At the start of the process, prices will be close to the starting point (called the *initial condition*). However, as time passes, a greater range of possible values becomes possible. The usual formulation is that percent changes in price are normally distributed. As a result, as prices start to fall, the price movements get smaller and will never fall below zero. (See Figure 3.9, Dispersion in a Random Series.)

There are two major factors that make Wiener processes important to financial mathematics. First, the dispersion of expected results accumulates in a manner that is easy to calculate mathematically. In this type of process, the variance accumulates linearly with time. As a result, volatility (the square root of variance) accumulates with the square root of time. The second factor is that, for many assets, this type of dispersion process is a reasonably good model for how prices actually change over time. (See Equation 3.7, Dispersion of a Wiener Process.)

For a Weiner process that follows N(0, σ):

$$\textit{Variance at time } T = \sigma^2 T$$
$$\textit{Standard Deviation at time } T = \sigma\sqrt{T} \qquad (3.7)$$

where

| | |
|---|---|
| N(0,σ) | **Normal Distribution.** A normal distribution with mean = 0 and volatility = σ |
| T | **Time.** The time that has passed |

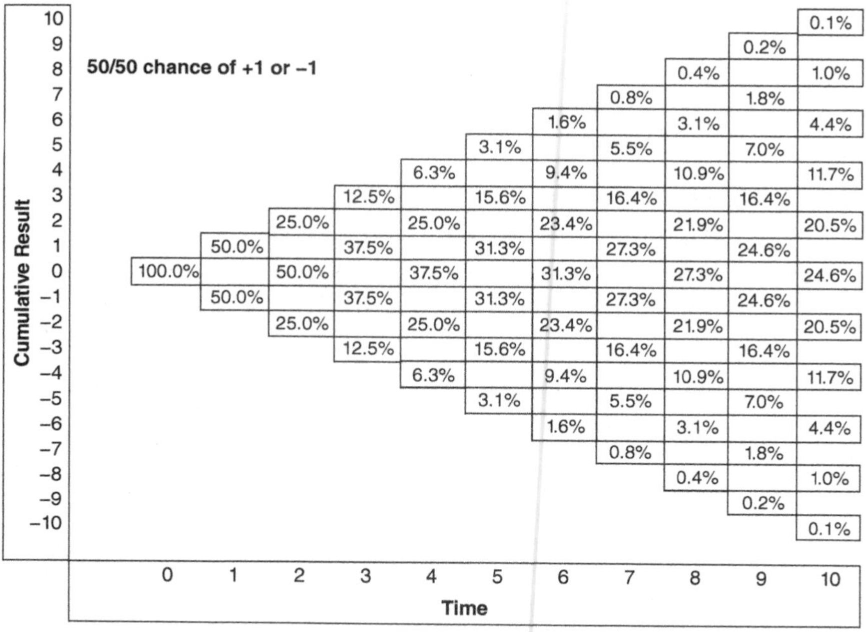

**50/50 chance of +1 or −1**

| Cumulative Result | 0 | 1 | 2 | 3 | 4 | 5 | 6 | 7 | 8 | 9 | 10 |
|---|---|---|---|---|---|---|---|---|---|---|---|
| 10 | | | | | | | | | | | 0.1% |
| 9 | | | | | | | | | | 0.2% | |
| 8 | | | | | | | | | 0.4% | | 1.0% |
| 7 | | | | | | | | 0.8% | | 1.8% | |
| 6 | | | | | | | 1.6% | | 3.1% | | 4.4% |
| 5 | | | | | | 3.1% | | 5.5% | | 7.0% | |
| 4 | | | | | 6.3% | | 9.4% | | 10.9% | | 11.7% |
| 3 | | | | 12.5% | | 15.6% | | 16.4% | | 16.4% | |
| 2 | | | 25.0% | | 25.0% | | 23.4% | | 21.9% | | 20.5% |
| 1 | | 50.0% | | 37.5% | | 31.3% | | 27.3% | | 24.6% | |
| 0 | 100.0% | | 50.0% | | 37.5% | | 31.3% | | 27.3% | | 24.6% |
| −1 | | 50.0% | | 37.5% | | 31.3% | | 27.3% | | 24.6% | |
| −2 | | | 25.0% | | 25.0% | | 23.4% | | 21.9% | | 20.5% |
| −3 | | | | 12.5% | | 15.6% | | 16.4% | | 16.4% | |
| −4 | | | | | 6.3% | | 9.4% | | 10.9% | | 11.7% |
| −5 | | | | | | 3.1% | | 5.5% | | 7.0% | |
| −6 | | | | | | | 1.6% | | 3.1% | | 4.4% |
| −7 | | | | | | | | 0.8% | | 1.8% | |
| −8 | | | | | | | | | 0.4% | | 1.0% |
| −9 | | | | | | | | | | 0.2% | |
| −10 | | | | | | | | | | | 0.1% |

Time

**FIGURE 3.9** Dispersion in a Random Series

For financial mathematics, the Wiener process is often generalized to include a constant drift term that pushes prices upward. The constant drift term is due to risk-free inflation (and described later in the chapter in the "time value of money" discussion). Continuous time versions of this process are called *Generalized Wiener Process* or the *Ito Process*. (See Equation 3.8, A Stochastic Process.)

A stochastic process with discrete time steps can be described as:

$$\frac{\Delta S_t}{S_t} = \mu \Delta t + \sigma \Delta W_t$$

or

$$\Delta S_t = \mu S_t \Delta t + \sigma S_t \Delta W_t$$

(3.8)

where

$\Delta S_t$      **Change in Price.** The change in price that will occur

$S_t$      **Price.** The price of an asset at time t

| μ | **Drift.** The drift term that pushes prices upwards. Commonly, this is a constant, but can be generalized to vary over time |
|---|---|
| Δt | **Change in Time.** Typically, finance uses convention that $\Delta t = 1.0$ is a one year passage of time. As a result, drift and volatility are represented as annualized numbers |
| σ | **Volatility.** The annualized volatility that is used to scale the change in the Wiener Process ($\Delta W_t$) to the asset being modeled |
| $\Delta W_t$ | **Change in the Wiener process.** A draw from a normal distribution scaled to the appropriate time step $$\Delta W_t = N(0,1)\sqrt{\Delta t}$$ |
| $N(0,1)$ | **Normal Distribution.** A draw from a normal distribution with mean = 0 and standard deviation = 1 |

These processes are historically significant because option pricing formulas are based on stochastic mathematics. As a result, a large portion of modern finance is based on these concepts. However, since most option formulas can be looked up in a book, these processes are not commonly used for either risk management or trading outside of Monte-Carlo simulation (which is discussed in Chapter 4).

## MEAN REVERSION

Mean reversion is the theory that prices will return to a long-run average price. For example, a model of crude oil prices might assume that prices revert to the cost of drilling for oil. Another common mean-reversion assumption comes from the hedge fund industry. In the hedge fund industry, a common strategy is based on the assumption that the price of a stock will not continually outperform its peer group—that economic conditions and overall outlook for the sector will be more important than any company-specific advantages.

Mathematically, the most common model of mean reversion is that the further a price moves from its long-term equilibrium price (the mean price) the more it gets pulled back to the long-run average. With continuous time steps, this is called the *Ornstein–Uhlenbeck* process. In mathematical terms, the stock price formula is modified by altering the drift term to incorporate a term that pulls prices back to the mean. (See Equation 3.9, A Mean-Reverting Process.)

A mean reverting process in discrete time steps can be described as:

$$\Delta S_t = \lambda(\mu - S_t)\Delta t + \sigma S_t \Delta W_t \tag{3.9}$$

where

$\Delta S_t$  **Change in Price.** The change in the price of the asset

$S_t$  **Price.** The price of an asset at time t

$\lambda$  **Reversion Speed.** Higher values for $\lambda$ will cause the series to revert to the mean more quickly

$\mu$  **Long Term Mean/Equilibrium Price.** The equilibrium price to which the series will eventually return. Commonly, this is a constant, but can be generalized to vary over time

$\Delta t$  **Change in Time.** Typically, finance uses convention that $\Delta t$ = 1.0 is a one year passage of time. As a result, drift and volatility are represented as annualized numbers

$\sigma$  **Volatility.** The annualized volatility that is used to scale the change in the Wiener Process ($\Delta W_t$) to the asset being modeled

$\Delta W_t$  **Change in the Wiener process.** A draw from a normal distribution scaled to the appropriate time step

$$\Delta W_t = N(0,1)\sqrt{\Delta t}$$

$N(0,1)$  **Normal Distribution.** A draw from a normal distribution with mean = 0 and standard deviation = 1

Like other stochastic processes, the most common use of mean reversion models is in Monte-Carlo computer simulations. Typically, mean reversion is added into a stochastic process so that simulations better match historically observed data.

## CORRELATION

Statistics is commonly used to describe the expected relationship between two assets. If two securities are correlated, the values are likely to change in the same way. For example, the stock price of an oil company might be correlated with crude oil. If crude oil prices rise, then the stock price of the oil company should also be likely to rise. When determining if two prices are correlated, it is necessary to compare changes in price rather than prices.

The most common way to measure the relationship between two assets is to calculate the *correlation coefficient* of their price changes. The correlation coefficient is a number between −1 and +1 that indicates the strength of

---

## KEY CONCEPT: CORRELATION

In the financial markets, the statement that "two assets are correlated" means "the price changes in the two assets are correlated" rather than the "prices are correlated." This distinction is very important because it is changes in value that determine the risk, profit, and loss of investments.

---

the relationship between the two data series. (See Figure 3.10, Positive and Negative Correlation.)

Some features of correlation are:

- **Positive Correlation.** A correlation coefficient equal to +1 means that the two series have behaved identically over the testing period.
- **Negative Correlation.** A correlation coefficient of –1 indicates that the series have been inversely proportional during the testing period. In other words, when one price rises, the other price falls.
- **Zero Correlation.** A correlation coefficient of zero indicates no relationship between the two values

The calculation of the correlation coefficient, $\rho$, is mathematically defined. (See Equation 3.10, Correlation.)

**Positive Correlation**      **Negative Correlation**      **Zero (Low) Correlation**

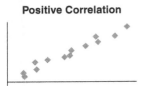 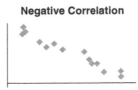 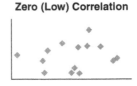

**FIGURE 3.10**   Positive and Negative Correlation

$$\rho = \frac{\sum^{(x-\bar{x})}(y-\bar{y})}{(n-1)\sigma_x\sigma_y} \quad\quad (3.10)$$

where

| | |
|---|---|
| x | **Data Set.** The first set of data |
| $\bar{x}$ | **Mean.** The average of the first data set |

$\sigma_x$           **Standard Deviation.** The standard deviation of the first data set

y            **Data Set.** The second set of data

$\bar{y}$            **Mean.** The average of the second data set

$\sigma_y$           **Standard Deviation.** The standard deviation of the second data set

n            **Number of samples.** The first and second data sets need the same number of values

Correlation is extensively used in risk management to examine the combined risk of multiple trading strategies and by trading desks to allocate capital between trading strategies. If two strategies are uncorrelated, there may be a benefit from investing in both (called *diversification*) that won't exist if they share the same risk profile.

## DIVERSIFICATION

Random numbers can often be combined to make them more predictable. This is the basis for the financial concept of *diversification*. In financial analysis, diversification is a way of reducing risk by making investments in more than one asset at a time. For example, the sum of two dice rolls (six-sided fair dice) is more predictable than a single roll. On a single roll, all numbers have an equal chance to appear. However, when two dice are rolled together and summed, the sum is more likely to be centrally distributed (seven) than an extreme event (like two or twelve).

The reason is that there are multiple combinations of events that can result in a seven. For example {1,6}, {2,5}, {3,4}, {4,3}, {5,2}, and {6,1} all sum up to seven. In other words, there are six opportunities to get a seven by rolling two dice. However, there is only one way, {1, 1}, to get an extreme event like a two.

The amount that diversification reduces uncertainty depends on the correlation between the random numbers. For example, if the first and second roll were always identical, there would be no diversification benefit. Investments work the same way—investing in non-correlated investments is likely to reduce risk more than investing in two very similar investments.

In a financial example, an investment manager might be deciding how to allocate money between two investments. The investment manager has two investments, and he needs to allocate a percentage of his capital to each asset. The assets might not have the same expected return, so the first step is to estimate the return of the combined investment. (See Equation 3.11, Expected Return from Combining Assets.)

The expected return from holding two assets is the return of each asset weighted by how much of the asset is in the portfolio.

$$\mu_{Portfolio} = w_1\mu_1 + w_2\mu_2 \tag{3.11}$$

where

$\mu_x$    **Expected Return.** The return expected from owning x. In this case, x represents an asset or a portfolio of assets

$w_x$    **Weight.** The weight of asset x. The sum of weights needs to equal 100%

The reason that it is important to look at expected returns is that diversification is often worthwhile even when returns are reduced. The expected variance of the portfolio is a more complicated calculation. The variance of the portfolio depends on asset weights, asset volatilities, and the correlation between assets. (See Equation 3.12, Portfolio Variance from Combining Assets.)

The variance of the portfolio (the square of the volatility) is a function of the asset weights, the asset volatilities, and the correlation between the assets.

$$\sigma^2_{Portfolio} = w_1^2\sigma_1^2 + w_2^2\sigma_2^2 + 2w_1w_x\rho\sigma_1\sigma_2 \tag{3.12}$$

where

$\sigma_x$    **Volatility.** The volatility of asset x

$w_x$    **Weight.** The weight of the asset x. The sum of weights needs to equal 100%

$\rho$    **Correlation.** The correlation between asset 1 and asset 2

The expected return and volatility of the resulting portfolio will depend on the weighting of the assets. As the weighting changes between assets, the risk/reward of the portfolio will also change. However, the path between the two assets won't be a straight line because of the non-linearity in the volatility calculation. (See Figure 3.11, Asset Allocation.)

On a trading desk, the temptation might be to assign all of the assets to the portfolio with the highest return. However, trading desks are typically limited by risk rather than capital. As a result, getting a better risk/reward relationship allows a trading desk to take on larger positions. In the Figure 3.11 example, both of the assets had an average return/volatility ratio of 2.0. By combining the assets, the return/volatility ratio could be improved to 2.3. To a trader that is limited by the amount of volatility rather than capital, this allows traders to improve their profits by 15 percent. (See Figure 3.12, Risk/Return.)

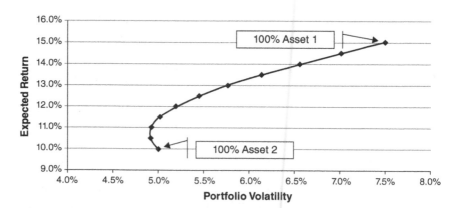

|  | Expected return ($\mu$) | Volatility ($\sigma$) | Correlation ($\rho$) |
|---|---|---|---|
| **Asset 1** | 15.0% | 7.5% | |
| **Asset 2** | 10.0% | 5.0% | 50% |

**FIGURE 3.11**    Asset Allocation

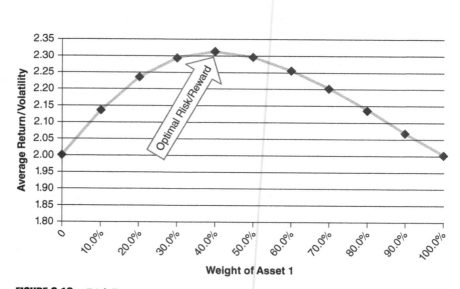

**FIGURE 3.12**    Risk/Return

## NORMAL DISTRIBUTIONS

In finance, the most important continuous probability distribution is called the *normal distribution*. This distribution is characterized by a bell-shaped curve that has the most weight in the center and that tapers off toward either end. Mathematically, the normal distribution is characterized by two factors—its mean, $\mu$, and its standard deviation, $\sigma$. (See Figure 3.13, Normal Distribution.)

The normal distribution is also called a *bell curve* or a *Gaussian distribution*. Mathematically, several features of the normal distribution are well known by most professional risk managers. For example, nearly all the values lie within three standard deviations of the mean. Approximately 68.3 percent of values are within one standard deviation of the mean, 95.5 percent are within two standard deviations, and 99.7 percent are within three standard deviations. Since standard deviation is commonly abbreviated by the Greek letter sigma, an observation (a random sample from a normal distribution) might be characterized by how far it is from the mean (a 1-sigma event, a 2-sigma event, etc.).

Some features of normal distributions that are commonly memorized by risk managers and traders:

- Approximately 68.3 percent of values are within one standard deviation of the mean
- Approximately 95.5 percent of values are within two standard deviations of the mean
- Approximately 99.7 percent of values are within three standard deviations of the mean

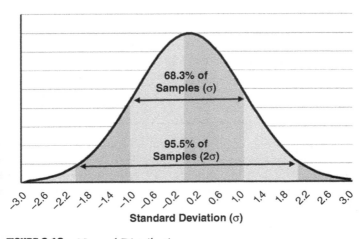

**FIGURE 3.13**   Normal Distribution

## LOG-NORMAL DISTRIBUTIONS

A second continuous probability distribution that is commonly encountered in financial markets is the *log-normal distribution*. A log-normal distribution is a continuous probability function of a random variable whose logarithm is normally distributed. Log-normal distributions are important to trading because they are commonly used as a simple model of prices. The intuition behind this model is that prices can go infinitely high but can't fall below zero. If percent returns are normally distributed (another common financial assumption), then prices are log-normally distributed. (See Figure 3.14, Log-Normal Distribution.)

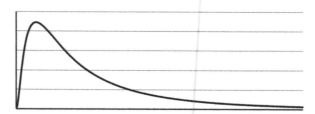

**FIGURE 3.14**   Log-Normal Distribution

## CALCULUS

Calculus is a branch of mathematics that studies how functions change. Calculus can solve a wide variety of problems. It is particularly useful for helping to price financial instruments, like options, whose value changes based on many underlying factors. Calculus provides a shorthand notation that makes describing risk factors much more concise. To communicate with traders and risk managers, it is necessary to learn the combined terminology.

There are two main mathematical operations in calculus—*derivatives* and *integrals*. These operations are the inverse of one another. Integration is the inverse of derivation.

---

📖 Note: In mathematics, the term *derivative* means something very different than it means in finance. In this section, the term derivative refers to the calculus meaning while the rest of the book uses derivative as a finance/ accounting term.

---

The two meanings of the term *derivative* are:

- **Derivative in calculus:** A derivative is a measure of how the output of a function will change due to some change in the input. Typically a "calculus derivative" will be described as a *first derivative, second derivative,* or *third derivative.*
- **Derivative in Finance:** In finance and accounting, a derivative is a financial instrument that derives its value from the value of some underlying asset.

## FUNCTIONS

Calculus will describe functions using notation like F(x) where F(x) is a function whose value depends on x. The choice of using *F* and *x* are arbitrary. Generally, an abbreviation that is easy to remember is used in place of *F* and *x*. For example, if a family tracked the location of their car on a trip, the location of the family car at a given point in time might be abbreviated L(t). By providing a point in time, t, the location of the car, L, could be determined.

## FIRST DERIVATIVE

A (calculus) derivative indicates how quickly a function is changing with respect to some other value. For example, on a car trip, velocity measures how quickly the location is changing at any point in time. In this case, velocity would be called the first derivative of location with respect to time.

There are two major types of calculus notation. One indicates an average over a period of time, and the other the values at a specific point in time. In the first case, the change in distance is divided by the change in time. This calculates the average change over that period (See Equation 3.13, First Derivative – Average Velocity.)

$$Average\,Velocity = \frac{\Delta L}{\Delta t} \quad \text{(Average velocity over a period of time)} \qquad (3.13)$$

where the capital Greek letter Delta, $\Delta$, means *change in*. For example, $\Delta X$ could be read either "Delta X" or "change in X." In this case, velocity is the change in location divided by the change in time. The resulting value, velocity, would be measured in units of distance divided by units of time (something like kilometers/hour, miles/hour, etc.).

Over the course of the hour, the velocity of the car may have changed many times. In addition to an average speed over some period, it is possible to describe the speed of the car at a specific point in time. To estimate the velocity of the car at a particular point in time, it is necessary to look at smaller time changes. Mathematicians might describe this as finding the value (in this case, abbreviated V for Velocity) for a very small change in time. This is called taking the derivative as $\Delta t$ goes to zero. Mathematically, a derivative at a specific point in time is abbreviated by lower case letter delta, $\delta$. (See Equation 3.14, First Derivative—Instantaneous Velocity.)

$$Velocity = \frac{\delta L}{\delta t} \quad \text{(Velocity at a point in time)} \qquad (3.14)$$

### Second Derivative

Just like a function can change over time, the first derivative of a function can change. For example, a vacationing family can also calculate how quickly their car is accelerating or decelerating given their data. Acceleration measures how quickly velocity is changing. In other words, it is the change in velocity over a given period of time or the derivative of velocity with respect to time. Since velocity is the derivative of location, acceleration is a derivative of a derivative, which is called a *second derivative*. (See Equation 3.15, Second Derivative – Acceleration.)

$$Acceleration = \frac{\delta Velocity}{\delta t} \quad \text{or} \quad \frac{\delta\left[\dfrac{\delta L}{\delta t}\right]}{\delta t} \quad \text{or} \quad \frac{\delta^2 L}{\delta t^2} \qquad (3.15)$$

In this example, acceleration is in units of velocity per unit of time. For instance, acceleration might be described "the car goes from zero to 60 miles per hour in 40 seconds." In other words, acceleration is measured in units of distance over units of time squared.

### Integration

Integration is a calculus technique that is the inverse of taking a derivative. In the example of a car trip, if the velocity of the car is known at every point in time, it would be possible to reconstruct how far the car traveled. In finance, integration is commonly used to analyze statistical distributions.

## CALCULUS INTEGRATION

One use of calculus is to analyze probability distributions. With a histogram (or other discrete distribution), it is possible to count how many observations are in each category. For example, if the height of 100 students was measured and placed in a histogram, it would be possible to calculate how many children had a height between 61 and 65 inches by counting how many were in each category. (See Figure 3.15, Calculating Discrete Probability.)

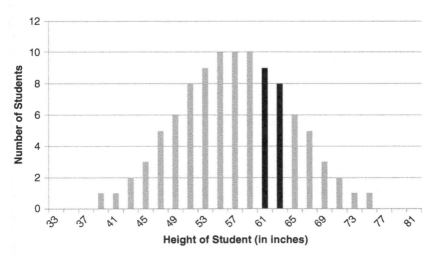

**FIGURE 3.15** Calculating Discrete Probability

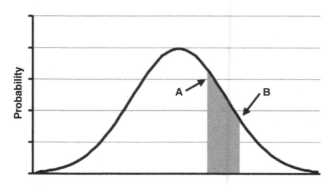

**FIGURE 3.16**   Calculating Continuous Probability

With a continuous probability distribution, a similar process is used. This process of finding the area under a continuous curve is called *integration*. The area underneath a frequency distribution represents the probability that a random draw from the distribution will be located in that part of the curve. For example, the shaded area between points A and B in the example can be used to determine the probability that a sample is drawn from that region. (See Figure 3.16, Calculating Continuous Probability.)

Mathematically, the notation for integration is similar to the notation used for calculating a sum. For continuous distributions (like a probability distribution), an integral operator (looks like a stretched-out S) will replace the summation operator ($\Sigma$). (See Equation 3.16, Discrete and Continuous Probability.)

Trying to find the number of samples in the range A to B.

$$Discrete\ Probability\ \sum_{x=A}^{B} S(x)$$
$$Continuous\ Probability = \int_{A}^{B} S(x)dx$$

(3.16)

where

A   **Lower Bound.** The lower bound of the range

B   **Upper Bound.** The upper bound of the range

$S(x)$   **Samples.** In discrete space, the percentage of samples in each category

dx   **Differential.** The axis (or variable) over which the integration will be performed

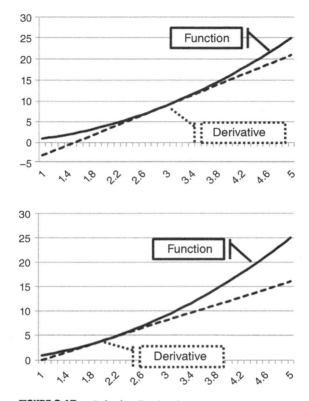

**FIGURE 3.17** Calculus Derivatives

## CALCULUS DERIVATIVES

In calculus, a *derivative* is a straight-line approximation of a curve at a specific point. More precisely, a derivative is the slope of the line tangent to a curve being analyzed at that point. (See Figure 3.17, Calculus Derivatives.) This is a very flexible analysis because it can be applied to almost any mathematical relationship. For example, if a mathematical relationship of the value of a bond and interest rates can be created, a derivative will make it possible to estimate how much the price of the bond would change for a given move in interest rates.

The process of taking a derivative is called *differentiation*. Differentiation calculates the rate at which a dependent variable, like a function or the value of a financial instrument, changes with respect to an independent variable like a price. The rate of change is called the derivative of the function

## KEY CONCEPT: MATHEMATICAL DERIVATIVE

A mathematical derivative is a linear approximation of a curve. The notation used to indicate a derivative looks like dy/dx (pronounced "dy over dx"). If the curve (a dependent variable or function) is named *y* and the independent variable is named *x*, then:

- *dy/dx* is the derivative of *y* with respect to *x*
- *dy* is an infinitesimally small change in *y*
- *dx* is an infinitesimally small change in *x*

To avoid confusion, the standard convention in mathematical finance is never to use the letter d as a variable name.

with respect to the input. If the function is called *y* and the independent variable *x*, it would be called the "derivative of y with respect to x."

In a series with discrete time steps, the slope of the line would be represented as the formula: slope = $\Delta y/\Delta x$. In other words, the slope at a specific point could be estimated by examining how much the dependent (y) value changes with a change in the independent (x) value. With a continuous line, the terminology changes a bit. Instead of the slope being $\Delta y/\Delta x$, the rate of change is described as dy/dx.

It is possible to take the derivatives of a derivative. This is called a *second derivative* and the rate of change is abbreviated $d^2y/dx^2$. Taking a derivative of the second derivative is called the *third derivative*, and so on. Finding derivatives of a function allows an approximate answer for the function to be calculated very easily. (See Equation 3.17, Calculus Abbreviations.)

There are several different types of notation used to indicate a mathematical derivative.

| Derivative | Abbreviation | Alternate Abbreviation | |
|---|---|---|---|
| Function | $f(x)$ | $f$ | |
| First Derivative | $f'(x)$ | $\dfrac{df}{dx}$ | (3.17) |
| Second Derivative | $f''(x)$ | $\dfrac{d^2f}{dx^2}$ | |
| Third Derivative | $f^{(3)}(x)$ | $\dfrac{d^3f}{dx^3}$ | |

## KEY CONCEPT: MATHEMATICAL AND FINANCIAL DERIVATIVES

The accounting term *derivative* refers to an asset which derives its value from another asset. The calculus term *derivative* refers to the tangent line to a function at a certain point. These are completely different concepts.

- **Accounting Derivative.** An accounting derivative is a type of financial contract whose value depends on an underlying asset.
- **Calculus Derivative.** A mathematical derivative is a linear approximation of a function at a particular point on the function.

## CALCULUS TAYLOR SERIES

When applied to financial mathematics, the process of calculating the value of a function can become very complex. However, if the derivatives of a function can be determined, an approximation of the function can be calculated. This process of making a numerical approximation of the function is called a Taylor Series Expansion. This is used to simplify a variety of complex calculations. (See Equation 3.18, Taylor Series Expansion.)

Solving for a f(x + Δx) if f(x) and the derivatives of f(x) are known:

$$f(x+\Delta x) = f(x) + f'(x)\Delta x + \frac{1}{2}f''(x)(\Delta x)^2 + \dots + \frac{1}{n!}f^{(n)}(x)(\Delta x)^n \qquad (3.18)$$

or in alternate notation ignoring third order and higher terms:

$$df = \frac{df}{dx}\Delta x + \frac{1}{2}\frac{d^2f}{dx^2}(\Delta x)^2$$

where

| | |
|---|---|
| $df$ | **Change in value of function.** That function will change in value when the variables in the function are changed: df = f(x + Δx) − f(x) |
| $\Delta x$ | **Change in Input.** The amount that the independent variable changes |
| $\frac{df}{dx}$ or $f'(x)$ | **First Derivative.** This is a number (the slope of a line) that had been previously calculated |
| $\frac{d^2f}{dx^2}$ or $f''(x)$ | **Second Derivative.** This is a number (the slope of a line) that had been previously calculated |

The number of factors in each Taylor expansion can vary. The approximation gets more accurate with more factors. However, this improved accuracy makes the formula more complicated to solve. As a result, using a Taylor Series to approximate a function value involves a trade-off between ease of calculation and accuracy. Taylor expansion can also be applied to solving functions that depend on more than one variable. If the independent variables are not functions of one another, different expansions can be added together. (See Equation 3.19, Taylor Expansion with Multiple Variables.)

For a function with multiple variables like $f(S, r, \sigma, \tau)$:

$$df = \frac{df}{dS}\Delta S + \frac{1}{2}\frac{d^2 f}{dS^2}(\Delta S)^2 + \frac{dr}{dS}\Delta r + \frac{d\sigma}{dS}\Delta\sigma + \frac{d\tau}{dS}\Delta\tau \qquad (3.19)$$

assuming that both the first and second derivatives (a second-order expansion) are needed for one factor (S) and a single order expansion is needed for other variables ($r, \sigma, \tau$)

The reason that a Taylor Series expansion on non-correlated variables is fairly simple is that the cross-derivatives can be ignored. The cross derivatives are much smaller than the first- and second-order terms. In many cases, the second-order terms can also be ignored. However, in a general case, this isn't always true. For example, if the variables are highly correlated, then it is necessary to consider the second-order and cross-relationship factors. For example, models of stochastic price processes commonly need additional terms to be considered. (See Equation 3.20, Generalized Taylor Series on Two Factors.)

Finding $f(x + \Delta x, y + \Delta y)$ for a function $f(x, y)$:

$$df = \frac{df}{dx}\Delta x + \frac{df}{dy}\Delta y + \frac{1}{2}\left[\frac{d^2 f}{dx^2}(\Delta x)^2 + \frac{d^2 f}{dy^2}(\Delta y)^2 + 2\frac{d^2 f}{dxdy}\Delta x\Delta y\right] \quad (3.20)$$

## TIME VALUE OF MONEY

Financial mathematics tends to base all of its calculations on the concept of money. However, they value of money is not constant. For example, a dollar in 2014 does not purchase the same amount of goods or services that the same dollar would have purchased in 1914. When looking at the value of money in the future, an adjustment has to be made to the value.

Additionally, even when ignoring inflation, a dollar on hand is worth more than the promise of a dollar in the future. The reason is that a dollar today can be used without waiting for it to be delivered.

Interest rates link the value of money today with the value of money in the future. An *interest rate* is a payment received by a lender for loaning someone else money for a period of time. The interest rate on a loan that is certain to be repaid is called the *risk-free* rate. If a loan has the possibility that it won't be repaid (that the borrower will default on the payment), then a higher interest rate will need to be charged to adjust for the risk. A loan to a counterparty that has a chance of not repaying the loan is called a *credit-adjusted rate*.

The mathematical formula that links the value of money today (the *present value*) to the value of money in the future (the *future value*) is called the *continuous compounding formula*. (See Equation 3.21, Continuous Compounding.)

$$FV = e^{rt}PV \tag{3.21}$$

where

FV   **Future Value.** The value of money at some point in the future

PV   **Present Value.** The value of money today

e    **Constant.** A mathematical constant (approximately 2.718281828)

r    **Interest Rate.** The convention is to use an annual interest rate

t    **Time.** The time period between the present and future dates. The standard convention is that $1.0 = 1$ year

A wide variety of interest rates can be observed in the financial markets. As a result, the primary decision is which interest rate to use. Typically, that will depend on the credit risk of the borrower. In addition, interest rates are typically reported for specific time horizons. As a result, to be usable, it is often necessary to interpolate interest rates into a smooth curve.

The most visible interest rate curve, and a common choice for the risk-free interest rate, is LIBOR. LIBOR is an acronym for the London Inter-Bank Offer Rate and is the interest rate that large banks will use when they loan money to one another. Another common choice for representing risk free interest rates in many textbooks is to use U.S. Treasury rates. (See Figure 3.18, Interest Rate Interpolation.)

| T | Rate | Source |
|---|------|--------|
| 0.0028 | 0.06% | Fed Funds |
| 0.0833 | 0.22% | Eurodollar Deposit |
| 0.25 | 0.28% | Eurodollar Deposit |
| 0.50 | 0.42% | Eurodollar Deposit |
| 1 | 0.32% | Libor (Interest Rate Swap) |
| 2 | 0.47% | Libor (Interest Rate Swap) |
| 3 | 0.79% | Libor (Interest Rate Swap) |
| 4 | 1.18% | Libor (Interest Rate Swap) |
| 5 | 1.57% | Libor (Interest Rate Swap) |
| 7 | 2.19% | Libor (Interest Rate Swap) |
| 10 | 2.79% | Libor (Interest Rate Swap) |
| 30 | 3.67% | Libor (Interest Rate Swap) |

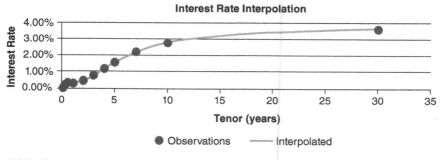

**FIGURE 3.18**    Interest Rates

## TEST YOUR KNOWLEDGE

1. What description best describes what the formula shown below is demonstrating?

$$df = \frac{df}{dx}\Delta x + \frac{1}{2}\frac{d^2 f}{dx^2}(\Delta x)^2$$

A. Stochastic Process
B. Taylor Series
C. Integration
D. Probability Density Function

2. In a normal distribution, approximately what percentage of samples is within two standard deviations of the mean?
   A. 50.0 percent
   B. 68.3 percent
   C. 95.5 percent
   D. 99.7 percent
3. How are variance and volatility related to one another?
   A. volatility = square root of variance
   B. volatility = square of variance
   C. $\Delta$ volatility = ($\Delta$ variance) + (1/2) ($\Delta$ variance)$^2$
   D. Insufficient information is provided to determine a relationship
4. How are the median and mean related for a log-normally (right-skewed) distribution?
   A. median = mean
   B. median < mean
   C. median > mean
   D. Insufficient information is provided to answer the question.
5. What is the excess kurtosis of a normal distribution?
   A. 0
   B. 1
   C. 2
   D. 3
6. With positive interest rates, what is the relationship between the value of a dollar today and the value of a dollar delivered in one year?
   A. dollar today > dollar future
   B. dollar today < dollar future
   C. dollar today = dollar future
   D. Insufficient information is provided to answer the question.
7. A trader might calculate the first derivative of a function at a specific point for what purpose?
   A. To determine the cumulative probability that the value is less than the point.
   B. To calculate the correlation of the function to a random variable
   C. To determine the probability that the function will equal that point.
   D. To develop a linear estimate of the function at the point.
8. What does the formula below mean?

$$? = \frac{1}{n} \sum_{1}^{n} x$$

   A. Determine the cumulative probability that the value is less than point n.
   B. Take an $n^{th}$ order Taylor series expansion of x.

      **C.** Find the natural log of x/n.

      **D.** Take the sum of all values of series x and divide them by the number of samples.

9. What does stochastic mean?

      **A.** Exhibiting random behavior

      **B.** Involving more than one variable

      **C.** A series of functions that has a well-defined mathematical derivative

      **D.** A series having zero variance

10. What is a characteristic of a mean-reverting series?

      **A.** It will be log-normally distributed.

      **B.** It will be normally distributed.

      **C.** It will get pulled back to a long-term average value.

      **D.** It will always have a positive first derivative.

## CHAPTER 4

# Backtesting and Trade Forensics

This chapter describes how hedge funds and other disciplined traders develop trading strategies. Trading is extremely competitive and the best way to avoid losing money is to make good investments. As a result, it is common for hedge funds and other trading groups to take a systematic, disciplined approach to investing. This involves testing ideas both before and after the transaction. Before a trade is made, traders use *backtesting* to test strategies against historical data before they make bets with actual money. After the trade, *trading forensics* are used to perform a post-mortem analysis that identifies how well actual performance matched predictions that were made at time of trading.

*Backtesting* is a set of techniques used to analyze how trades would have performed over some historical period. This doesn't guarantee that trades will perform the same way in the future. However, testing can give substantial insight to the potential behavior of the trade—anything that has been observed in the past has a reasonably good chance to happening again. Trading forensics re-analyzes the trade and additionally provides another layer of control for trading management to review the trading process.

For trading desks, the decision to invest money into a trading strategy is a core element of the decision to "accept risk" or to "avoid risk." This is a strategic decision. It defines the risks that will be voluntarily taken on even if, or perhaps especially if, each strategy is highly successful. These techniques are often grouped into a category called *strategic risk management*.

## SYSTEMATIC TRADING

Many professional traders follow a systematic approach to trading which they call a *trading strategy*. The goal of a trading strategy is to remove emotion from investing and rigorously test an idea before placing an investment. There are several phases to developing trading strategies. Each stage is designed to test the trader's preconceptions about the market before a trade is executed and quantify how the strategy might have worked under different market conditions.

The starting point for a trading strategy is typically the development of a trading idea. For example, "I want to buy electricity call options in the Texas power market because prices always spike in the summer." Once the idea for a trading strategy has been developed, it can go through several phases of testing. The first test is typically a *backtest*. A backtest examines the trade to see if a trade would have been successful in prior years.

To a risk manager, this testing is important since it allows targeted analysis into some of the major trading risks. For example, many trades can be divided into the categories of "trader believes this consistently happens" and "trader believes something has changed in the market." The test results should be consistent with this description. For example, if the proposed trade would have lost the trader money each of the last three years, a proposal predicated on "it always happens this way" should be viewed skeptically.

## DATA VALIDATION

There are two large hurdles to successfully modeling the financial markets. The first hurdle involves getting the raw material, the data, necessary to evaluate a strategy. The second hurdle involves keeping an open mind so that data can be understood without biasing the results with preconceptions or emotions.

There are many reasons why getting data may be a problem for a trader. It might not be available if no vendor is tracking and accumulating the information. Alternately, the data might be expensive or hard to use. Most of the time, all of these problems come into play. Furthermore, even if the raw data is available, the job is only partially completed—it still must be examined and understood before any meaningful work can be completed.

There are several items to consider with data:

- **Availability.** In some cases, data may not be available, or only a small part of the necessary data might be available.
- **Timing.** To be used in a simulation, the data would have to be available at the time the simulated trading decision would have been made. It is often difficult to determine exactly when historical data would have been available on the day that it was produced.
- **Stale Data.** Prices and similar data represent information at a specific point in time. Data that is infrequent may have a substantial lag between

when it was valid data and when it is superseded. In that intervening period, the data might be *stale*—not representative of the markets between those two points.

- **Errors.** Any data set can contain errors. This bad data must often be filtered out before it can be used.

Some indications of bad data are infrequent data points or large step changes in prices. There are a variety of mathematical tests that can determine if something has fundamentally changed in the data set. However, it is difficult to automatically determine if the unusual data is actually bad or if there was a reasonable explanation for the unusual behavior. Determining how to handle bad data is a decision that generally has to be made after understanding the cause of the unusual data.

## STRATEGY TESTING

Disciplined traders will typically test their strategies against historical data to see how they performed. This process consists of several phases, ranging from using historical data to performing small scale transactions.

Some of the common phases associated with testing trading strategies are:

- **Backtesting.** *Backtesting* is the process of testing a trading strategy or idea over prior time periods.
- **Out-of-Sample Backtesting.** *Out-of-sample backtesting* splits the historical data into two portions—a portion that is used to develop the strategy and a portion used to test the data. This reduces some issues associated with strategies that look good in testing but can't be repeated.
- **Paper Trading.** *Paper trading*, also called phantom trading, is simulated trading that attempts to duplicate the actual process of making trades, recording profits and losses, and estimating transaction costs in a live simulation.
- **Live Testing.** Live trading is the process of using small-sized trades to test the feasibility of the transaction under real-life conditions.

The purpose of testing is to identify potential problems with a trading strategy and to gain insight into whether the ideas could be profitably applied in the future. This does not prove that a strategy will be successful in the future. No one knows the future. However, it is possible to eliminate a large number of potentially bad investment ideas. Typically, only strategies that have a good backtest are considered for real life implementation.

The largest weakness in the backtesting approach is that, given enough attempts to develop a strategy, eventually it is possible to find some combination of investment that gives good returns over any historical timeframe. Computers make this very easy since they can quickly process historical tests. It does not take long to identify the combination of investments that would have maximized returns over a historical period and develop some rule that would have led to those investments. However, those rules are seldom useful for identifying opportunities in the future.

Historical testing also has a selection bias because of the strong relationship between risk and return. The best trading strategies typically demonstrate consistent good performance with very low risk. In other words, successful trading strategies have a better risk/return relationship than other investments. However, because these strategies aren't taking on the most risk, they are seldom the most profitable strategies. Typically the top-performing investment in any given historical period is a very risky investment that happened to get lucky. The selection of a strategy that maximizes the profits for one period without making them apply to other periods is called *curve fitting* or *over-fitting*.

### KEY CONCEPT: SIMULATION ACCURACY

*Past performance does not necessarily guarantee future returns!*
Looking good in a backtest does not imply that the strategy will actually be predictive of the future. While it's reasonably safe to assume that a recently observed problem might recur several times, the opposite is not true. Backtesting can easily fail to identify potential problems.

In almost every set of historical financial data, some investment will have out-performed other investments. Given enough attempts to find a profitable strategy, eventually it is possible to select a way to pick assets that would have worked for that period. For example, it would be possible to develop a stock-picking strategy to rank stocks based on the initials of their CEO cross-referenced to the number of visible sunspots at the start of the month. Given enough attempts, a computer optimizer could identify which values resulted in the most profitable trades. However, this does not indicate that the approach will work in the future.

## KEY CONCEPT: RISK AND RETURN

Risky investments are likely to have periods where they are both more profitable and have greater losses than safer investments. As a result, if trading tests only look at profitability, the top-performing investment in any given historical period might be an extremely risky investment that just happened to get lucky.

### Historical Backtesting

Historical backtesting is the process of using financial data for prior periods to develop and examine potential trading strategies. Inherent in the backtesting process is a bias to selecting high-risk investments. This is due to the fact that traders will keep testing ideas on the same set of data until they find an idea that looks profitable. To reduce the risk of selecting bad strategies, traders typically try to quantify testing in several ways. For example, in addition to just looking at profits, traders might examine:

- What percentage of trades is expected to be profitable? Does this percentage vary over time or is it stable?
- What is the expected return on each trade? Has this been declining over time or holding steady?
- How quickly should a trade make money on average?
- How sensitive are profits to transaction costs? If transaction costs are higher than expected, does this make the strategy unprofitable?
- Are losses randomly distributed or correlated?
- What kind of losses can be expected, on average, once a month?
- What is the worst case scenario for a drawdown? (A drawdown is a peak to trough decline in profitability).

Typically, traders will look for strategies that have good performance and a consistent trading profile. These are not necessarily the most profitable strategies, but the ones where a high percentage of trades are profitable and the losses can be controlled.

### Out-of-Sample Testing

A common way to improve the backtesting process is to conduct tests on a set of data that is different from the one used to originally develop the strategy. This will identify the most obvious cases of *curve fitting*.

## KEY CONCEPT: DATA MINING AND OVER-FITTING

Backtesting is commonly associated with *data mining* and *technical analysis*. These are both types of investing associated with analyzing historical price movements to predict future price movements. Because these strategies use historical data to design the strategy, both of these approaches are highly vulnerable to *over-fitting*.

Over-fitting is the process of making a historical simulation or model look better by optimizing its performance over a historical time period. Alternately, over-fitting can be used to describe the process of including parameters in a model that improves performance over the fitting period but does not improve the future performance. Either way, over-fitting can affect out-of-sample data sets if enough attempts are made on the testing on both the initial fitting and out-of-sample periods.

This is not a perfect solution since, given enough attempts, it is possible to find a random strategy that will work in multiple periods. Essentially, running enough tests on the out-of-sample data set converts it into in-sample data.

Another use of out-of-sample testing is to examine how the strategy works under different market conditions. For example, an out-of-sample test might analyze whether a strategy is expected to work well under both rising and falling markets. It might also analyze how the strategy reacts to market volatility or extreme events like market crashes.

### Forward Testing/Paper Trading

After historical testing is concluded, the next step in the development of a trading strategy is to simulate the strategy in conditions that are as close to real life as possible. This step is called forward testing, phantom trading, or paper trading. In the paper-trading stage, the strategy is run in real time each day. However, instead of executing real orders, simulated orders and simulated executions are created. This data can then be analyzed for reasonability. The purpose of this step is to identify and address issues that might not be found during historical testing.

Simulating and testing the strategy as it would be executed once actual trading begins allows the strategy developer to identify implementation problems. For example, with historical testing, pricing data already exists.

## KEY CONCEPT: TRANSACTIONS COSTS AND TIMING

Two items that are hard to model from historical data are the costs associated with making trades and timing of when market data arrives.

**Transaction Costs.** Many strategies look profitable in simulation because no trades have occurred to bring prices back to equilibrium. The only way to fully determine if a *price* represents a transaction opportunity is to find someone willing to transact at that price during actual trading.

**Timing of Data.** Trading strategies need to use data that is available at the time of trading.

As a result, historical simulation often doesn't identify problems associated with the timing of when data is available to the market. Paper trading might identify that the trader assumed that the trade could be executed a half hour before the necessary data had arrived.

Paper trading is also a way to help estimate transaction costs that might be incurred in the execution process. For example, a model might assume that the trader might pay a bid/ask spread based on typical market conditions. Paper trading allows the model to observe the bid/ask spread at the expected time of trading under realistic conditions.

After becoming familiar with handling the model during the day, it is time to start practicing with the model with limited amounts of money.

### Live Testing

The final stage of the testing process is typically to make small-sized trades in the market. This stage will attempt to replicate the process that was used for historical testing and paper-trading in the market. It is common for real-life problems that did not show up in historical testing to appear when trading is attempted in real life.

## TRANSACTION COSTS AND SLIPPAGE

Models of trading strategies rarely work as well in practice as they do in simulation. A common reason for underperformance is the inability to get an execution at the desired market price. The root problem is that the market price is typically a historical price (perhaps the price of a recent transaction).

**TABLE 4.1**  Transaction Costs and Slippage

| Type of Problem | Description |
| --- | --- |
| Bad Market Price | If the market price was set by a mistake, made under duress, or news has just been released, the previous market price may not represent the *market view* as to a fair price. In other words, it is not always possible to transact at that price. |
| Transaction Costs | Immediate transactions (market orders) are typically made against the best limit order available at the time of the execution. For example, a buy market order will be executed against the lowest offer price in the market rather than the market price. |
| Slippage | The best available limit order may not have enough size to completely fill the desired transaction. That means that the order will be executed against progressively worse prices until enough trading is done to complete the order. |

There is no guarantee that someone else will be willing to trade at that price. (See Table 4.1, Transaction Costs and Slippage.)

The usual benchmark for a trade price is the price from recently observed transactions. Recent transactions are often used because they are available and the data is usually of reasonably good quality. As part of a legal contract, there is often a definitive historical record of transaction prices. Transactions also provide proof that someone was actually willing to transact. In the absence of transactional data, prices might be estimated from quotes provided by brokers, clearing prices set by exchanges, or surveys of market participants. Particularly for closing prices, where trading will not resume until the morning, these prices are only indications of where prices might start up in the morning.

In many cases, trades will look profitable in simulation but be unprofitable in real life. Unless it is possible to trade at the same prices assumed by the model, actual trading may underperform the simulation. This is especially common for simulations dependent on fast trading. For example, a breaking news story might be released. Trades entered just prior to the release of the news story are completed and time-stamped just after the story release. In addition, the clocks from the news provider and the trade data provider might not perfectly synchronize—they might be a couple of seconds off. In a simulation, it might appear that lightning fast trades made just after the news story release could make a quick profit. This might not

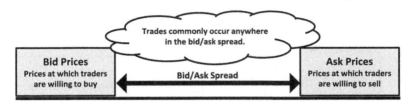

**FIGURE 4.1** Bid/Ask Spread

actually be possible. The only way to see if they are actually profitable is to try it in real life.

A related issue is that there are a limited number of people willing to buy or sell any single asset at any given time. If traders who wish to buy and traders who wish to sell could have agreed on a mutually acceptable price, a transaction would have already occurred. As a result, in most market situations, there is one price where traders are willing to buy (a bid price) and a higher price where people are willing to sell (an ask price). The difference between the two prices is called the *bid/ask spread*. Transactions often occur within the bid-ask spread. (See Figure 4.1, Bid/ Ask Spread.)

Another practical issue that is hard to model is the tradeoff associated with paying for an immediate execution versus waiting for a more motivated trading partner. An immediate execution will lock in a price (usually crossing the bid/ask spread). Waiting gives the opportunity to make a trade in the middle of the bid/ask spread, but risks the market moving before the trade is completed.

Waiting for an execution is similar to giving the market a free option on a trading strategy. If the financial security moves in the direction predicted by the strategy, the opportunity to trade at a good price will often be lost. If the stock moves opposite to expectations, the investment will always be bought, but the trade will be losing money. In other words, the risk is asymmetric and the odds are stacked against the trader. (See Figure 4.2, Risk Associated with Waiting for Execution.)

The alternative to waiting for a trade is to pay money for an immediate execution. For example, if a trader wants to buy an asset, there is usually the option of paying the asking price. This will lead to an execution that is at the asking price rather than in the middle of the bid/ask spread. Later, if the asset is sold for immediate execution, the transaction will take place at the bid price. In other words, the *round trip transaction cost* from buying and selling will be approximately equal to the bid/ask spread in many cases.

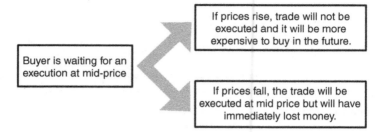

**FIGURE 4.2**   Risk Associated with Waiting for Execution

For extremely liquid products, spreads are often small. However, for less liquid products, transaction costs can often approach 5 percent of the value of the asset being traded. (See Figure 4.3, Crossing the Bid/Ask Spread for Immediate Execution.)

A final complication is that there is sometimes insufficient volume to fully complete an order at the bid or ask price. The highest bid price and the lowest ask price form what is known as the *inside quote*. These prices are formed by buyers and sellers wishing to transact at those prices. However, even though some trading is possible at a given price, there may be limited volume available for transactions. As a result, a trader wishing to trade a large volume might need to agree to progressively worse prices (*slippage*) to complete a transaction.

## KEY CONCEPT: SLIPPAGE

*Many trades look much more profitable before transaction costs are considered.*

Trading requires both a buyer and a seller. Although not every market has a well-developed concept of bid and ask prices, they are all composed of buyers and sellers. The intuition that trading can cost more than expected is shared between all markets.

Financial models (and accounting) commonly assume that there is a single price for an asset. However, in the market, there isn't a single price—buying a security requires finding a seller willing to transact with you and agreeing on a price; the opposite is true for selling. A trading strategy might identify that a trade would be profitable if someone were willing to transact at the *market price* (typically the price of a recent transaction), however that does not mean that it is possible to make a trade at that price.

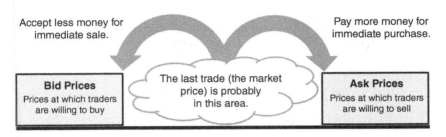

**FIGURE 4.3**  Crossing Bid/Ask Spread for Immediate Execution

## MONTE CARLO TESTING

An alternative to testing a trading strategy with historical data is to use a simulation. This approach is called *Monte Carlo* modeling. Monte Carlo models were first developed in the 1940s and 1950s shortly after electronic computers were first popularized. The concept is that sometimes it is faster to use computer time to calculate possible outcomes rather than attempting to solve the problem with math. The development of the hydrogen bomb is a famous example of Monte Carlo modeling.

A familiar example of a problem suited to Monte Carlo analysis is figuring out how often it is possible to win the one-player card game, solitaire, with a standard 52-card deck. It is impossible to win every game of solitaire. There are so many permutations of cards that it is extremely difficult to mathematically calculate an answer. However, if it were possible to play enough games of solitaire, it would be possible to use statistical sampling techniques to estimate the number of winning games. This is a task that is well suited to a computer. It requires a minimum amount of mathematics— only a good computer programmer, knowledge of the rules, and a relatively fast computer.

Another advantage of Monte Carlo simulation is that it allows a thorough examination of whether one strategy is better than another. For example, the computer can be programmed to try a variety of strategies. Each strategy can be tested to see how many games are won using that strategy. Then, this data can be summarized to identify the key decisions that led to success.

Monte Carlo methods provide an alternative to solving a mathematical equation. The problems still need to be set up in much the same way as any other problem. For example, Monte Carlo won't predict the future. However, it might allow someone to analyze what might happen if several uncorrelated events occurred simultaneously.

There is no single approach to Monte Carlo methods. Each simulation has to be individually modeled. In many cases, this is as much art as science. Even so, there are several common features in most Monte Carlo models:

1. Develop random inputs
2. Generate a simulation using the random inputs
3. Calculate the result of trading with the strategy
4. Run the simulation multiple times and aggregate the results.

### Develop Random Inputs

Monte Carlo simulations are driven by random inputs. A common choice for an input is a model that adds random movement onto an existing price (this is called *stochastic process*). For example, gold prices might be modeled assuming they start at the current price (observed in the market today) and then follow a random walk into the future where each day a random adjustment is applied to the price from the previous day.

These inputs are typically a professional judgment—and not all model inputs will work out equally well in real life. To minimize some of the judgment, inputs are typically calibrated by analyzing historical data. This helps guarantee that a model at least matches historical observations.

### Generate Simulation

The simulation phase of a Monte Carlo analysis implements the logic that makes decisions based on the random inputs. Typically, this logic is deterministic. For example, if X and Y inputs are at certain levels, take some action.

### Calculate Results

Once a simulation is completed, the results of the simulation can be calculated. For example, a trading simulation might calculate the average daily profit, the largest cumulative loss (called a drawdown), or the volatility of daily returns.

### Aggregate Results

Finally, a Monte Carlo simulation will be run a large number of times (commonly 10,000 times or more). The results from each simulation will be tabulated and analyzed. This data will be used to describe the expected daily returns and risk of a strategy *assuming that the initial assumptions were accurate.*

# MODEL RISK

With both historical and Monte Carlo analysis, there is a risk that either the methodology or assumptions used in the analysis of the trading strategies are incorrect. This is called *model risk.*

Models are simplifications of actual events and involve a tradeoff between simplicity and complexity. Compared to complex models, simple models are quicker to develop, easier to understand, and have fewer moving parts that can break. In addition, having only a few assumptions in a model makes it easier to review the model at a later point to ensure that all the assumptions are still valid.

The downside to simplification is that certain things will have to be ignored when the model is created. This creates a risk that the models might not have enough factors to accurately describe reality. Increasing the complexity of a model will allow more factors to be incorporated. However, complexity causes its own set of issues. For example, it is often difficult to identify when a complex model stops working properly. Compared to simpler models, complex models are hard to understand and it is difficult for anyone not intimately familiar with the model to verify that it is working properly.

There are three common reasons for model failure:

1. Initial assumptions were incorrect.
2. Market data used to analyze the model has errors.
3. The process for parameterizing the model is flawed.

## Bad Assumptions

Incorrect initial assumptions are a major cause of modeling errors. If the basic assumptions in a model are wrong, every conclusion made afterward can be affected. For example, many models are based on assumptions about typical market behavior. These assumptions might be invalid if atypical markets are being examined for trading opportunities. This might also occur if a strategy is profitable in one market and it is ported to a second market to grow the size of trading.

## Bad Market Data

Another common problem encountered during model development is related to bad market data. Market data varies in reliability and can contain bad data and errors. For example, a trade might initially be reported with a bad price. Although this may be corrected at a later point, a simulation based on the data may or may not have picked up the correction. This might look like a very profitable trading opportunity in a simulation even though there was actually no opportunity.

Other problems are old or stale data. In an illiquid market where no one trades regularly, there can be an extended period between trades. If enough time passes, trading might not be possible at the price of the previous transaction. A historical simulation might need to correct this by modeling an expected trade price by looking at prices of more liquid financial instruments or industry benchmarks.

### Parameter Estimation Errors

Still another modeling problem concerns the estimation of parameters. For example, a model might use historical prices to estimate volatility of an asset. If the calculation is done incorrectly, even if the underlying data is correct, the conclusions from the model might not accurately reflect reality.

## COMPARING STRATEGIES

Traders and risk managers will use a variety of techniques to analyze potential trading strategies. The most common of these measures involves comparison between the risk and return of a trading strategy. Typically, these calculations are expressed as an expected average return divided by the volatility of returns.

The reason that these measures are commonly used is because trading limits are typically determined by a value at risk (VAR) calculation. Since VAR measures volatility of returns, for traders to maximize their profits they need to maximize returns for a given level of volatility. In other words, trading success for most traders is measured by the amount of profit that they can make given a limited amount of return volatility.

There are several common formulations for risk/reward formulas. The simplest metric is called a *Sharpe Ratio*. The Sharpe Ratio measures average excess returns (returns above the risk-free rate) divided by the standard deviation of returns. (See Equation 4.1, Sharpe Ratio.)

$$Sharpe\ Ratio = \frac{P * Average\ (Excess\ Daily\ Return)}{\sqrt{P} * StdDev\ (Excess\ Daily\ Returns)} \tag{4.1}$$

where

| | |
|---|---|
| P | The time period adjustment for the Sharpe Ratio |
| **Excess Daily Return** | The average daily return minus an appropriately scaled risk free rate. For example: |

$$Excess\ Daily\ Return = daily\ return - risk\ free\ rate$$

Most commonly, Sharpe Ratios are calculated based on daily returns and then annualized. This is done assuming that returns are normally distributed. Average returns over a period are calculated by multiplying the daily expected return by the number of days. For example, for a security that has 252 trading days per year and an average profit per day of 0.01 percent, the annual profit will be 2.52 percent. Standard deviations (for normally distributed returns) scale with the square root of time. (See Equation 4.2, Annualized Sharpe Ratio.)

$$Annualized\ Sharpe\ Ratio = \frac{252 * [Average(daily\ return) - Risk\ Free\ Rates]}{\sqrt{252} * StdDev\ (daily\ returns)} \quad (4.2)$$

The Sharpe Ratio formula is called an *Information Ratio* when excess returns are calculated with respect to some value other than the risk-free rate. For example, a stock portfolio might calculate excess return above the S&P 500 (a well-known index of large capitalization U.S. stocks).

A weakness of the Sharpe Ratio/Information Ratio methodology is that scaling volatility with the square root of time requires a stable portfolio with independent price moves and constant volatility. In cyclical markets with mean reversion or variable volatility, this scaling won't work well. As a result, these analytics work better for some trading strategies than others. For example, a diversified portfolio of assets that is bought and then held for a year might be well approximated by these assumptions. However, a macro-economic strategy that makes lightning fast, short term investments around infrequent news releases might have a harder time using Sharpe

---

## KEY CONCEPT: SHARPE RATIO AND INFORMATION RATIO

Sharpe Ratio and Information Ratio compare risk and return by calculating average returns divided by the standard deviation of returns (volatility). Higher ratios indicate more profitable strategies. Hedge funds will often achieve Sharpe Ratios in the range of 1.0 to 3.0 for extended periods.

**Sharpe Ratio.** Average returns are calculated as the average excess return above risk-free rates.

**Information Ratio.** Average returns are calculated as the average excess return above some benchmark.

ratios because its variable volatility. Strategies with large moves that happen infrequently are also difficult to test.

A second weakness of a Sharpe Ratio/Information Ratio is that it can take a long observation period for accurate statistics to be measured. For example, taking a random strategy with a daily 5 percent chance of a $0.95 profit and a 95 percent chance of a $0.05 loss, the numbers don't converge particularly quickly. Even over the course of the year, there can be a large variation in estimate results. (See Figure 4.4, Option Strategy Payoffs.)

When the distribution of returns is not clustered around a typical result (like a normal distribution) or an insufficient time horizon is available to measure results, statistics does not do a good job of describing typical behavior. For example, with an option book consisting of frequently observed small profits and the occasional large loss, the average return doesn't describe either the small profits or the large losses—it estimates an intermediate value.

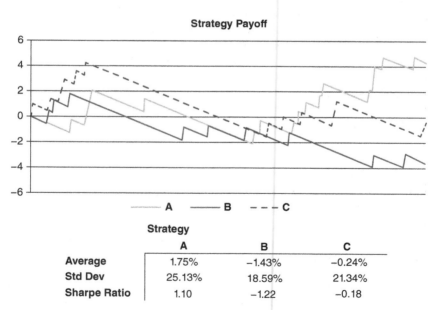

| Strategy | A | B | C |
| --- | --- | --- | --- |
| Average | 1.75% | −1.43% | −0.24% |
| Std Dev | 25.13% | 18.59% | 21.34% |
| Sharpe Ratio | 1.10 | −1.22 | −0.18 |

**FIGURE 4.4**  Option Strategy Payoffs

## KEY CONCEPT: RANDOMNESS AND RESULTS

*When returns are not clustered around a typical value, it takes much longer to estimate the distribution.*

While it is fairly common for trading desks and risk managers to treat every distribution as a normal distribution, not all distributions are normal.

- Compared to a normal distribution, many more samples are needed to estimate the mean of non-normal distribution. This is especially pronounced in the case of a bi-modal distribution where some rarely observed values are very large and most values are very small. This is doubly a problem when the rarely observed large result has a different sign than the common small result—like small losses from buying lottery tickets and a large profit if the lottery is won.
- Using an insufficient number of samples can lead to overestimating or underestimating the expected returns and risks of a strategy.

## COMBINING STRATEGIES

Determining the optimal strategy is more complicated than just choosing the most profitable strategy. Instead of investing in just one strategy, it is possible for trading desks to invest in multiple strategies. As long as the strategies are not highly correlated, traders can use diversification to reduce the overall risk of the portfolio. Not only does this lead to a potentially improved risk/return relationship, this has a big impact on profitability since the size of the portfolio is typically measured as a VAR number.

## KEY CONCEPT: TRADING DESKS AND RISK TOLERANCE

Trading desks are typically limited by risk tolerance rather than capital. This is due to the fact that most trading desks can achieve a high degree of leverage by borrowing money, taking on leveraged trades, and similar activities.

For example, if a trading desk with a $1 million VAR limit is trying to allocate investment between two uncorrelated strategies with the same Sharpe Ratio, the VAR limit for each investment (the size of the investment) will not be $500,000 each. Diversification will reduce the combined VAR of the strategies. As a result, the trading desk might be able to give each strategy a $700,000 VAR limit. In other words, compared to investing in a single strategy, diversification might allow the trading desk to increase its expected profit by 40 percent.

Combining multiple trading strategies is an example of an asset allocation problem. Mathematically, the core concept behind diversification is that variance (the square of the standard deviation) is additive. (See Equation 4.3, Portfolio Variance.)

$$\sigma_P^2 = \sigma_A^2 + \sigma_B^2 + 2\rho\sigma_A\sigma_B \qquad (4.3)$$

where

$\sigma_P$   Dollar Volatility of the combined portfolio
$\sigma_P$   Dollar Volatility of strategy A
$\sigma_P$   Dollar Volatility of strategy B
$\rho$   Correlation between strategy A and strategy B

## TRADE SURVEILLANCE

After a trade is made, it is common for trading firms to monitor the trading process to ensure that firm policies are being followed. The process for detecting possible trading problems is called *trade surveillance*. Some goals of trade surveillance are to protect the reputation of the firm from allegations of market manipulation, prevent rogue trading (trading in a manner that is disallowed by firm policy), and to minimize operational errors in the trading process.

Trade surveillance can encompass a wide variety of measures. Some common types of measures include ensuring that firm management has accurate data, that various aspects of risk are considered, and that there is monitoring for unusual behavior during the trading day. (See Figure 4.5, Trade Surveillance.)

### Accurate Data

The first line of trading surveillance is to ensure that trading positions are completely and correctly entered into trading and risk systems. In addition

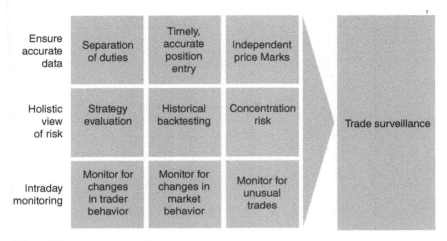

**FIGURE 4.5**   Trade Surveillance

to accuracy, timeliness is also important. Trades that have been verbally accepted but not entered into firm systems on the day of trading have been anecdotally linked to many situations of *rogue trading*. Rogue trading occurs when a trader makes unauthorized trades on the behalf of their firm. Ensuring that all trades are in the firm's systems largely prevents this risk. As a result, ensuring that traders are completely and accurately representing trades is a common way to eliminate many types of potential issues. (See Table 4.2, Examples of Rogue Trading.)

A second common approach to improving data accuracy is to ensure that trades are correctly priced. This is commonly accomplished by keeping

**TABLE 4.2**   Examples of Rogue Trading

| Year | Institution | Loss | Details |
|------|-------------|------|---------|
| 2008 | Societe Generale | $7.0 billion | A junior trader, Jerome Kerviel, who specialized in European stock indices, lost several billion dollars. Trades were hidden by offsetting them with falsified hedge trades that didn't actually exist. Before joining the trading desk, Jerome Kerviel had worked in the back office. His knowledge of the firm's systems gained from that period was largely blamed for his ability to circumvent the firm's controls. |

*(Continued)*

**TABLE 4.2** (*Continued*)

| Year | Institution | Loss | Details |
|------|-------------|------|---------|
| 1996 | Sumitomo | $2.6 billion | Sumitomo's head copper trader, Yasuo Hamanaka, lost several billion dollars trying to corner the copper market. The positions were recorded in an account to which the firm claimed that only Hamanaka had knowledge or access. |
| 2011 | UBS | $2.3 billion | A trader in European stock indexes, Kweku Adoboli, avoided recording trades for an extended period while positions lost billions of dollars. The losing trades were disguised by entering false offsetting transactions into the firm's systems. |
| 1995 | Barings Bank | $1.3 billion | A futures trader in the Singapore office of Barings Bank utilized the firm's error account (accounts used to correct trading mistakes) to hide increasingly large trading positions. |

the responsibility for marking prices separate from the trading desk. This process has some nuances that are important. First, traders will have more insight than mid-office groups into the prices where trading is possible. Second, independent teams responsible for pricing trading positions can be subject to their own incentives and pressure to smooth out earnings. As a result, this process works best when both traders and the independent pricing group have a way to escalate concerns to an oversight team that is independent of both groups.

## KEY CONCEPT: ROGUE TRADING

Rogue trading is a common allegation made against traders when losses occur and their trades were not correctly entered into the firm's systems. Whether the losing trades were actually unauthorized is often difficult to prove. There is some evidence that management was aware of the trading in several rogue-trading cases and intervened only when losses occurred. However, without having the trades accurately recorded, the traders are considered negligent of their responsibilities. As a result, systems that accurately capture trading positions help to protect both the firm and the traders working at the firm.

## KEY CONCEPT: REVIEWERS

Trading issues need to be handled by someone with sufficient time, familiarity, authority, and accountability to get results. The level of the review needs to match the level of the reviewer.

- **Time.** The reviewer needs enough time to understand the issues and talk to the teams involved. The trade surveillance process needs to consider how much time reviewers will have available to dedicate to reviews.
- **Familiarity.** The reviewer needs sufficient familiarity with the markets to make informed decisions on the topic being reviewed.
- **Authority.** The reviewer needs sufficient authority to take action and resolve issues.
- **Accountability.** The reviewer needs to be accountable for the review. For example, if a reviewer is too senior or if reviews are done by committee, the reviewer may not be personally affected if a review is done improperly.

The oversight team responsible for identifying issues and clearing exceptions is commonly tiered so that smaller, more common, issues can be cleared at the trading-desk level and larger issues get escalated to more senior individuals in the firm. The goal is to make sure that someone with the right level of information and ability to take action is directly involved in the process at all times. For example, senior managers in a firm might lack the detailed reports and knowledge of day-to-day operations to resolve small issues effectively. However, more junior managers might lack the authority to make decisions that affect the entire firm.

### Holistic View of Risk

A second pillar of trade surveillance is getting an assessment of risk that incorporates the whole set of risks that might face a trader or trading desk rather than focusing on specific elements. A common problem with risk measurement is that it focuses on one or two elements of risk. Focusing on specific elements of risk allows risks to be categorized and aggregated. A benefit of this approach is that a single approach can be used for all known risks. However, a disadvantage of focusing only on expected risks is that no effort may be spent looking for unexpected risks.

## KEY CONCEPT: RISK MANAGEMENT

The best way to prevent losses is to make good trading decisions. Risk management can contribute to that process. However, risk management is commonly implemented as a way to provide summarized reports to senior management rather than as a way to help traders make better trades.

On the level of a trading desk, it is important for traders to understand the risks of their trading to ensure that there is enough expected profit for each transaction. This commonly requires looking at risk in more detail than would appear in a risk management report or summary for executive management.

Some common steps followed by professional traders are:

- **Strategy Evaluation.** Regular review of trading strategies can identify risks that might fall through the cracks of a typical market, credit, or operational risk framework.
- **Valuation Model Reviews.** Some trading strategies, particularly those that invest in complicated options or physical assets, rely on valuation models to calculate the value of the investment every day. Assumptions that were appropriate when a model was first created can become invalidated over time and need to be regularly re-examined.
- **Forward testing.** Similar to backtesting, forward testing is performed over a period when a strategy was actually being traded. This allows an ongoing side by side comparison of actual results to simulation results.
- **Concentration Risk.** A strategy that is heavily invested in a single asset or assets that share a similar characteristic has a risk of being less diversified in practice than it has been over some historical backtesting period. Risk management tends to describe risk under typical conditions very well, but is less accurate at predicting rare or unusual events that might impact a small number of people.
- **Liquidity Risk.** In most markets, the ease at which trading can be done (liquidity) changes over time. Many strategies are built on the presumption that trading is always possible without shifting the market. Even when this is true most of the time, it may not be true on the day that traders want to transact—for example, during the early part of a market crash or similar unusual event.

- **Trade Repository.** Requiring traders (and counterparties) to report contract details to a registered trade repository allows computer systems to automatically verify trades. This keeps position systems up to date and prevents traders from failing to enter trades into the firm's systems because if the counterparty reports a trade without a matching transaction from the trader, a notification is created.
- **Gross and Net Positions.** Most risk management combines positions to calculate a net final position. A common trading problem comes when a spread position (or other long/short portfolio) has a small net position but a large gross position. For example, a $1 billion long by $1 billion short position is a lot riskier than a $1 million long by $1 million short position even though they have the same net exposure (zero exposure). Ensuring that netting operates on a strategy level can identify potential risks that are obscured in a firm-wide risk management system.

## Pre-Trade and Intraday Monitoring

Intraday trade surveillance consists of processes and technology that detect trading rule violations and prevent trading errors during the trading day. Generally, these systems are designed to make it easier for traders to do their jobs and stay in compliance with firm requirements.

These systems typically block or prevent trading if an unusual event is identified. These systems are set up so that overrides can be used to re-enable trading. These overrides are commonly tiered to work at a variety of levels. At the lowest level, the system can be overridden by the traders (possibly the head trader for the desk). A higher level of unusual activity can be approved at higher levels in the firm—typically after consultation with the appropriate risk management group. Finally, a third level of approvals will be required for the largest variations.

Some common monitoring systems include:

- **Position Limits.** The effects of trades can be tested prior to trading to ensure that position limits won't be violated. Authorizations to exceed limits are usually tiered so that the trading desk can increase certain limits themselves, a risk management team increases limits to a higher level, and senior firm management to a third level.
- **Short Sale Restrictions.** In many markets, borrowing and selling short is only allowable when it is possible to obtain the item being sold. In other cases, restrictions may apply if it will be difficult to obtain the asset at a later point. Short sales can be prevented in entities or instruments where it is difficult to borrow the asset.

- **Restricted Lists.** Trades in certain entities or instruments can be automatically prevented. For example, an investment bank might prevent its traders from executing trades in a company that the bank is advising in a merger and acquisition situation.
- **Counterparty Credit Limits.** Limits may be placed on the total size of transactions allowed with other traders. This reduces exposure in case those other traders go bankrupt. Authorizations to exceed limits are usually tiered so that the trading desk can increase certain limits themselves, a risk management team increases limits to a higher level, and senior firm management to a third level.
- **Unusually High Volumes.** With execution commonly done through computers, there is always a risk that a trader will type in the wrong size of trade. Systems can be designed to prevent execution of unusually large volumes or unusually sized transactions without the proper authorization override.
- **Recommended Execution Strategies.** Trading systems can be designed to monitor market conditions and recommend trading strategies. For example, a system might recommend that a large trade be broken into several pieces and traded over several hours rather than all at once.
- **Changes in Market.** Automated systems can provide warning to identify large changes in prices, volumes, the credit rating of a trading partner, or other changes in market behavior to help traders get ahead of changing markets.
- **Pattern Recognition.** Unusual trading behavior can be identified using pattern recognition. For example, a trading system might identify simultaneous purchases and sales in the same asset (wash trades) that are often an indicator of market manipulation.

## TEST YOUR KNOWLEDGE

1. Sharpe Ratios and Information Ratios both measure what?
   A. The ease of liquidating trades
   B. Expected excess returns divided by volatility (standard deviation of returns)
   C. The theoretical price of the asset if held to maturity based on commonly accepted financial assumptions like non-existence of arbitrage and time value of money.
   D. The maximum expected drawdown of a trading strategy
2. What is the primary benefit of out-of-sample backtesting?
   A. It allows the strategy to be modeled with normally distributed returns.
   B. It decreases volatility of the strategy.

C. It increases the expected returns of the strategy.

D. It reduces the likelihood of over-fitting a model.

3. Richard, the head of a trading desk, is examining the possibility of incorporating a new trading strategy into the trading desk operations. He has four possible strategies for which he calculated Sharpe Ratios and correlation with existing strategies. Which is the best strategy for Richard?

A. Sharpe Ratio −0.5, correlation = 0

B. Sharpe Ratio −0.5, correlation = 1.0

C. Sharpe Ratio = +0.5, correlation = 0

D. Sharpe Ratio = +0.5, correlation = 1.0

4. Chang, a trader at a hedge fund, is examining two trading strategies. Strategy A has a 2.0 Sharpe ratio, Strategy B has a −0.1 Sharpe Ratio, and the strategies have a −1.0 correlation. What is the best combination of strategies?

A. Only Strategy A

B. Only Strategy B

C. An equal weight combination of Strategy A + Strategy B

D. A combination of Strategy A and B, with a larger investment in Strategy A than Strategy B

5. What is a way to reduce trading risk?

A. Require all trades to be recorded with a trading repository that ensures that trades are accurately recorded on the day of entry.

B. A system to prevent unusually large computerized trades without approval by a human.

C. Perform suitability checks on trades, like credit risk approval and restricted lists, to ensure that approved instruments are being traded in approved sizes.

D. All are ways to reduce risk.

6. Which answer best describes the term *slippage* in the context of a trading strategy?

A. The risk that the price obtained from trading will be different than the price expected when the order was sent to the market.

B. The risk that the strategy works less well over time due to copycat trading.

C. The risk that the order won't be transmitted quickly and that another trader will get the best transaction.

D. The risk that risk management systems won't get updated reports to decision makers in a timely manner.

7. What is rogue trading?

A. A trader that is making trades with someone else's money that he/she is unauthorized to make and makes money.

    **B.** A trader that is making trades with someone else's money that he/she is unauthorized to make and loses money.

    **C.** A trader that is making trades that he/she is authorized to make but has not reported the trades to the teams responsible for trading oversight.

    **D.** All of the above.

8. What is an example of pre-trade monitoring?

    **A.** Checking a restricted list to determine if the trader is allowed to make a trade in the asset.

    **B.** Checking a counterparty credit report to make sure that additional trading is allowed with the counterparty.

    **C.** Checking that the size of the transaction is reasonable—allowable under current position limits and at a size that can be transacted in the market without moving prices too much.

    **D.** All of the above.

9. What is model risk?

    **A.** The potential volatility in Sharpe Ratio calculations due to asymptomatic approximations of variance.

    **B.** The risk that a model has not been properly reviewed.

    **C.** The risk that a model fails to perform as expected.

    **D.** All of the above.

10. What is a likely repercussion of using data in a model that was assumed to be available at 8 a.m. on the day of the transaction but was actually available at 6 p.m.?

    **A.** There is no major difference as long as it is available the same day.

    **B.** Actual trading results are likely to under-perform the simulation.

    **C.** Actual trading results are likely to out-perform the simulation.

    **D.** Insufficient information is provided to answer the question.

## CHAPTER 5

# Mark to Market

O nce a trade has been made, traders have to calculate profits and losses on a regular basis. Commonly, this is done daily by comparing recent transaction prices to the previous day's price. For some financial instruments, finding the current price is as simple as checking the last traded price from an exchange feed. For other investments, finding the current value requires complex modeling.

For investments that can't be easily liquidated, trying to calculate a market price is both challenging and risky. In these cases, market prices may not be representative of the true value of the asset. Traders holding an illiquid position might not have the ability to trade at prices being reported by other traders. These positions are particularly vulnerable to market panic or manipulative transactions made by other traders. A large number of financial disasters have resulted from nuances of mark-to-market accounting and risk management limits.

A daily process of valuing trading positions is a way to control risk. By understanding what is occurring each day, business leaders can track the performance of each trading strategy as well as the firm's overall results. That allows business leaders to make decisions on whether to increase or decrease each investment or pay to transfer some risk to other parties.

## PROFITS AND LOSSES

Mark-to-market accounting, sometimes abbreviated MTM, is a type of fair-value accounting used to value many tradable assets. It uses current market prices to calculate accounting profits and losses. It is the most common way to account for derivatives and tradable financial instruments. MTM accounting is based on the premise that pricing data is available and conveys information that reflects the fair value of the financial instruments. For instruments that get traded regularly, the mark-to-market price is usually the last reported trade price.

Some common terms used in calculating profits and losses are:

- **Mark.** To record for accounting purposes
- **Market.** A mechanism (like an exchange) that allows traders to convert assets or liabilities into cash or vice-versa
- **Fair Value.** At a high level, the price where a trade could be liquidated under current market conditions. In less liquid markets, a fair price might also take into account the respective advantages and disadvantages that each trader would obtain from the transaction.

Mark-to-market accounting has a large effect on trading and risk management because it determines prices. These prices are then used to make trading decisions, create risk management reports, and ultimately drive profits or losses. When prices are readily available, and markets liquid, there is a well-developed concept of a market price for an asset. However, in markets where trading is intermittent, illiquid, or when prices are not readily available, the methodology for determining a price becomes very important.

Mark to market works by looking at recent transaction prices to set prices for accounting purposes. In cases where recent transaction prices are not available, quotes from brokers may be used. The appeal of mark-to-market accounting is that it forces everyone in the market to have an updated price for an asset. Prices need to be based on some data observed in the market. As a result, mark-to-market accounting is an effective way to prevent accounting fraud associated with mis-marking positions.

On the downside, reducing one risk (accounting fraud) creates a new set of risks that have to be managed. An increased likelihood of market panics, temporary disappearance of liquidity, and bank failures have all been linked to mark-to-market accounting. The underlying reason for this is that only a small portion of assets that exist are bought or sold on any given day. As a result, a small volume of trading can have a disproportionate effect on market prices. Since risk management limits, margin, and capital requirements all incorporate prices as their primary input, these price movements can cascade into a variety of other problems.

Mark to market can also cause a divergence between theoretical values predicted by financial mathematics and actual traded prices. Financial analysis makes a lot of assumptions about markets. For example, some common financial assumptions are that time value of money links current and future prices, that markets are efficient, and so on. None of that really matters in the trading market—traders can agree to trade at any price that they want. In other words, it only takes a single irrational trader (defining irrational as any trade that doesn't try to maximize profit) to set an irrational price for the whole market.

For example, on a Friday before a holiday weekend, after several days of losses, a trader might be told by the head of trading at his firm to liquidate his investment by the end of the day or get fired. Selling into a falling market, the trader runs out of buyers who are willing to buy enough of the asset. Under pressure from company management who threaten to fire the trader if the book isn't closed that day, the trader agrees to sell the final 1000 contracts at a substantial discount to earlier prices. Given the lack of buyers, this is highly likely to be the last trade of the day. As a result, everyone who owns a position in the asset has to mark a substantial loss onto their balance sheets. This will occur even if the low price is likely to rebound as other traders come back from vacation the following business day.

Since the firm who is forcing the trade is not under distress and the market is operating normally, it may not be possible to quantify the trade as an outlier (since the preceding sales pushed prices down). The trade would also not be considered a forced or distressed sale since the firm voluntarily decided to make the trade. As a result, because of mark-to-market accounting, the final price of the day will be used for everyone in the market.

Even investors who were not transacting on that day will be required to use the mark-to-market price to value their books. This can have a cascading effect on the market. For example, a large loss in value of an asset might trigger a margin call for other traders holding that asset. Needing to raise money, those traders would then be required to sell assets or reduce their positions. As more assets start being sold to cover losses, the sell-off could cross several markets and snowball into a market crash.

## MARKET PRICE

Two of the most important risks facing investors, market risk and credit risk, depend on being able to price securities. Mark-to-market accounting is the process of using the current market price to value securities. The *market price* is the price at which an asset could be liquidated or a liability removed if transacted on that day. In practice, for securities with an active trading market, this usually means that prices are based on prices published by exchanges or brokers on the valuation day. In cases of less-liquid securities, where published prices aren't available, the portfolio may be marked to a theoretical price called a *mark-to-model* price.

The primary advantage of mark-to-market accounting is that the concept is fairly intuitive for a wide variety of securities. Mark-to-market accounting also recognizes profits or losses when they occur. For example, if an asset is purchased for $100 and then rises in price to $110, the profit

## KEY CONCEPT: MARK-TO-MARKET TERMINOLOGY

This should be indented similar to other items. The market price is the expected transaction price of a security if liquidated on the valuation date. In practice, this is typically the price of the most recently observed transaction.

**Mark-to-Market Accounting.** Mark to market is an accounting practice that records the price or value of a security to reflect the current market value rather than its acquisition price.

**Mark-to-Model Accounting.** Mark to model is an accounting practice that records the price or value of a security according to internal assumptions or financial models. This is commonly done in situations where market prices for an asset are unavailable.

**Liquid Market.** A liquid market has a high volume of trading where buyers can easily find willing sellers and vice versa. A key feature of most liquid markets is that market prices can be easily determined.

**Illiquid Market.** An illiquid market is one where it is difficult or impossible for a buyer to find a willing seller or vice versa. Since transactions don't occur very often, it can be difficult to identify a price at which both buyers and sellers are willing to conduct a transaction.

under mark-to-market accounting will be $10. This gives regular feedback to the owner of the asset or liability.

One of the key assumptions behind mark-to-market accounting is that a price always exists for every security. In other words, that price exists independent of buyers and sellers. However, in real life, prices are based on a negotiation that requires both a buyer and a seller. Without both a buyer and a seller, it is impossible to exit a transaction—and that means that there isn't really an exit price. Mark-to-market accounting also assumes that securities are readily transferable to another party.

The impact of assuming that an exit price exists without being able to make a transaction can vary. In many cases, recent transaction prices remain good indicators of future transaction prices even when there are temporary interruptions in trading. However, for other types of markets, like an intermittent auction, the prior price might not be indicative of the future price. For example, in annual auctions to obtain electricity transmission rights, the time between auctions and the sensitivity of the final price to small changes in supply and demand can make past results a poor indicator of future results.

A more extreme example of market illiquidity is a market where reselling is restricted or sales are primarily from wholesaler to retail customer.

## MARKET PRICE

The market price is the expected transaction price of a security if liquidated on the valuation date. This makes sense when a security is tradable. However, when in illiquid markets the accounting guidance may be at odds with market reality.

For example, a restaurant chain might enter a contract to buy propane at a fixed price from a local supplier. While there is a wholesale market for propane, there might be no way for an end-user, like the restaurant, to transfer the contract or resell the propane.

## MARKET LIQUIDITY AND MARK TO MARKET

Market liquidity affects mark to market in a variety of ways. For many securities, only a small percentage of the outstanding volume in that security is traded on any given day. In addition, unless it is obviously an outlier, the market price is almost always the latest transaction price. The purpose of mark-to-market accounting is to remove the ability to set prices from traders by giving it to the market, which is dominated by the traders transacting at that moment. As a result, common sense does not necessarily apply to mark-to-market prices. The quality of prices depends on the traders transacting at a specific point in time.

- **Liquid Market.** A market characterized by frequent trading and a large number of trading partners willing to both buy and sell.
- **Illiquid Market.** A market characterized by infrequent trading and difficulty finding trading partners.

For liquid markets with a lot of trading, new transactions tend to occur at a high enough frequency that new prices are frequently observed. As a result, bad prices tend to get replaced very quickly because newer transactions continuously occur. In addition, because there is a large volume of buyers and sellers, it is difficult for any single trader to move prices very far.

In illiquid markets, trades are less frequent. Prices that are not indicative of market conditions can persist for long periods. It is possible to have a trade at a bad price set the market price. For example, even if a trader thinks that a recent price was too low, it may be impossible for him to find another

## KEY CONCEPT: ILLIQUID MARKETS CAN HAVE PERSISTENT BAD PRICES

*Bad mark-to-market prices don't represent arbitrage opportunities.*

For example, an illiquid asset might pay its owner $1 million whenever it is exercised. The asset can be exercised at any time. There is no credit risk and the risk-free rate is zero. A trader incorrectly types a $1.1 million price into his trading system when he attempts to buy one unit. Not unsurprisingly, he finds a willing seller and a transaction occurs. This is not enough of a move to be considered an outlier. However, it does set the market price of the asset to $1.1 million.

To an outside observer, this might look like an arbitrage opportunity to sell more of this asset. Market prices are at $1.1 million for an asset worth only $1 million. However, this is only an arbitrage opportunity if a second buyer can be found at that price. Without a buyer willing to pay $1.1 million for the asset, there is no opportunity to sell. More importantly, with zero interest rates, no credit risk, and exercise at any time, traders have little incentive to buy or sell the asset at its theoretical fair value of $1 million. As a result, because there is little incentive for a trade at the fair price, nothing resets the market price to $1 million and the bad price sets the market price for a period of time.

trader willing to sell at that price. As a result, a new trade might not occur for a long period. Illiquid markets are also more vulnerable to the possibility that a single trader will be able to disproportionately affect prices.

## MTM AND MARKET CRASHES

Mark to market has been linked in some studies to market crashes. While this link has never been completely proven, the unintended consequences of mark-to-market accounting can cause serious business risks. For example, many investment funds force a mandatory liquidation when risk limits are exceeded or prices fall below certain levels. These limits can enable one trader, trading a small volume, to force other market participants to liquidate large volumes or scramble to raise cash. This generally leads to a larger number of people selling into the market and leads to progressively larger price disruptions. Eventually, enough forced liquidations can snowball, leading to or exacerbating stock market crashes and similar market panics.

For this to occur, mark-to-market accounting must typically be combined with rules that will trigger some actions when certain things happen to prices. For example, banks might be required to maintain a certain amount of cash on hand or traders might be required to liquidate positions once risk limits are exceeded. In this case, illiquid markets allow unexpected price movements on small volume to force large numbers of investors to behave irrationally as they liquidate assets (defining rational as an investor who tries to maximize wealth).

Price movements can trigger a large number of actions that can exacerbate market crashes or other panics. These actions may be mandated by regulators or firm management giving traders no ability to override these actions.

Some of the items that can create risk when combined with mark to market accounting are:

- **Margin Calls.** Margin is a good faith deposit. Large price movements can force market participants to margin calls. This can trigger panic selling to raise the necessary cash.
- **Risk Limits.** Traders often have risk limits that constrain the size of their portfolios. If these limits are exceeded, trading firms may have a policy of forced liquidations.
- **Hedging Requirements.** Many trading strategies, particularly options portfolios, might require the trader to keep a balanced book at all times. Price moves can rapidly trigger a large number of trades in quick succession.
- **Asset Restrictions.** Many investment funds have restrictions on the assets that they own. For example, a fund might be restricted from owning stocks with a price lower than $10.

## Example: How a Market Panic Is Created

*A study in possible unintended consequences if houses were marked to market and subject to the same risk management as derivatives.*

A private, gated community has passed rules that members of the community must maintain a minimum level of assets or be forced to sell their house and move out of the community. Members of the community can include the value of their house among their assets, but the rules indicate that the value of the house must be marked to market.

One member of the community is offered the opportunity to invest in a technology start up that will give massive, guaranteed returns. To raise money, he agrees to sell his house at a below-market price. This event starts

*(Continued)*

a chain reaction. Since houses in the community are marked to market, the immediate consequence is that every other homeowner in the town now has a large mark-to-market loss on their house.

This causes a quarter of the homeowners to fall below the minimum threshold for assets required by the community and forces them to sell their houses. In other words, despite the fact that every homeowner is still able to pay their mortgage, and no one else wanted to move, the restrictions on minimum assets and mark to market created a massive oversupply of houses being sold on the market.

As a result, even if the homeowners are given sufficient time to sell their houses (maybe three to six months), without an influx of buyers to offset the amount of selling, prices will be forced to decline. As prices go down, a vicious cycle emerges, with additional sellers emerging every time a house is sold. In other words, the adoption of mark-to-market accounting along with risk management designed to protect the community has created a market sell-off.

## MTM ACCOUNTING

The concepts of fair value and mark to market come from the accounting community. For example, the U.S. Financial Accounting Standards Board defines fair value in its accounting standards codification (FASB ASC). One part of that codification, ASC 820 (Fair value measurements), defines fair value as the "price that would be received to sell an asset or paid to transfer a liability in an orderly transaction between market participants at the measurement date." In other words, fair value is based on the concept of an *exit* price that could be obtained during an orderly market.

It should be noted that an orderly market is not necessarily an active market. An orderly transaction is characterized by having a sufficient amount of time allocated to make the transaction. An active market is a market where transactions occur with sufficient frequency and volume to provide pricing information on an ongoing basis. Both orderly and active typically relate to the market in a particular security (like a stock) rather than a trading venue (like a stock exchange). For example, even though the New York Stock Exchange (NYSE) is an active market, it is possible for some stocks listed on the exchange (those with infrequent trading) to be considered inactive.

Because a lack of general market liquidity is not considered a disorderly market, prices could diverge substantially from what would be considered reasonable. For example, a risk-free bond that pays $100 in five days may be trading for $0.01 (in defiance of typical assumptions about market efficiency and time value of money). Traders are free to transact at any price where they can find a trading partner. The traded price would still be considered a fair price if transactions are occurring.

It is possible to exclude specific transactions from fair value calculations if those trades were forced or made under distress. However, the market as a whole can't ever be considered to be distressed. In other words, as long as the market is transacting as usual, market-based prices have to be considered in the valuation process. Specifically, it is not acceptable to calculate the value of the asset based on a *hold to maturity* approach (by discounting expected future cash flows) or use assumptions based on *normalized* market conditions.

Guidance on ASC 820:

> *Even if there has been a significant decrease in the volume and level of activity for the asset or liability and regardless of the valuation technique(s) used, the objective of a fair value measurement remains the same. The glossary defines fair value as the price that would be received to sell an asset or paid to transfer a liability in an orderly transaction (that is, not a forced liquidation or distressed sale) between market participants at the measurement date under current market conditions.*

**Source: FASB ASC 820-10-35-51D**

Two types of disorderly prices are typically defined—*distressed sales* and *forced sales*. In a distressed sale, the seller is in or near bankruptcy, experiencing severe cash shortage, or having assets repossessed by creditors. In a forced sale, the seller is required to sell to meet legal or regulatory requirements or

---

### FAIR VALUE

Accounting guidance states that fair value is based on the exit price in an orderly market. An orderly market may still exhibit unusual market conditions.

- Fair Value is defined as *exit price* under current conditions
- Inappropriate to use *hold to maturity* assumptions around pricing
- Inappropriate to use exit price under *normalized* conditions

## KEY CONCEPT: DISTRESSED AND FORCED TRANSACTIONS

Market data based on *distressed* or *forced* transactions should generally not be used to calculate the fair value of an asset. Some indications of disorderly transactions:

1. **Insufficient marketing time.** An inadequate exposure to the market for a period of time prior to transacting compared to customary periods for similar trades under current market conditions indicates a disorderly sale.
2. **Single Buyer.** The seller marketed the asset only to a single market participant (even if a customary marketing period was used).
3. **Distressed Sale.** The seller is in or near bankruptcy, experiencing severe cash shortage, or having assets repossessed by creditors.
4. **Forced Sale.** The seller is required to sell to meet legal or regulatory requirements or has entered into a supervisory agreement with regulators.
5. **Outlier Price.** The transaction price is an outlier when compared to other recent transactions for the same (or similar) securities.

has entered into a supervisory agreement with regulators. A sale by a firm whose internal policies require selling is not considered a forced sale.

Illiquid markets increase the likelihood of distressed transactions or forced transactions. Quoted prices are generally less reliable in these circumstances. Some indications of distressed transactions are rushed transactions, transactions offered to a single party rather than the broader market, and transactions done at a price much higher or lower than contemporaneous transactions.

Some signs of illiquid markets are infrequent prices being released or substantial differences in prices being released by market participants. For example, in a broker-based market, having two brokers quoting prices that vary substantially from one another is an indicator of market problems. Another warning sign is very few transactions or releases of data. Infrequent pricing might indicate that prices are not based on current information

## HIGHEST AND BEST USE

The market price of an asset is based on *the highest and best use* of that asset. The highest and best use of an asset is the use that would maximize the value of the asset (or the group of assets) for market participants. To be considered a possible use, the use has to meet certain criteria:

- **Legal.** The use must be legal.
- **Physically Possible.** The use must be physically possible to achieve.
- **Financially Feasible.** The use must maximize the value of the asset.

Liquidation price is also a consideration in determining the highest and best use of an asset. Derivative fair value is based on the price that another market participant would pay to acquire the asset or be paid to transfer a liability. As a result, the concept of highest and best use relates primarily to the highest and best use for other market participants rather than yourself.

## FAIR VALUE HIERARCHY

Accounting guidance recognizes that the ability to transact will vary by market and market participant. For example, trading crude oil for delivery along the U.S. Gulf Coast will have higher liquidity than trading crude oil for delivery in the middle of Canada. In addition, some market participants will have access to some markets that other market participants might not have. For example, a major bank might be able to trade currencies (foreign exchange trades) on an inter-dealer market unavailable to traders at a hedge fund.

To address concerns associated with different types of markets and market participants having different access to markets, a significant element in ASC 820 is the use of a three-level fair value hierarchy that describes the quality of the inputs used in the valuation. The fair-value hierarchy preferentially depends on *observable inputs*. Observable inputs are data obtained from an independent source that is publicly available to a wide group of investors. The process for generating the data should be reliable, documented, and available to a broad audience.

In the ASC 820 fair-value hierarchy, level 1 fair-value inputs are highly observable inputs—typically prices directly from an exchange. Level 2 inputs are more subjective and often result from fragmented markets where trading is spread out between multiple venues. Level 3 inputs are unobservable and associated with markets with limited liquidity. (See Table 5.1, Classification of Fair Value Inputs.)

Securities are described as Level 1, Level 2, or Level 3 depending on the market data used to price them. For example, Level 1 securities are based on Level 1 market data inputs. A Level 1 security would typically trade in a single venue (like a stock exchange) that publishes official closing prices every day. For most Level 1 securities, a majority of market participants will be able to

**TABLE 5.1** Classification of Fair Value Inputs

| Level | Description |
| --- | --- |
| Level 1. All market participants agree on a single price. | Level 1 fair value inputs are based on highly observable prices. These are typically prices directly observable in the market where everyone agrees on a single price. For example, the closing price of a stock on the New York Stock Exchange or the settlement price of a futures contract would be considered highly visible market data. |
| Level 2. A tight range of prices exists in the market. | Level 2 fair value inputs are ones on which market participants can agree on a tight range of values even though they don't all agree on an exact price. For example, when prices are estimated from broker quotes, every broker may have slightly different prices. Depending on which brokers are surveyed, every market participant may have a slightly different market price, but they would tend to be in a tight range. |
| Level 3. A wide range of price estimates exist in the market. | Level 3 fair value inputs consist of unobservable data whose perceived value is likely to vary substantially between market participants. These inputs are typically heavily modeled or based on illiquid markets where transactions are infrequent. |

access the primary market. In addition, there will be sufficient trading volume that the reported fair value (price) is representative of an active market.

When trading is not concentrated in a single venue, or adjustments have to be made to Level 1 market data, securities are described as Level 2. For example, the value of a restricted class of stock might be based on the price of common stock less a liquidity premium. Even though the price of the common stock is a Level 1 market data input, adjusting the price makes the restricted stock a Level 2 security. Another example of a Level 2 input is the price of a commodity that is similar to an exchange traded commodity but of a slightly different quality or location. In these cases, the non-standard asset might be priced by adjusting the exchange traded price to create a Level 2 security.

Many derivatives fall into the category of Level 2 securities. For example, interest rate swaps, vanilla call or put options, and other standard products are often Level 2 securities. These securities typically incorporate models or modeled data like interpolated interest rates or an option pricing model. To be considered a Level 2 security, these models must be widely accepted, non-proprietary, and use observable data. Market data estimated by use of widely accepted, non-proprietary models is called *indirectly observable* data. For example, option prices might be used to estimate implied volatility data that is used to price similar, but not identical, options.

## KEY CONCEPT: FAIR VALUE CLASSIFICATION

In many cases, the fair value classification of a security is fairly obvious. However, in other cases, fair value classification is subjective and needs to be made by the management of each firm.

For example, the firm's management needs to understand the source of the market data inputs—whether they are based on transactional data, modeled, or based on surveys of market participants. In addition, firm management must understand whether models are used to price the security and determine if those models are proprietary or widely used across the industry.

Typically, firms will need to disclose their reasoning for classification when they file their financial reports for shareholders. Firms will also need to disclose to shareholders any significant Level 2 and Level 3 inputs and models that affect the value of any securities held by the firm.

Level 3 securities involve more complicated modeling, proprietary models, or incorporate various amounts of non-observable data when compared to Level 2 securities. Some Level 3 securities might be described as "mark to model" or be based on markets with limited or intermittent transactions. (See Table 5.2, Fair Value Classification.)

**TABLE 5.2**   Fair Value Classification

| Level | Description |
|---|---|
| **Level 1.** Valuations based on observable prices on identical securities. | Level 1 securities are based on unadjusted market data directly from a primary trading venue on which the security is actively traded.<br>*Quoted price is directly observable in an active market<br>*Prices on identical securities<br>*Prices are not adjusted (regardless of significance)<br>*Prices are available on the valuation day |
| **Level 2.** Valuations include some indirectly observable data or are based on widely accepted, non-proprietary models. | Level 2 securities are partially based on data that is not directly observable or pricing incorporates widely accepted, non-proprietary models.<br>*Inputs are observable (directly or indirectly)<br>*Quotes and indirectly observable data corroborated by use of multiple data sources<br>*Includes adjustments made to a directly observed price |

*(Continued)*

**TABLE 5.2**   (*Continued*)

| Level | Description |
|---|---|
| | *Limited to using only widely accepted, non-proprietary models<br>*Typically less liquid than Level 1 securities |
| Level 3. Values are based on non-observable inputs or proprietary models. | Level 3 securities are valued using significant unobservable inputs or models that vary substantially between market participants.<br>*Significant unobservable inputs<br>*Infrequent or intermittent trading |

In some cases, a security may sit on the borderline between two classifications. In those cases, the management of each firm is responsible for designating securities into a Level 1, Level 2, or Level 3 category. This decision should incorporate that firm's ability to access the markets and the observability of the market data to which it has access. This designation can also change over time. For example, if trading on a security is halted or infrequent on the primary exchange, a security may temporarily go from a Level 1 to a Level 2 security. When trading resumes or picks up again, this classification might be reversed. Different market participants may have different classifications for securities.

## EFFICIENT MARKETS

Market efficiency is commonly cited as support for market-based pricing. A common assumption in the academic literature on financial modeling is that market efficiency should make it impossible to predict the future. This concept is based on the idea that market participants either attempt to maximize their personal wealth or will be driven out of business. The thinking is that when someone can predict the future, they will do so as often as possible and attempt to trade on that knowledge. When that occurs, buying and selling will eventually push prices into equilibrium where no one has better knowledge than anyone else.

This concept makes possible a wide variety of common financial calculations. For example, time value of money is based on the concept that the fair value of something today is based on its value in the future less some premium for risk or convenience. For example, a riskless asset worth $100 in one year's time should be worth approximately $98 today if annual risk-free rates are 2 percent (and the asset can be held to maturity). However, if the investment cannot be held to maturity, this relationship does not hold. This is important to risk managers because mark-to-market accounting assumes immediate sale and does not allow pricing based on the assumption that assets get held to maturity.

A break down between an *exit price* and a *held-to-maturity* price can occur any time there are a limited number of trading partners. Enough buyers and sellers competing to maximize profits should mean that someone can hold the asset to maturity and competition should drive prices to theoretical values.

However, if market prices are not tradable, there may be no possibility for arbitrage to drive actual prices back to theoretical prices. This can occur with stale prices. Observable prices used as inputs into a mark-to-market process are typically historical prices or non-binding quotes from brokers. Historical prices indicate the price of the last transaction—not necessarily transactions that are currently possible. Since transactions require both a buyer and a seller, there is no guarantee that someone else can be found to transact at the same price.

Trades occur at whatever price that buyers and sellers agree to transact. Trading prices don't have to be equal to the theoretical fair value. Additionally, while accounting guidance generally allows exclusion of prices thought to be unreliable, as long as trades are made in the normal course of business in an orderly manner, trade prices are used for marking to market–not the theoretical prices. This is important because there are lots of reasons that might force someone to sell an asset (like a need cash for an even better

---

### KEY CONCEPT: FAIR VALUE

Fair value is based on the concept of *exit price* and not value if held to maturity. Even in orderly markets, the *exit price* and *held to maturity price* of assets can diverge if there are an insufficient number of market participants.

- Fair Value is based on the concept of exit price
- Exit price can be anything that traders agree upon—it is not restricted by time value of money, no-arbitrage restrictions, or any other typical valuation methodology associated with rational investing.
- Exit price is typically based on observed (historical) transactions which may not be achievable by other market participants.

opportunity or the need to liquidate a college fund to make a tuition payment, etc.). Highly motivated buyers and sellers might force transactions that might normally be considered illogical that still would not constitute a sale under duress.

Risk management policies commonly trigger actions based on price movements. For example, one common risk management policy is a *position limit* that prevents further trading, or forces liquidation, on an account once the risk limit is exceeded. These risk limits are typically based on historically observed price volatility. As a result, when a big price move occurs, volatility goes up and prevents traders from trading. As a result, market liquidity can vanish overnight. A similar, but more extreme, problem can occur when risk management policies force a liquidation of a portfolio.

Related problems can also occur with margin accounts or the requirement to maintain a certain amount of capital to cover losses. In this case, a transaction (which may be the result of a very small trade) might cause a large move in the market. Requirements for additional margin or additional equity to cover potential losses can trigger sales in other assets. As a result, the *contagion* caused by a single trade can spread between multiple markets.

## KEY CONCEPT: SPECULATORS AND MARKET STABILITY

*Markets with a lot of speculators are less risky than markets without speculators.*

The risk of a combined mark-to-market and risk management policy causing a panic can be effectively mitigated with more market participants. The more people that are ready to buy and sell on short notice, the more quickly that transaction prices will come back to normal trading patterns. In markets without a large number of investors willing to transact, differences between the held to maturity value and the liquidation value become more likely. This exacerbates market swings.

When speculators get blamed for market swings, it is usually in an illiquid market without other speculators. Limited liquidity and lack of competing speculators makes it much easier for a single speculator to a force a liquidity-based sell-off. However, when a large number of traders are willing to step into the market to arbitrage the smallest trading opportunity, markets stay very efficient.

# DOMINANT TRADERS

Mark to market is particularly risky to companies that have dominant market positions. A dominant trader is one that has a monopoly on a market or much larger trading positions than any other market participant. While the dominant trader has a lot of market power and ability to set prices, they also take on a lot of risk. The reason is that when the trader who is providing all the liquidity in the market attempts to get out of his positions, there may not be anyone else willing to transact.

Dominant traders are also vulnerable to prices set by other market participants. In particular, dominant traders are at substantial risk of other traders making manipulative trades. For example, if trader A has a dominant position in the market (maybe a $50 billion investment), and traders B and C both are betting on price declines, trader B and C can *fix* prices by transacting between themselves at a lower price. In other words, they can create mark-to-market losses for the first trader in the hopes of triggering a distressed sale created by margining requirements, the need to comply with minimum asset levels, or a violation of risk limits.

A large number of companies with dominant positions in their respective markets have gone bankrupt or suffered massive trading losses due to price movements considered impossible or implausible by risk managers. A common thread between many of these events is that immediately prior to these losses, market prices in a market dominated by a single trader were observed to move in a manner that was seemingly at odds with rational markets. As a result, the dominant trader suffered mark-to-market losses, was unable to get out of their positions, and prices rebounded after the forced liquidation of the dominant market participant.

## Long Term Capital Management

Long Term Capital Management (LTCM) went bankrupt in 1998 following a panic in Asian and Russian bonds. The hedge fund was the darling of Wall Street in the 1990s after being founded by the former vice-chairman of Solomon Brothers, John Meriwether, and included Nobel Prize winners Myron Scholes and Robert Merton on its board of directors.

LTCM was the dominant holder in several varieties of Russian bonds. Many of these bonds had identical payoffs differentiated by different rules on trading prior to expiration. If held to maturity, these bonds would have provided a guaranteed profit. However, instead of prices converging, prices started to diverge. While reports attribute the price movements to a *flight to quality* rather than market manipulation, LTCM was caught unable to trade out of its positions, eventually going bankrupt due to mark-to-market losses.

After the LTCM bankruptcy, as predicted, the bond prices converged. The end result was a massive profit for the firms who bet against LTCM and later acquired their positions during the bankruptcy proceedings.

### JP Morgan's London Whale

In 2012, JP Morgan announced multi-billion dollar losses in its portfolio of credit-default swaps (CDS). JP Morgan had dominant market position in these assets, and the London-based head trader of the book, Bruno Iksil, was nicknamed the London Whale due to the size of the CDS portfolio. Prior to 2012, the business consisted of both buying and selling CDS portfolios. However, toward the end of 2011, trading became more one sided with JP Morgan holding positions opposite the rest of the market.

The JP Morgan bet was essentially that the world economy would emerge from lows observed in the period between 2008 and 2011. Although this would later prove to be a correct assumption, before the trade could become profitable, large mark-to-market losses on the portfolio forced JP Morgan to liquidate the portfolio at a loss. This in turn prompted government investigations and forced the resignation of several senior members of the firm charged with trading oversight.

### TEST YOUR KNOWLEDGE

1. Under mark-to-market accounting, how is a fair value market price defined?
   A. The price that would be received to take on a liability or price paid to acquire an asset.
   B. The price that would be received to sell an asset or paid to transfer a liability to another market participant.
   C. The theoretical price of the asset if held to maturity based on commonly accepted financial assumptions like non-existence of arbitrage and time value of money.
   D. The expected price of the asset if sold under normal market conditions.
2. Andrew, an energy market analyst, is helping the financial control/accounting team on the natural gas trading desk determine the proper level for natural gas trades in the fair value hierarchy. The trades are located 50 miles from the futures settlement point. This distance adds a $0.01 spread to the cost of the natural gas over the futures price.
   A. Level 1 Asset
   B. Level 2 Asset

C. Level 3 Asset

D. Insufficient information is provided to answer the question.

3. Brianna, a junior trader at MegaHedgeFund, needs to mark some bonds to market. They are 10-year risk-free bonds paying a 15 percent coupon every month (a 60 percent annual interest rate!). For the last two weeks, multiple transactions have been made pricing the bonds at 2 cents on the dollar ($20 per $1000 of face value). Not only is this an extremely low price for a risk-free high coupon bond, the observed market price is a fraction of the next coupon payment. With risk free rates at 3 percent, Brianna calculates that the fair value should be $3,773 per $1,000 of face value. How should these bonds be marked to market?

A. $20

B. $1000

C. $1600

D. $3773

4. What is NOT true about mark-to-market accounting?

A. It is commonly used to value derivatives.

B. It is based on the concept of an exit price under current conditions.

C. It is used only to price assets traded on the primary exchange (or the most advantageous venue if the asset is traded on multiple exchanges).

D. A major goal of mark-to-market accounting is to protect shareholders from fraud related to earnings announcements.

5. What is a feature of illiquid markets?

A. Market participants use limit orders more than market orders.

B. Credit risks are much higher than normal.

C. It is difficult for a trading desk to raise money.

D. It is difficult to find trading partners and make trades.

## CHAPTER 6

# Value-at-Risk

Risk is a way to describe the size of an investment. Trading desks use risk limits to restrict the size of investments that their traders can make on behalf of the firm and the firm's investors. Limiting the size of investments is one of the primary ways that traders *control risk*. This is not just a matter of restricting capital since many investments (like futures) only require a small amount of money to initiate a trade. Instead, position limits are commonly based on a volatility-based estimate of size called value-at-risk, abbreviated VAR.

Trading desks typically have several VAR limits. The first limit, a *soft limit*, indicates the target size of the trading portfolio. The second limit, a *hard limit*, indicates a size which trading positions are not allowed to exceed. Trading desks use these limits to ensure that traders are following trading rules set by the firm and to ensure that diversification is working properly.

Value-at-risk was originally designed as a way to apply consistent size limits across any type of investment. It has been expanded since that time to estimate the size of large losses and as way for banks to determine the amount of money they need on hand (their regulatory capital requirements). From a decision perspective, the multiple uses of VAR complicate the most common usage for VAR on a trading desk—limiting the size of trading portfolio.

VAR is both a source of risk and a way to control risk. VAR has been expanded over time. Some of the ways that VAR has been expanded have allowed it to react to changes in market conditions very quickly. In some ways this is helpful—it estimates the potential size of gains or losses that day. In other ways, a rapidly changing VAR calculation makes it harder for traders to keep within position limits. A VAR that moves quickly (when traders keep the same trades) makes forced liquidations more likely because hard limits are more likely to be hit. This can cost trading desks a lot of money since any type of trading that isn't intended to maximize trader profit, like portfolio liquidation, tends to be very expensive. Other traders quickly realize they are trading with someone who doesn't care what price is received and that traders are only trading to get under risk limits. This makes Value-at-Risk both a helpful tool and a source of danger to traders.

## POSITION LIMITS

Value-at-risk was first invented to describe the size of a risk. Trading desks will often use VAR to limit the size of trades and investments. Prior to VAR, the head of a trading desk might want to limit maximum positions for each trader on the desk by setting product specific limits. For example, limits might be set: "You can own no more than 25 Crude Oil futures" or "You can own no more than $2.5 Million in XYZ stock." This works on the level of a trading strategy. However, having different types of limits for each type of security complicates a comparison of relative size of each investment.

The complication to setting position limits for each instrument is that there are multiple units (contracts, size of stock positions, and so on). A common unit of measurement is needed if multiple types of investments are to be compared across trading desks. For example, prior to VAR, if the goal was to give both stock and futures traders the same limits, it might be necessary to calculate how many crude oil futures contracts are equivalent to owning a certain amount of stock. This is complicated because futures are more highly leveraged than stock. Futures can be purchased with a relatively small good-faith deposit per contract, called *margin*. As a result, for the same cash outlay, a trader can take on a lot more risk with futures than stock.

Value-at-risk was created to simplify the comparison. It is based on the concept that all investments have something in common—every investment changes in value every day. As a result, a common way to compare sizes of investments is by examining how much their value is likely to change over a period of time. This is now the most common way to compare sizes of investments. When first implemented, the goal of VAR was to have a quick way to answer the question "How much money does the firm have at risk" within 15 minutes of the market close. Since that time, value-at-risk has become a standard way to describe the size of trading positions.

VAR is a not a comprehensive measure of risk. However, it is a good starting point. For example, if your long-lost relative dies and leaves you an inheritance, your first question is likely to be "how much money?" rather than "what is it invested in?" or "is it fully diversified?". VAR answers the question "How much money?". Those other questions are important to answer, and might make a good follow up, but the headline number is the size. VAR gives you that headline.

VAR has evolved over time and is now used for a variety of purposes. In addition to describing the size of risk, VAR is commonly used for regulatory purposes (to calculate required cash reserves) and by senior management (to estimate the worst-case losses for trading/investment positions). As a result, it's fairly common for a firm to have a single VAR number used by different departments for very different purposes. There is some risk to this—firms have encountered problems trying to use a single metric for a variety of purposes. VAR built for one use might not be the best way to meet requirements for every other use.

On a trading desk, a common use for VAR is to describe the size of investments. When used to describe size, VAR is relatively tolerant to modeling error. A description of size doesn't have to be especially accurate to be meaningful. For example, when describing the risk of a retirement account, there is almost the same risk facing a $195,000 account as a $225,000 account, even though these numbers are 15 percent apart. It is only larger differences in size (perhaps 50 percent or 100 percent different) that the differences become significant. As a measure of size, VAR typically performs well.

When used to calculate regulatory capital or to describe worst case losses, VAR becomes less effective. For one thing, if VAR determines funding costs, then the difference between $195,000 and $225,000 becomes significant. The difference is a 15 percent higher or lower funding cost. For an international investment bank, a 15 percent reduction in funding costs can add up to a lot of money. As a result, firms that use VAR to calculate regulatory capital requirements have an incentive to minimize their VAR to reduce their funding costs.

Finally, VAR is often used by senior managers to estimate the worst case scenario for an investment or trading book. This has limited accuracy. VAR is not much better than any other measure of size at estimating worst case scenarios. In almost all cases, the worst case scenario will be a total loss (perhaps a meteor hits the planet and destroys all life). Rare events (almost by definition) don't occur very often. As a result, they are difficult to predict. It is relatively easy to predict the typical range of price movements on an ordinary day. However, it is much harder to accurately guess the size of an extremely rare move. Rare moves are not well described by typical behavior because they have different root causes than normal price moves.

## WHAT IS VALUE-AT-RISK?

Value-at-risk uses a factor common to all financial instruments (daily changes in value caused by mark-to-market accounting) to establish an apples-to-apples comparison of size across a wide variety of instruments. It is typically pronounced "var" and rhymes with "car." In some cases, it is abbreviated VaR or V@R to distinguish it from the mathematical abbreviation for variance, which is commonly abbreviated var.

---

**KEY CONCEPT: VALUE AT RISK (VAR) IS DEFINED MATHEMATICALLY**

---

Value-at-risk is typically defined as the maximum expected loss on a financial instrument, or a portfolio of financial instruments, over a given period of time and a given level of confidence. It is a description of an investment's size and not whether it is a good or bad investment.

Examples:
- **95 percent 1-Day VAR.** The company has a 5 percent chance of losing more than the VAR amount over the next day.
- **99 percent 5-Day VAR.** The company has a 1 percent chance of losing more than the VAR amount over the next five trading days.

---

As a measure of size, value-at-risk is a fundamental building block of risk management. A common use for VAR is to compare two investments to see which one is putting the firm at more risk. Another use for VAR is tracking the size of an investment over time. VAR is also commonly used to establish consistent position limits across a trading firm—from individual traders, to trading desks, to entire divisions of a company.

Mathematically, VAR is defined as a threshold value where the probability of a loss exceeds the threshold over a given time horizon and probability level. For example, if a bank has a $1 million, 95 percent one-day VAR, the bank has a 5 percent probability of losing $1 million in the next 24 hours. In this example, 95 percent is the given probability level, 5 percent probability of loss comes from 100 percent minus the given probability level, and the given time horizon is one day.

VAR is a forward-looking measure that attempts to estimate likely price movements that will happen in the future. Because the future is unknown, VAR is never an exact measurement. As a result, two equally qualified risk managers can come up with slightly different estimates for VAR. In addition, there are several common approaches to estimating VAR. These approaches can include using historical price movements, forward implied volatility from options markets, or a variety of statistical models.

One common approach used to estimate VAR is to assume that percentage changes in price (called *percent returns*) are normally distributed. Historical data would then be used to estimate the size of a typical price move. This assumption used in the model (that percent returns are normally distributed and can be described by a single parameter called *volatility*) would give the model its name (this is called a *parametric* model). In addition, the frequency at which different moves would be observed could be graphed and described

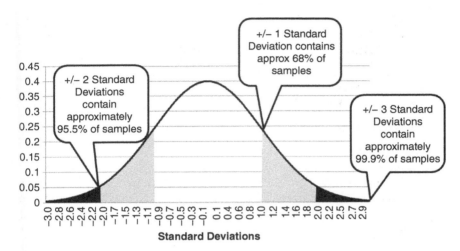

**FIGURE 6.1**  Normal Distribution

by a single factor, the standard deviation of the distribution. (See Figure 6.1, Normal Distribution.)

Statistical terminology is used to describe VAR regardless of how it is actually calculated. There are two major factors that are used to describe VAR. First, a VAR calculation needs to define the length of time over which percent returns are calculated. Two common choices for timeframe are one-day and one-week time horizons. Longer periods are possible, but become progressively harder to calculate due to the large amount of data required. Second, a VAR calculation needs to define the probability that a certain price move will be observed during that period. This is called the *confidence level*. The confidence level indicates how often a loss larger than the VAR number will be observed. (See Figure 6.2, Understanding VAR.)

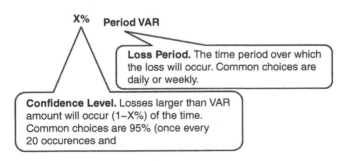

**FIGURE 6.2**  Understanding VAR

## Example: VAR

Rafaela, a risk manager at an investment bank, is calculating the VAR of a trading portfolio. Rafaela calculates that the one-day forward volatility is 5 percent. The portfolio is $100,000 in size. What is the one-day VAR at a 95 percent confidence level, assuming normally distributed percent returns?

**95 Percent One-Day VAR** = 1.645 × $100,000 × 5 percent = **$8,225**

**Explanation:**
Assuming normally distributed returns, a 95 percent VAR can be found by multiplying the one-day standard deviation in P&L by 1.645. The 1.645 is chosen because of how a normal distribution works—5 percent of values are less than 1.645 standard deviations away from the mean. This relationship is a property of the normal distribution. Finally, the standard deviation of the P&L can be converted into dollars by multiplying the portfolio size (in dollars) by the daily volatility.

Some common choices for VAR calculations are:

- **95 Percent Daily VAR.** A daily loss exceeding this number will occur approximately once every 20 days (since 5 percent of the time = 1 out of every 20 observations). In other words, a loss greater than this VAR amount will occur approximately once a month since there are approximately 21 trading days a month. If returns are normally distributed, this VAR will be 1.645 standard deviations.
- **99 Percent 5-Day VAR.** A cumulative weekly loss exceeding this number will occur approximately once every 100 weeks (since this is a weekly VAR and 1 percent of the time equals 1 out of 100 observations). In other words, since there are 52 weeks a year, this type of loss will occur once every two years. If returns are normally distributed, this loss will be larger than 2.326 standard deviations.

Because of its statistical nature, VAR does better comparing investments and describing events *on the average* than it does describing extremely rare events. In this regard, it is similar to other measures of portfolio size. For example, compared to a half million dollar portfolio, a $1 million stock portfolio will typically have larger daily price movements—perhaps double. However, that comparative description does not give accurate information about the likelihood that either portfolio will suffer a massive loss that might occur due to a stock market crash.

Extreme events are difficult to predict using VAR for several reasons. First, VAR is based on a *common denominator* that crosses commodity,

## KEY CONCEPT: VALUE-AT-RISK IS A MEASURE OF SIZE

*Value-at-risk* is way to describe the size of a trading position. It does this by describing how the value of trading positions is likely to change over time. As a measure of size, VAR doesn't give much insight into the specific risks facing a trading position.

- Value-at-risk is a measure of size.
- VAR is commonly used to set position limits.
- As a measure of size, VAR does not describe whether a transaction is likely to be a good or bad investment. Larger investments will have more risk than smaller investments. However, a large investment is not necessarily better or worse than a small investment.
- VAR does not describe worst-case losses very well. VAR gives approximately the same level of detail on extreme events as other measures of size. For example, different risk managers might calculate an *extreme loss scenario* for one day loss on a $100,000 diversified portfolio of stocks as being between a 30 percent and 100 percent loss. Despite the wide range, all those estimates might be equally correct.
- VAR obscures detail. Any description of size by itself, like VAR, lacks important details. Knowing the size of a stock investment doesn't give information like the geographic location of the company, its industry, or the specific challenges facing that stock.

industry, and geographic boundaries. It works by eliminating details needed to understand specific risk factors. Second, extreme events are relatively rare. There is no reason to believe that they will occur with the same frequency at which they were historically observed. Third, the worst-case scenario is almost always a total loss. Knowledge that a complete loss is possible usually isn't very useful to most traders since it is difficult take action on that information.

## TRADING LIMITS

The most common ways to control risk are to limit the size of investments and ensure that enough money is available to fund any losses. Both of these actions require knowledge about the size of the investment. As a result, a common problem facing risk managers is how to describe the size of an investment. Once the size of an investment can be described, then it is possible to create limits about the maximum size of investments.

Describing the size of an investment is often difficult because trades have different levels of *leverage*. Leverage, when used in finance, is a term that describes various ways to increase the size of an investment while still using the same amount of capital. One way to do this is by using borrowed money. For example, one way to create a leveraged investment is for a private investor to trade stocks using a margin account.

In addition, even without borrowing money, some investments are inherently more highly leveraged than other investments. For example, a company might agree to swap 10,000 barrels of oil for $1 million in one year's time. If the contract represents a fair exchange (if a barrel of oil is worth $100), neither side has to put down money at inception of the trade. The risk is similar to buying $1 million of crude oil (for every dollar the price rises, the trader would make $10,000), except that there is no initial investment.

Finally, even for similar investments of the same size, some investments are inherently more risky than other investments. For example, comparing a diversified stock portfolio that mimics the S&P 500 index against a single stock, the risk of having all of one's investment in a single stock is much higher. If the goal is to equally compare trading portfolios, the methodology shouldn't encourage traders to make large bets in the riskiest assets.

To solve these problems, value-at-risk describes size by typical changes in value (expected profits and losses) rather than in terms of money used to make the investment. VAR has largely replaced position limits and capital requirements based on the concept of number of shares, number of contracts, and other measures of size.

## PERCENT RETURNS

The mathematical concept of *volatility* is used to calculate how much positions are likely to change in value. In finance, volatility is typically defined as the standard deviation of continuously compounded returns over some timeframe. Over a discrete period, returns can be calculated by examining the percent change in an asset over that period of time. (See Equation 6.1, Discrete Returns.)

$$Return_t = \frac{Price_t}{Price_{t-1}} - 1$$

or (6.1)

$$Return_t = \frac{Price_t - Price_{t-1}}{Price_{t-1}}$$

where

Return$_t$     **Discrete Period Return.** The percent change in value between the current period and the prior period

Price$_t$      **Price.** The price in the current period

Price$_{t-1}$   **Price.** The price in the prior period

As progressively smaller periods of time get chosen, it becomes possible to calculate the continuously compounded return of the asset. This can be calculated using the same approach as for continuously compounded interest. (See Equation 6.2, Continuously Compounded Returns.)

$$Return_t = ln\left(\frac{Price_t}{Price_{t-1}}\right) \tag{6.2}$$

where

Return$_t$     **Continuously Compounded Return.** The continuously compounded percent change in value between the current period and the prior period

ln()       **Natural Logarithm.** The natural logarithm function

Price$_t$      **Price.** The price in the current period

Price$_{t-1}$   **Price.** The price in the prior period

The volatility of a set of observations can be calculated by taking the standard deviation of continuously compounded returns. The timeframe is an important component of the calculation. For example, daily, monthly, and annual volatility can be calculated by examining daily, monthly, or annual changes in price respectively. The typical convention is to always present volatility as an annualized number. In cases where a different unit is used, a key word like *daily volatility* will be used to indicate the difference.

As long as returns are independently distributed, volatility will scale with the square root of time. As a result, it is possible to scale volatility for one time frame (like daily volatility) to another time frame (like annual volatility). This is because variance is additive over time for these types of distributions. Variance is the square of standard deviation. When returns are independent, the variance of the sum of daily returns is equal to the sum of the variances. (See Equation 6.3, Converting Volatility between Timeframes.)

| Timeframe | Formula |
|---|---|
| Weekly (5 trading days) | $Weekly\ Volatility = \sqrt{5}\ Daily\ Volatility$ |
| Monthly (21 trading days) | $Weekly\ Volatility = \sqrt{21}\ Daily\ Volatility$ |
| Annual (252 trading days) | $Annual\ Volatility = \sqrt{252}\ Daily\ Volatility$ |
| Monthly from Annual (12 months a year) | $Monthly\ Volatility = \dfrac{Annual\ Volatility}{\sqrt{12}}$ |
| Weekly from Annual (52 weeks a year) | $Weekly\ Volatility = \dfrac{Annual\ Volatility}{\sqrt{52}}$ |

$$(6.3)$$

## PARAMETRIC VAR

There are two main types of VAR, *parametric VAR* and *non-parametric VAR*. The difference between the two is that parametric VAR assumes that returns will be normally distributed in the future. This substantially simplifies the math involved in combining positions into large portfolios and in converting between types of VAR. Non-Parametric VAR allows more realistic assumptions but is typically more complicated and involves large-scale computer simulation.

Because it is simpler to use, and the limitations of parametric VAR are relatively unimportant for the purpose of setting position limits and calculating capital requirements, parametric VAR is the more common form of value-at-risk calculation. Common assumptions associated with parametric VAR are that returns are independent, identically distributed (have the same volatility each day), and normally distributed.

The assumptions for parametric VAR are:

- Percent returns are normally distributed.
- Percent returns are independent from one day to the next (i.e., there is no mean reversion).
- Returns are identically distributed (i.e., every day has the same volatility).

A *parameter* is a term in a mathematical function that defines the specific form of some function. In the case of a normal distribution, there are two parameters that define a specific type of normal distribution—the mean of the distribution and the standard deviation. For financial products, the expected percent return (the mean value) is close to zero (time value of money inflation) and the same for every financial instrument. As a result, the normal distribution is primarily defined by a single parameter, the standard deviation. This looks

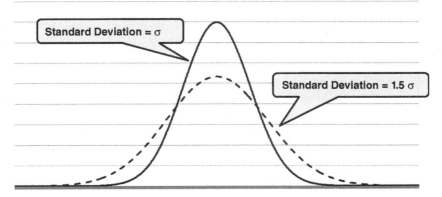

**FIGURE 6.3** Normal Distributions with Different Standard Deviations

like a bell curve whose width is determined by the standard deviation. (See Figure 6.3, Normal Distributions with Different Standard Deviations.)

Because a normal distribution is primarily defined by the standard deviation, traders can easily convert between different confidence levels. Some of these mathematical relationships are summarized below. (See Table 6.1, Important Normal Distribution Relationships.)

### Example

Austin, a portfolio manager, wants to calculate a one-day VAR at a $90, 95,$ and $99$ percent confidence level for a portfolio whose standard deviation of historical profits and losses is +/− $2 million a day.

- **90 Percent One-Day VAR = $2MM × 1.282 = $2.564MM**
- **95 Percent One-Day VAR = $2MM × 1.645 = $3.29MM**
- **99 Percent One-Day VAR = $2MM × 2.326 = $4.652MM**

If parametric VAR at one confidence level is known, it is possible to scale this to other confidence levels. Since VAR levels are all multiples of the same volatility term, traders can calculate the model parameter (the standard deviation) and use that parameter to find the other confidence levels.

It should be noted that the different confidence levels all contain the exact same information. This makes calculations easy, but it is also the reason that parametric VAR does not describe rare events very well. All of the calculations are based on scaling a typical P&L movement (the standard deviation), rather than analyzing exceptional moves.

**TABLE 6.1**    Important Normal Distribution Relationships

| Confidence Level | Probability that Loss is Greater than VAR | Standard Deviation Associated with Confidence Level |
|---|---|---|
| 90% | 10% | −1.282 |
| 95% | 5% | −1.645 |
| 99% | 1% | −2.326 |

**Example**

Graisen, a risk manager needs to convert a 95 percent one-day VAR into a 99 percent one-day VAR. The 95 percent one-day VAR is $3.29MM.

- **Standard Deviation**      = $3.29/1.645      = $2 MM
- **99 Percent One-Day VAR**  = $2MM × 2.326   = $4.652MM

**Example**

The annualized volatility of gold is approximately 15 percent. Truman, a trader, manages a $200MM portfolio invested in gold. He wants to calculate a one-day 95 percent VAR and a one-month 99 percent VAR. (See Equation 6.4, Moving from Annual to Daily VAR.)

**1-day 95% VAR**
- Daily Volatility                = 15%/$\sqrt{252}$        = .945%
- 1-Day 95%                       = .945% * 1.645        = 1.554%
  Confidence Volatility                                                            (6.4)
- 1-Day 95% VAR              = $200MM * 1.554% = $3.11MM

*Answer = $3.11MM*

Approximately once a month (one out of every 20 business days), Truman should expect a loss greater than $3.11MM. (See Equation 6.5, Moving from Annual to Monthly VAR.)

**1-month 99% VAR**
- Monthly Volatility      = 15%/$\sqrt{12}$                      = 4.330%
- 1-Month 99%            = 4.330% * 2.326              = 10.072%
  Confidence                                                                        (6.5)
- 1-Month 99% VAR    = $200MM * 10.072%   = $20.144MM

*Answer = $20.144MM*

Approximately once every 100 months, Truman should expect to have a monthly loss greater than $20.144MM.

**Note:**
The 1.645 (for a 95 percent confidence level) and 2.326 (a 99 percent confidence level) are a feature of normal distributions.

## ESTIMATING VOLATILITY FOR PARAMETRIC VAR

VAR is a forward-looking estimate of volatility. As a result, estimating future volatility requires a prediction or assumption about how the future will develop. As a result, there are a number of methods that are used to estimate volatility for VAR calculations. There are advantages and disadvantages to each approach. While certain approaches have worked better in certain situations, there is no guarantee that any single method will be better than other methods in the future.

The two main ways to estimate volatility are to look at what has happened in the past (historical volatility) or to use information from the option markets (implied volatility). Using historical information is based on the premise that the future will look like the past. In other words, if a loss was recently observed, there is a fairly good chance that a similar-size loss could happen in the future. The alternative is to use information based on options market prices using the assumption that traded option prices represent a consensus estimate of likely future volatility.

Within these two general categories of volatility estimates, there are a variety of sub-categories describing specific calculations. These are each described by specific terms like *equally weighted historical volatility, exponentially weighted historical volatility,* or *GARCH volatility.* (See Figure 6.4, Types of Volatility Estimates.)

The choice of methodology generally balances some operational needs (getting numbers quickly in the hands of decision makers and minimizing modeling risk) against other goals (better estimates of unlikely events).

Some methods to calculating volatility are:

- **Equally Weighted Historical Volatility.** The easiest method of calculating historical volatility.
- **Exponentially Weighted Historical Volatility.** More recent estimates are weighted more than older estimates.

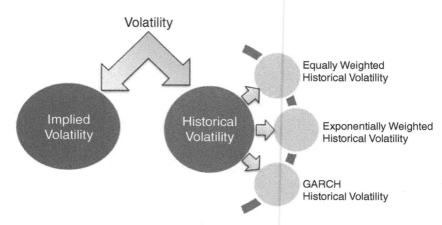

**FIGURE 6.4** Types of Volatility Estimates

- **GARCH Historical Volatility.** Short for *Generalized Auto-Regression Conditional Heteroskedacity*, GARCH introduces a mean-reverting term into an exponentially weighted calculation.
- **Implied Volatility.** Implied volatility from options markets is used to estimate returns.

### Equally Weighted Historical Volatility

For a single asset, parametric VAR requires estimating a single parameter—the volatility of asset prices. The easiest way to do this is to calculate the historical volatility of the returns, weighting all observations equally. This can be performed with standard mathematical functions. Due to the ease of this calculation, this is the most common approach to estimating volatility.

One complication in this calculation is that the size of the investment being analyzed needs to be held constant over the entire period. VAR measures likely changes in value of the portfolio on the calculation date. Holding the size of the investment constant allows the analysis to be applied to the calculation date. Volatility can be calculated by finding the standard deviation of continuously compounded returns. (See Equation 6.6, Continuously Compounded Returns.)

$$x_t = ln\left(\frac{S_t}{S_{t-1}}\right) \qquad (6.6)$$

where

$x_t$      continuously compounded return at time t

$S_t$      price at time t

$S_{t-1}$     price at time t − 1 (the observation immediately prior to time t)

ln()     natural logarithm function

**Note:** In later calculations, the sign of t will switch so that t = 0 will be the latest observation, t = 1 will be the prior observation, and so on.

For financial assets like stocks or bonds, this calculation is typically performed on historical spot prices. For physical commodities that have strong seasonal variation in prices, the calculation is typically done on futures contracts corresponding to the delivery month. Regardless of the source of the underlying prices, volatility is calculated by taking the standard deviation of the returns. (See Equation 6.7, Volatility Calculation with Equal Probability.)

$$\sigma = \sqrt{\frac{1}{N} \sum_{t=0}^{N-1} (x_t - \mu)^2} \qquad (6.7)$$

where

$x_t$     continuously compounded return at time t

N     number of samples

t     time, where t = 0 is the most recent sample

μ     mean return. This is calculated by the formula:

$$\mu = \frac{1}{N} \sum_{t=0}^{N-1} x_t$$

## Case Study: Which Is the Best VAR to Use? The Collapse of Barings

In February 1995, the oldest bank in the United Kingdom, Barings, collapsed due largely to extremely large trades made by one of its traders, Nick Leeson. Trading out of the Singapore office, Mr. Leeson lost $1.3 billion on unauthorized investments on the Singapore International Money Exchange (SIMEX). These losses wiped out the firm's entire equity capital and ultimately led to its collapse.

At the time of the collapse, even under normal market conditions, this position would have had a 95 percent monthly VAR of approximately $835 million. This amount exceeded the equity capital of the firm. While different VAR approaches would give different estimates of size and some might be better than others, it's likely that *any* type of firm-wide VAR calculation would have identified the outsized trades and prevented the bankruptcy of Barings.

Choosing the number of samples needed to calculate volatility is a judgment call. Most statistical estimates require 30 to 50 samples to be valid. Long time horizons can incorporate events that only occur infrequently. However, the longer the time frame, the less important recently observed events become to the calculation. VAR calculations commonly use between three months and two years of data.

Another issue with equally weighting all samples is that VAR can change due to items coming into or out of the sample set. For example, if an extreme event occurred on January 1, 2010, and a one-year horizon was used to calculate volatility, a year and a day later that large value would drop out of the VAR calculation. When that happens, the calculated volatility could undergo a dramatic change even though there were no major movements recently observed.

The effect of large movements causing large swings in volatility calculations can be seen below. (See Figure 6.5, S&P 500 Historical Volatility.) In this example, a 252-day moving average of prices is used to calculate volatility. The problematic area occurs in late 2009. In mid-2012, the volatility estimate drops dramatically because the large move drops out of the sample set.

## Exponentially Weighted Volatility

Exponentially weighting returns is similar to equally weighting returns, except that more recent values are given higher weighting in the volatility calculation. This complicates the calculation, but eliminates the problem of large values dropping out of the calculation. As large values get further away, they have a progressively smaller impact on the calculation.

Exponentially weighted returns use a decay factor, commonly called lambda ($\lambda$) that progressively decreases the weight of each sample as the samples get

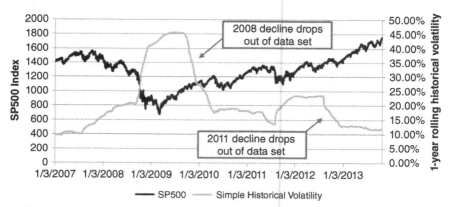

**FIGURE 6.5**    S&P 500 Historical Volatility

further back in time. For example, the current day's sample (t = 0) receives a 100 percent weighting. The earlier samples get progressively less weighting in the volatility calculation. (See Equation 6.8, Exponential Weighting.)

$$p_t = \lambda^t \tag{6.8}$$

where

$$p_t \qquad \text{weighting at time t}$$

For example, if $\lambda = .94$, then

$p_0 \quad = (.94)^0 \quad = 1.0000$

$p_1 \quad = (.94)^1 \quad = 0.9400$

$p_2 \quad = (.94)^2 \quad = 0.8836$

$p_n \quad = (.94)^n \quad \text{(and so on)}$

Including a weighting factor slightly complicates the volatility calculation. (See Equation 6.9, Volatility Calculation with Different Probabilities.)

$$\sigma = \sqrt{\frac{\sum_{t=0}^{N-1} p_t (x_t - \mu)^2}{\sum_{t=0}^{N-1} p_t}} \tag{6.9}$$

where

$x_t \qquad$ log return at time t

$p_t \qquad$ weighting at time t

$N \qquad$ number of samples

$t \qquad$ time

$\mu \qquad$ mean return, calculated by the formula:

$$\mu = \frac{\sum_{t=0}^{N-1} p_t x_t}{\sum_{t=0}^{N-1} p_t}$$

Compared to equal-weighted historical volatility, exponential weighting places much more emphasis on recent events. When a very large return enters the dataset, the volatility estimate will immediately have a large change. As time passes, that value has less and less effect on the volatility calculation. As a result, the volatility estimate won't suddenly drop when the extreme value drops out of the estimate.

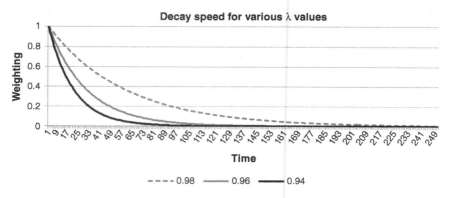

**FIGURE 6.6**   Exponential Decay Speeds

Exponential weighting produces a *soft limit* to the number of samples used in the equation because the weights will eventually get so small that the value has a negligible effect on the volatility calculation. For example, when lambda equals 0.94, observations older than 75 days are weighted less than 1 percent of more recent observations. At a lambda equals 0.96, this occurs after 113 days, and at lambda equals 0.98, it occurs after 228 days. After those points, increasing the length of the simulation period has little effect on the volatility calculation. (See Figure 6.6, Exponential Decay Speeds.)

### GARCH Historical Volatility

The same calculations used for exponentially weighted historical volatility can be used with any type of weighting. The choice of an exponential decline in weight is fairly arbitrary and various methods have been adopted to improve the choice of how volatility is weighted. One of the most important

### KEY CONCEPT: RECURSIVE CALCULATIONS

The process of calculating both equally weighted and exponentially weighted calculations can be substantially sped up if the values calculated for the previous day are used rather than recalculating the entire series. For example, the difference between a sum of values today and the previous sum is the addition of today's value and the subtraction of whatever value is dropping out of the calculation.

methods is called *generalized autoregressive conditionally hetroskedastic* models (GARCH).

The term GARCH comes from the following abbreviations:

- **Generalized (G).** This term means that the model is generalized to describe a set of models rather than a specific model. As a result, GARCH models typically need some additional information to define which model in the set of possible models is being used. For example, a GARCH(1,1) model describes a specific model with the two parameters needed to describe the model each equal to 1.
- **Autoregressive (AR).** A term used to describe a generalized random process where future movements are affected by the current value and values trend to a long-term mean value.
- **Conditionally Hetroskedastic (CH).** A term meaning that the underlying data has different variances (different volatility). This is different than other models of volatility discussed in this section that assume volatility is the same in all periods.

Some of the major criticisms of volatility calculations that have previously been discussed are they assume that volatility is constant over their calculation period. However, empirical studies of market volatility show that volatility appears to change over time and contains a mean-reverting component. GARCH models address those criticisms by allowing volatility to change over time—moving away from the average and then reverting.

Mean reverting means that volatility can diverge from its long-run average over time, but eventually comes back. The speed of reversion is commonly based on historical observations. For example, if volatility is high today it is likely to be higher than normal tomorrow as well. However, tomorrow's volatility is likely to be less high than it is today—it typically moves in the direction (reverts) toward the long-run average (mean).

GARCH models estimate the current volatility as a function of several factors—the weighted average long-term variance (abbreviated $\omega$), various historical volatilities (abbreviated $\sigma$), and various square residual errors (abbreviated $\varepsilon$). The most widely used GARCH model is called a GARCH(1,1) model. The (x,y) in parenthesis specify the number of volatility ($\sigma$) and residual error ($\varepsilon$) terms in the equation. (See Equation 6.10, GARCH(1,1) Model.)

A GARCH (x,y) model estimates volatility as a function of two variables ($\sigma$, $\varepsilon$). The x value in the model definition indicates how many $\sigma$ variables are in the model. The y value in the model definition indicates how many $\varepsilon$ variables are in the model.

$$\sigma_t = \omega + \alpha \varepsilon_{t-1}^2 + \beta \sigma_{t-1} \tag{6.10}$$

where

$\sigma_t$      volatility at time t

$\omega$      weighted average long term variance (a constant)

$\varepsilon_t^2$      squared residual error at time t. The residual error can be calculated: $\varepsilon_t^2 = \left(\sigma_t - \sigma_{t-1}\right)^2$

$\alpha$      a constant

$\beta$      a constant

The three constants in the equation ($\omega$, $\alpha$, $\beta$) are typically solved using an optimizer to best fit the volatility patterns that have been historically observed over some fitting period.

In practice, a GARCH model will work much like an exponential weighted model where the best weighting is determined based on algorithms specific to each asset. This uses a disciplined method to estimate parameters that is missing from simpler models. The downside of GARCH models is that they involve much more computation than simple models and they are harder to understand by laymen. This means results get in the hands of decision makers more slowly and problems take longer to resolve.

### Implied Volatility

An alternative to using historical VAR estimates is to use forward volatility implied by trading in the options market. Theoretically, this method is appealing since it provides a forward-looking, market-based expectation of volatility. The concept is that since traders are putting their own money at risk, market prices represent a consensus view of volatility. In addition, because the value is observed rather than modeled, there are relatively few

### KEY CONCEPT: CHOOSING THE BEST MODEL FOR A TASK

Complex models often inspire overconfidence in the users of those models. All historical models share a common problem—they assume that the future will look like the past. In some ways this is good—if a large move has recently been observed, there is a good probability it will happen again. However, if something unexpected occurs, it is likely that all historical models will fail—and the more complex models won't necessarily work better than simpler models in these cases.

modeling decisions that need to be made. That makes this approach easy to implement.

On the downside, there is no real evidence that forward markets provide better volatility estimates than historical models. In any market, prices are set by relative supply and demand for the assets being traded. In the options market, selling options is risky. Because of that risk, the number of potential sellers is typically less than the number of option buyers. This introduces a complexity into forward volatility calculations—prices are typically set by where people are willing to sell.

Another factor could be the reasons that traders transact in the option markets. Buying an option is a way to place a highly leveraged bet on prices. It is also a way to reduce risk. This creates the possibility that option buyers might be less price sensitive than sellers. For example, someone looking to reduce risk might be willing to pay an above market price to reduce some exposure. However, there is only one reason to sell options and take on additional risk—because the price of the option is sufficiently high.

An empirical comparison of equal weighted historical volatility to forward implied volatility shows that both methods give similar estimates. Market-implied volatility generally has more day-to-day variation than historically calculated volatility. It also responds (both up and down) more quickly than historical volatility. (See Figure 6.7, Implied Volatility.)

More sensitive numbers can be helpful in some cases to give an early warning about possible market volatility. However, it can also cause operational problems that exacerbate risky situations since a major use of VAR is to set position limits and calculate regulatory capital requirements. These are both calculations that can exacerbate financial crises because they can force portfolio liquidations.

For example, if value-at-risk is being used to limit the size of trading positions, a sharp rise in volatility will force traders to start liquidating positions to get under trading limits. Because it is a forced move, the traders are no longer price sensitive—they have to take any price offered in the market. As soon as other traders realize this fact, the traders who are being forced to transact will have a much harder time transacting at good prices.

## CALCULATING PORTFOLIO VAR

When two assets are not perfectly correlated, the combination of the two assets will be less risky than either asset alone. For example, if a coin is flipped, it will have a 50 percent chance of landing on heads and a 50 percent chance of landing on tails. Flipping the coin twice will reduce the uncertainty because the results of the coin flip are not correlated. If a coin is flipped twice,

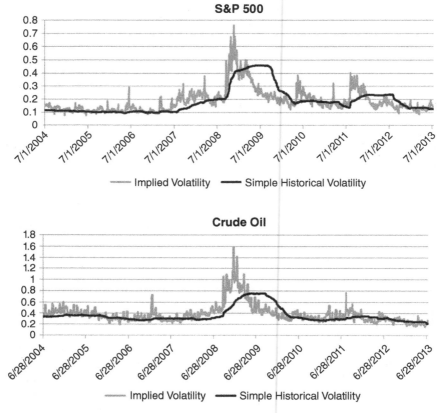

**FIGURE 6.7** Implied Volatility

## KEY CONCEPT: HOW SENSITIVE DOES VAR NEED TO BE?

One of the highly touted *advantages* of exponential historical volatility, GARCH, and implied volatility compared to simple historical VAR models is that the more complicated models react much more quickly to changes. In practice, this can be a self-fulfilling prophecy and exacerbate losses in periods of volatile markets.

VAR is commonly used to limit the size of trading positions. When volatility suddenly spikes, the practical effect is that traders begin selling their positions into the market to get back under their trading limits. This simultaneously reduces liquidity (most institutions use VAR, so every trader is trying to sell at the same time) and creates an incentive for the few price-sensitive traders (those still willing to buy) to drive prices as low as possible.

Markets are efficient when all traders are attempting to maximize their own profit. Operating efficiently, the price of an investment represents consensus on the true value of that asset. However, when one side suddenly becomes insensitive to price, market prices and value can diverge quickly. This doesn't mean that more complicated models are bad, but it does underscore the importance of common sense in risk management.

there is a 25 percent chance of two heads and a 25 percent chance of two tails. There is a 50 percent chance that a head and a tail have been observed. In other words, the chance of flipping a combination of heads and tails is more likely than flipping only heads or only tails.

The amount of diversification gained by combining multiple assets depends on the relationship between the assets. At one extreme, if two assets are identical (maybe two shares of the same company), then there is no diversification benefit. At the other, two assets may have moves of identical magnitude, but be opposite in direction. For example, an agreement to buy a barrel of crude oil will offset the risk of an agreement to sell a barrel of crude oil. *Correlation* is the mathematical term that describes the strength of the relationship between two assets.

The formula for combing two assets into a portfolio is shown below. (See Equation 6.11, Portfolio VAR.)

The square of the portfolio VAR is equal to the sum of the squares of the component VARs plus a correlation adjustment. The portfolio VAR can be calculated by taking the square root of the sum on the right side of the equation.

$$VAR^2_{portfolio} = VAR^2_A + VAR^2_B + 2 * \rho * VAR_A * VAR_B \qquad (6.11)$$

where

$VAR_{portfolio}$    VAR of the portfolio (in units of currency, like dollars)

$VAR_A$    VAR of investment A (in units of currency, like dollars)

$VAR_B$    VAR of investment B (in units of currency, like dollars)

$\rho$    correlation between A and B

The major complication in this calculation comes from the need to estimate the correlation between the individual investments. Two of the practical problems associated with using correlation estimates are instability of results and the averaging effect.

- **Instability.** Historically calculated correlation varies widely over time. For example, two assets might move together because they were touted on the same investment talk show on TV for several months and the same investors rushed to purchase both assets. Looking at historical prices, the reason why to investments are behaving alike may be impossible to determine. The risk is that this correlation may break down in the future because there is no lasting relationship between the two assets.
- **Averaging.** Correlation often focuses on extreme rather than average behavior. For example, crude oil is separated into gasoline and diesel fuel. When crude oil prices move suddenly, both gasoline and diesel prices tend to move too. However, when crude prices are stable, supply and demand in the individual markets for gasoline and diesel determine prices. As a result, in stable markets, there may be very low correlation between gas and diesel.

Another complication of combining a large number of positions together is that the difficulty of the calculation goes up as additional items are added. As a result, it is common to identify a limited number of risk factors that are used to calculate risk. For example, interest rates, crude oil prices, and broad stock market indices are common risk factors.

Actual exposures commonly get *mapped* to these risk factors and then grouped together into buckets. For example, publically traded stocks might be split into Value Stock and Growth Stock exposures and then aggregated together to form two buckets. The assignment of financial instruments into categories is called *mapping*. The simplification of positions causes the calculations to lose some precision. However, the benefit of mapping is that it reduces the calculation from around 1,000 factors (the number of well traded stocks) to two factors (Value and Growth buckets). This simplifies the calculations and can help summarize the key exposures to interested parties.

---

### KEY CONCEPT: VAR IS ALWAYS GREATER THAN OR EQUAL TO ZERO

VAR is a measure of uncertainty or risk. An investment might involve no risk or uncertainty and result in zero VAR. There can never be negative uncertainty.

## VARIANCE/COVARIANCE MATRIX

When more than two assets are combined, the formula to calculate the combined volatility becomes complicated. To simplify this calculation, the calculation is often represented as a matrix of variance and covariance calculations. Volatility is calculated this way because the square of the volatility, called *variance*, is additive. The variance of the combined portfolio is calculated by adding together the cross variances of all assets in the portfolio. This can be reconverted into a volatility number by taking the square root of the portfolio variance. This can either be calculated in dollars (as shown earlier in the chapter) or per investment dollar (as shown in this section).

A variance/covariance matrix contains the list of assets on both the top and left side. Each axis has the same list of assets. Each cell contains the correlation between the pair of assets corresponding to its row and column multiplied by the weight of the assets (as a percentage of total dollars invested) by the volatility of each asset. A two-asset variance/covariance matrix is shown below. (See Equation 6.12, Variance/Covariance Matrix.)

For a portfolio of two assets (named asset A and asset B), the volatility per dollar in the portfolio can be represented: The value in each cell will be equal to: (correlation between 1 and 2) (weight of 1) (weight of 2) (volatility of 1) (volatility of 2). This is often represented in tabular form:

|   | A | B |
|---|---|---|
| A | $\rho_{AA} W_A W_A \sigma_A \sigma_A$ | $\rho_{AB} W_A W_B \sigma_A \sigma_B$ |
| B | $\rho_{BA} W_B W_A \sigma_B \sigma_A$ | $W_B W_B \rho_{BB} \sigma_B \sigma_B$ |

$$(6.12)$$

The variance of the portfolio is the sum of each of the cells in the matrix.

where

$\sigma_A, \sigma_B$     **Volatility.** The volatility of a series is the standard deviation of the elements within series. In financial situations, the series is commonly a series of logarithmic returns or dollar changes in value.

$\sigma_X^2$     **Variance of X.** Variance is the square of the volatility. This is an alternate way to represent volatility that has a useful mathematical property – the ability to add component variances together to calculate a combined variance.

$\rho_{AB}$     **Correlation.** The correlation between A and B

$W_A$,      **Portfolio Weights.** When volatility is calculated
$W_B$       per dollar, then it is necessary to weight the
            calculation by dollars invested in each asset. The
            total of all weights needs to sum to 100%.

This equation is often simplified to make it easier to read. First, the correlation between any asset and itself is always equal to 100 percent. This allows the correlation term to drop out of the diagonal. In addition, the term (correlation) × (volatility of asset 1) × (volatility of asset 2) already has a specific name, called *covariance*. A simplified form of a variance/covariance matrix is shown below. [See Equation 6.13, Variance/Covariance Matrix (alternate notation).]

For a portfolio of two assets (named asset A and asset B), the notation involved in calculating the variance of the portfolio can be simplified a bit.

|   | A | B |
|---|---|---|
| A | $W_A{}^2\sigma_A{}^2$ | $W_A W_B Cov(A,B)$ |
| B | $W_B W_A Cov(B,A)$ | $W_B{}^2\sigma_B{}^2$ |

(6.13)

As a formula, the variance per dollar in the portfolio would be calculated:

$$\sigma^2_{Portfolio} = w_A^2\sigma_A^2 + w_B^2\sigma_B^2 + 2w_A w_B Cov(A, B)$$

**Note:** The volatility can be found by taking the square root of the portfolio variance.

where

   $Cov(A,B)$   **Covariance of A and B.** The covariance of A and B is usually an intermediate step to calculating correlation. However, if the correlation is known, the covariance can be found by multiplying the correlation by the volatilities of A and B.

$$Cov(A,B) = \rho_{AB}\sigma_A\sigma_B$$

An important property of covariance is that the order of the parameters doesn't matter. This allows $Cov(A,B)$ and $Cov(B,A)$ to be combined into a single term.

$$Cov(A,B) = Cov(B, A)$$

Mathematically, variance is a special type of covariance. The variance of an asset A, $\sigma_A$, is the covariance of A with itself.

$$\sigma_A = Cov(A, A)$$

Covariance is a common mathematical formula standard in most spreadsheets. If it has to be done by hand, the calculation of covariance is very similar to the calculation used to calculate variance and standard deviation. If A and B are series with n elements each, the covariance is the sum of the differences multiplied by one another.

$$Cov(A, B) = \sum_{1}^{n}(A_n - \bar{A})(B_n - \bar{B})$$

When combining two assets, there isn't a real advantage to using a matrix—it's easier to use the equation (6-11) described above. However, where there is more than one asset, displaying the information in matrix form makes it much easier to keep track of which elements need to be in the final calculation. For example, if there are 500 assets being combined into a portfolio, the calculation becomes quite complex. An example of a four-element variance/covariance matrix is shown below. (See Equation 6.14, A Four-Element Variance/Covariance Matrix.)

|   | A | B | C | D |
|---|---|---|---|---|
| **A** | $W_A^2\sigma_A^2$ | $W_A W_B Cov(A,B)$ | $W_A W_C Cov(A,C)$ | $W_A W_D Cov(A,D)$ |
| **B** | $W_B W_A Cov(B,A)$ | $W_B^2\sigma_B^2$ | $W_B W_C Cov(B,C)$ | $W_B W_D Cov(B,D)$ |
| **C** | $W_C W_A Cov(C,A)$ | $W_C W_B Cov(C,B)$ | $W_C^2\sigma_C^2$ | $W_C W_D Cov(C,D)$ |
| **D** | $W_D W_A Cov(D,A)$ | $W_D W_B Cov(D,B)$ | $W_D W_C Cov(D,C)$ | $W_D^2\sigma_D^2$ |

(6.14)

## NON-PARAMETRIC VAR

One criticism of parametric VAR is that real-life returns are not necessarily normally distributed. In fact, there may be no single distribution that accurately describes the behavior of the financial markets. The primary alternative to using the statistical distributions used for parametric VAR is to use some type of simulation that generates prices. The two most common types of simulations are *historical simulation* and *Monte-Carlo simulation*. These models are called non-parametric because they are not defined by their parameters (like mean and standard deviation) in the same way as the parametric models.

Historical simulation is straightforward. Instead of characterizing historical returns by their mean and standard deviation, the returns will be directly sampled to find the value that corresponds to the desired confidence level. For example, if 10 years of historical S&P 500 returns

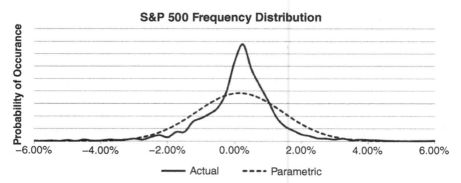

**FIGURE 6.8**   S&P 500 Frequency Distribution

were analyzed, it is possible to graph the estimated parametric distribution side-by-side with the actual distribution. (See Figure 6.8, S&P 500 Frequency Distribution.)

Calculating the actual distribution of VAR will lead to different VAR numbers. For example, in the S&P 500 example, the actual returns are more peaked and have a wider dispersion of results than a normal distribution. Looking at actual numbers, 1 percent of the days had losses greater than 3.75 percent (a 99 percent one-day VAR). The comparable parametric estimate would have estimated a 99 percent one-day VAR of 3 percent. (See Table 6.2 S&P 500 VAR.)

An advantage of non-parametric VAR compared to parametric VAR is that non-parametric VAR is fairly easy to implement. Additionally, non-parametric VAR does not rely on average parameters estimated over a period of time, mapping to benchmarks, or complex correlation/covariance calculations.

On the downside, large scale non-parametric VAR simulations might require a large amount of computer power. Additionally, non-parametric VAR depends on the quality of model used in the analysis. Finally, historical VAR shares the primary weakness associated with Parametric VAR—it assumes that future returns will be similar to historically observed returns.

**TABLE 6.2**   S&P 500 VAR

| Type of Volatility Model | 99% One-Day VAR | 95% One-Day VAR |
|---|---|---|
| Historical Simulation | −3.75% | −1.75% |
| Parametric | −3.00% | −2.00% |

## KEY CONCEPT: NON-PARAMETRIC VAR

Statistical sampling techniques can be used to extend historical simulation in a variety of ways. When this is done, returns are randomly selected from a sample set and then used to construct a frequency distribution. However, all of the returns do not need to be equally likely to be selected. For example, nearby results can be weighted more heavily. This would make them more likely to be selected.

Returns don't necessarily need to be historical daily returns either. They could be historical 10-day returns or the returns could come from some type of model. This would allow the model to incorporate concepts of mean reversion or various types of stress scenarios.

The main steps in this process are:

1. Choose a return from the set of possible returns.
2. Repeat a large number of times.
3. Calculate the frequency distribution of returns.
4. Find the value that corresponds to the desired VAR probability.

**Correlation.** If the VAR for multiple assets is being calculated, having the same observation date used for each asset will allow VAR to be calculated without making assumptions about correlation. Rather than assuming a correlation, the actual movements of each asset on that day can be analyzed.

**Multi-Day VAR.** VAR for a multi-day period can be calculated piecemeal (10 samples to construct a 10-day VAR) or based on actual historical results (where the return is based on the price 10 days earlier). Calculating multi-day returns piecemeal assumes that returns are independent. This can make mathematical operations (like constructing a distribution) easier. However, using actual historical 10-day returns allows factors like mean reversion and correlation between days not to be separately analyzed.

**Monte Carlo.** When the set of possible returns is estimated based on something other than observed history, it is called Monte Carlo VAR. Monte Carlo VAR is typically based on models that can incorporate complicated features like mean reversion, step changes in volatility, and similar extensions to generate the set of possible future returns. The quality of VAR results depends on the model chosen for returns.

## VAR LIMITS IN PRACTICE

Generally speaking, VAR is a description of size. A large VAR number means a large-sized investment. The size of the investment does not imply either a good or a bad investment. For example, a large retirement account may have the same investments, better investments, or worse investments when compared to a smaller retirement account. The actual investment choices, and not the size of the investment, determine the success of each investment.

VAR uses changes in value to compare different types of financial instruments. This leads to VAR calculations that are sometimes fairly complicated. Fortunately, it is relatively easy to monitor to make sure that VAR is working effectively. For example, it is possible to compare actual results to the VAR that was calculated on that day. For a 95 percent confidence level, approximately 1 in 20 values should be outside the VAR limit.

Traders and risk managers monitor VAR by comparing actual trading results to those estimated by VAR calculations. If VAR is working poorly, it will be observable by looking at past data. In this kind of analysis, VAR thresholds (usually indicated by solid black lines) are compared to actual results (gray marks). (See Figure 6.9, VAR Backtest.)

This data can be analyzed to see if the number of samples outside the VAR estimate matches the confidence level of the VAR calculation. For example, in the NYMEX WTI graphic, 5.58 percent of the days had losses greater than the VAR threshold for the day. Given the 2200 daily observations in the backtest, this indicates that losses are more common than the 5 percent of samples estimated by VAR.

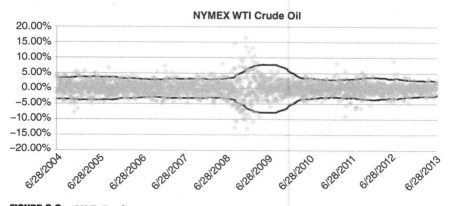

**FIGURE 6.9**   VAR Backtest

## THE MISUSE OF VAR

A major problem with VAR is that VAR gets used for multiple purposes. For example, VAR is commonly used to calculate regulatory capital requirements and is viewed by senior management as a comprehensive measure of risk. These purposes can distract from the goal of using VAR to manage trading operations.

VAR is a statistical measure of risk that does a good job when price movements are clustered around the most likely movements. However, VAR doesn't do as well describing portfolios or investments with the possibility for a large outlying loss. The relative frequency of large losses is obscured by the VAR estimate. For example, if an option trader sells options, he might have a 99 percent chance of making $1 each day and a 1 percent chance of losing $199 each day. Using a 99 percent VAR calculation could give the impression that it's impossible for this strategy to lose money when, on average, it is expected to lose $1 per day on average.

When portfolios have the potential for large losses, it is possible to game VAR calculations by combining or separating portfolios to limit the frequency of large moves. For example, if there are two strategies that each have a chance for a large negative payoff, the probability of the large negative events might individually be below the chosen VAR threshold. However, when the strategies are combined, the probability of loss is now likely enough that a 99 percent VAR is a -$198 loss. (See Figure 6.10, Daily P&L for Two Strategies.)

In other words, it is often possible to manufacture a VAR number of a specific size by changing how positions are aggregated. Being able to game the system damages the ability of traders to use VAR as the primary control over trading losses.

Solving this issue is not as simple as using wider VAR estimates like using a 99.99 percent VAR. One reason is that this would fail at the goal of comparing sizes of investments. For example, comparing two strategies:

Strategy A: 99 percent chance of $1 profit, 1 percent chance of $199 loss

Strategy C: 50 percent chance of $100 profit, 50 percent chance of $199 loss

| Strategy | Day 1 | 2 | 3 | 4 | 5 | 6 | 7 | 8 | 9 | ... |
|----------|-------|-----|-----|-------|-----|-----|-----|-----|-----|-----|
| A | −$199 | $1 | $1 | $1 | $1 | $1 | $1 | $1 | $1 | $1 |
| B | $1 | $1 | $1 | −$199 | $1 | $1 | $1 | $1 | $1 | $1 |

**FIGURE 6.10** Daily P&L for Two Strategies

While neither strategies A nor C are profitable, strategy C is expected to lose money 50 times as much as Strategy A. While it would be possible to change the VAR probabilities so that strategy A showed the same VAR as Strategy C, this doesn't really describe what is being observed. Strategy C is much riskier.

Even so, the real problem comes when high-probability VAR is used to measure capital charges or position limits. Having the same VAR for these two strategies would encourage the trader to pick the riskier strategy. For example, if the numbers were all multiplied by millions, a trader might reasonably decide to take a 50/50 chance at making $100 million on a one-day bet. In other words, by setting an extremely high probability VAR to solve one problem, risk managers could create a worse problem.

### Expected Shortfall

Expected shortfall is a risk measure that may end up replacing VAR at some point in the future. Mechanically, it is calculated much the same way that VAR is calculated. Instead of being the threshold value for the expected loss like VAR, expected shortfall is the expected value of the losses below the VAR threshold. (See Figure 6.11, Expected Shortfall.) Like VAR, expected shortfall is described by a confidence level and time horizon.

Because it is constructed in the same way as VAR, expected shortfall and VAR share many characteristics. Both VAR and expected shortfall present risk as a single number. Both are also relatively easy to calculate and can be applied to any type of financial instrument. Both have similar weaknesses. In exactly the same way as VAR, the calculation depends on the left tail of return distribution. This tail is calculated by looking at a small number of samples (historical VAR)

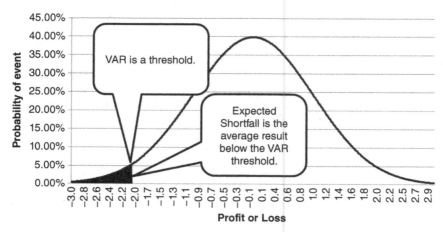

**FIGURE 6.11** Expected Shortfall

## KEY CONCEPT: EXPECTED SHORTFALL MEASURES SIZE

Expected shortfall, like VAR, describes whether the size of an investment is large or small rather than whether it is good or bad. If an investor has two investments, a $10 million investment in a single stock, and a $1 million investment in the same stock, the expected shortfall on the bigger investment will be larger since there is more money to lose. That doesn't mean that the large investment is a worse investment. If given the choice of receiving either investment for free, investors would almost universally choose the larger investment. This is because the larger investment has the potential to both make and lose more money than the smaller investment.

or is assumed to be a certain shape (parametric VAR). This limits the ability of expected shortfall to predict what will actually happen in the future.

Expected shortfall, like VAR, is primarily a measure of size. A large risk number indicates potential for large losses, and a smaller number indicates a potential for smaller losses. However, a complete loss can occur with either a large or a small investment. In other words, expected shortfall isn't insurance or a guarantee that losses will be limited to the expected shortfall. For one thing, expected shortfall is an average loss rather than a worst-case loss. For another, predictions on the far extreme of a probability distribution aren't particularly accurate.

The reason that expected shortfall may replace VAR is that it is *sub-additive*. Sub-additive means that when two risks are combined, the combined risk is equal (if the portfolios are correlated) or less risky (if the portfolios have less than 100 percent correlation) than the sum of the two component VAR numbers. This doesn't happen all the time with a VAR calculation. With VAR, when two portfolios are added together, the combination can result in a higher VAR number than if the component VAR numbers are added together. This commonly happens when each component has a large, but infrequent, possibility of loss.

## TEST YOUR KNOWLEDGE

1. With a 95 percent one-day VAR, approximately how often would a risk manager expect a loss greater than the VAR be observed?
   A. Once a day

    **B.** Once a week

    **C.** Once a month

    **D.** Once a year

2. Colin, a risk manager needs to convert a 99 percent one-day VAR into a 95 percent one-day VAR. The 95 percent one-day VAR is $5MM. What is the 99 percent one-day VAR?

    **A.** $3.5MM

    **B.** $4.2MM

    **C.** $4.7MM

    **D.** $7.0MM

3. If two assets are combined, asset A has a 95 percent one-day VAR of $1MM, and asset B has a 95 percent one-day VAR of $2MM. The sum of the VAR numbers will be:

    **A.** less than zero.

    **B.** between zero and $1MM.

    **C.** between $1MM and $3MM.

    **D.** greater than $3MM.

4. What are criticisms of the historical VAR approach?

    **A.** Many return series are not normally distributed.

    **B.** The timeframe is arbitrary.

    **C.** Equal weight is given to each return and extreme returns cause large changes to VAR when they enter and exit the sample.

    **D.** All of the above.

5. Why is VAR used as a measure of portfolio size rather than the cash spent to enter the investment?

    **A.** Many financial instruments (like FX swaps and commodity forwards) commonly have zero fair value and large risks associated with them.

    **B.** The value of an investment doesn't measure the leverage inherent in that investment.

    **C.** Similar investments with the same price might have very different volatility and risks associated with them.

    **D.** All of the above.

6. Emily, a portfolio manager, is comparing two trading strategies with the same VAR. How do the risks of the portfolio compare to one another?

    **A.** The two strategies are likely to be equally profitable.

    **B.** The daily returns from each trading strategy should be of similar magnitude.

    **C.** The traders who manage each portfolio have a similar outlook on the market.

    **D.** All of the above.

7. Keith, a risk manager, has calculated the standard deviation of expected daily returns for an investment. He used one year of data. How does he create an estimate of annual volatility assuming lognormal prices, 12 months a year, and 21 trading days a month?

   A. Do nothing—he already has the annualized volatility.

   B. Multiply the standard deviation of daily returns by the square root of 12.

   C. Multiply the standard deviation of daily returns by the square root of 252.

   D. Insufficient information is provided to calculate an answer.

8. Anna, a risk manager at a hedge fund, wants to estimate the worst-case move for the portfolio. Which measure of VAR is best suited to calculating an extreme result?

   A. A 95 percent one-day VAR

   B. A 99 percent one-day VAR

   C. A 99 percent one-day VAR

   D. These measures all contain the same information scaled differently

9. What type of VAR model is well suited to a GARCH approach?

   A. A VAR calculation that needs to rapidly react to short-term changes in market volatility.

   B. A VAR calculation that needs to filter out the effect of recent market volatility to focus on long-term trends.

   C. A VAR calculation that uses forward implied volatility estimated from recent option transactions.

   D. GARCH is not useful for VAR modeling.

10. What are the implications of an exponentially weighted VAR calculation?

    A. VAR limits on trading books will change rapidly and potentially lead to a costly cycle of forced liquidations and repurchasing of assets.

    B. VAR will react quickly to recent market behavior.

    C. Both A and B.

    D. Neither A nor B.

11. What information does VAR convey?

    A. The worst-case loss for a trading strategy.

    B. Whether a trading position is a good or bad investment.

    C. The exposure of the trading position to changes in implied volatility.

    D. The size of an investment.

12. Steve is a programmer working at a hedge fund. He is reading a technical documentation manual describing how a certain calculation was calculated. He wants to check the output from the calculation on a spreadsheet.

Calculation Description: daily_return = $\ln(\text{price}_1 / \text{price}_{t-1})$
What does the "ln" mean?

A. It is a variable that is probably defined somewhere else in documentation.
B. It is the inverse normal distribution function.
C. It is a variable that means "last night's price."
D. It is the natural logarithm function.

## CHAPTER 7

# Hedging

Traders can make trades that reduce the risk of other investments. This process is called *hedging*. Hedging locks in profits and losses in one investment by taking an offsetting position in a similar tradable investment. Hedging is commonly done to allow tradable instruments (like crude oil futures) to offset the price risk associated with operating a non-tradable asset (like an oil well). This allows the oil well owner to lock in a fixed sale price for oil that is expected to be produced at some point in the future.

Hedging is a way to *transfer risk*. Traders often use hedging to protect against risks when liquidating their trading position would be difficult or impossible. In the oil well example, the owner doesn't wish to sell the oil well—just to reduce the uncertainty of his future earnings by locking in prices. Of course, this will remove the potential for additional profit along with limiting potential losses.

Hedging often involves both tradable and non-tradable investments. This creates accounting issues because the hedged item (like the crude oil that is expected to be produced) may not be valued the same way as the hedge (the futures). As a result, special accounting rules can be used to delay recognizing profits and losses of the hedge. This allows the trader to match the profit and loss reporting for the hedge (a tradable financial instrument) and hedged item (the non-tradable investment).

## HEDGING

A *hedge* is an investment intended to offset potential profits and losses that might be incurred by another investment. Some common reasons for hedging are to improve the risk/reward relationship of a portfolio or protect profits from an ongoing business. This is typically done by taking a short position (a position that gains in value when the price of an asset declines) to offset a long position (a position that gains in value when prices rise) or vice versa.

Hedging often occurs when the risk being hedged is an intrinsic part of a company's business. For example, an oil well exposes its owner to uncertainty around future prices of oil. When oil is removed from the well, its owner can sell it at market prices. However, fluctuating oil prices will make the oil more valuable at various points in time. This uncertainty can be reduced by arranging to sell a quantity of oil at a fixed price. The oil well is the *hedged item*. The contract selling the oil at a fixed price is called a *hedge* for the oil well.

While hedging is often viewed like buying insurance, it can be very risky. Hedging involves risk much like a speculative trade. Hedges can be very large positions—as large as the business they are intended to offset. In addition, they are often in the opposite direction relative to the initial investment. This is dangerous because hedges may not receive the same level of scrutiny as the initial investment. Commonly, hedging is delegated to quantitative employees who may not have familiarity with trading. The lack of experience is compounded when senior managers fail to fully examine trades because they are described as *hedges* with a risk management purpose rather than *speculative* positions. However, the risk of a hedge is identical to a speculative trade—it is only the intent of the trade that is different.

In the case of the oil drilling company, the company is giving up potential profits if oil prices rise. If the oil well was purchased based on the belief that prices would rise, locking in current prices might be a bad idea. This problem can be compounded if a lot of money is spent on hedging. Certain financial instruments, like options, cost a tremendous amount of money. Traders have to weigh the benefit of removing uncertainty against the cost of hedging.

In addition to its role in trading and risk management, hedging is also an accounting concept. If an investment qualifies as a highly effective hedge for accounting purposes, the hedging company can get beneficial accounting treatment by combining the gains and losses from the hedge and the

### KEY CONCEPT: HEDGING IS A WAY TO TRANSFER RISK

Hedging is a way to transfer some or all risks from a position to another trader. It has a protective purpose. This is similar to how the term is used in a garden. In gardening, a hedge is a line or wall of closely spaced shrubs and trees. Hedges might be planted around a garden or a house for protection the same way that a wall might be built. In finance, a hedge is also intended to protect something. A hedge is an investment whose purpose is to reduce the uncertainty of another investment (the hedged item) by offsetting potential profits and losses.

underlying investment. This is important because hedges often use financial investments subject to mark-to-market rules (like financial futures) to offset a physical obligation (like owning oil in an oil well) which does not need to be marked to market.

## HOW IS HEDGING USED?

On a trading desk, hedging is used for a variety of purposes. A common example is to reduce uncertainty in an existing line of business. For example, an airline might use hedging to reduce its exposure to jet fuel prices by arranging to buy fuel at fixed prices. In other cases, it means to transfer or offset risk. Hedge funds were originally called hedge funds because they had the ability to take both long and short positions.

There is sometimes a fine line between trading for a profit, called *speculation*, and hedging. For example, a jet fuel trader might make a speculative bet that jet fuel prices will rise. This will be done using the same type of transaction as the *hedger* who is trying to reduce exposure to jet fuel prices. Particularly if the speculator is working on an airline's trading desk, the only difference will be the intent of the trade.

Hedging can also be used to make targeted investments. For example, a trading desk might put on both long and short trades to bet that one asset will outperform another asset. As long as the assets are reasonably similar, this will largely remove exposure to the broader market.

Some common reasons for hedging include:

- **Asset Hedging.** Hedging can be used to offset, or lock in, cash flows from some asset. This gives the owner of the asset less variation in future cash flow.

### Example

Marc, the manager of a $100 million hedge fund that invests in the U.S. stock market, is concerned that upcoming government unemployment announcements will cause the stock market to crash. Given the size of his portfolio, he doesn't have time to close down his positions before the announcement. However, there is sufficient liquidity in the futures markets that he could sell futures based on major market indexes prior to the announcement. If he makes the transaction to hedge his strategy, he will give up the possibility of profit (good news being announced) to protect himself against potential losses (bad news being announced).

- **Macro-Economic Hedges.** Trading desks can take positions to protect against (or speculate on) macro-economic factors like the overall health of the economy or changes in interest rates.
- **Long/Short Strategy.** A common trading strategy is to take long and short positions in related instruments. This allows the assets to be traded against one another, removing most of the risk associated with the broader market. The trader will be affected by changes in the size of the spread between the two prices.

## HEDGING COSTS MONEY

Hedging has drawbacks. It will either reduce the potential for both profit and loss or it will cost a substantial amount of money. Either situation has the potential to lead to a worse outcome than having an unhedged position.

When hedging with futures, hedging will reduce the potential for both profits and losses. This may be beneficial if an extreme event could lead to bankruptcy. However, hedging can also limit the ability of a company to make money if market conditions improve. For example, an airline might hedge to lock in fuel prices. This will protect it from bankruptcy if fuel prices rise. However, if prices for jet fuel fall, the airline might lose business, and potentially go bankrupt, because its competitors are able to purchase cheaper fuel and offer lower fares.

When hedging with options, the asymmetric payoff of options can eliminate the possibility of losses while allowing profits. However, with options, the cost of the hedge becomes a large factor. Options are typically very expensive. As a result, the decision on whether to hedge often needs to consider the cost of hedging. In some cases, it makes sense to pay money to reduce a potential loss. However, as the cost of hedging rises, the benefit (relative to the cost) of hedging becomes smaller. At an extreme, it makes no sense to replace the possibility of a loss with a certain loss of the same size.

### KEY CONCEPT: REMOVING RISK IS NOT ALWAYS SMART

Reducing risk is not always a smart business decision. For example, a certain loss of $100 is not preferable to a 50/50 chance of losing $100. While the certain loss has no uncertainty in its final result, and therefore no risk, it also guarantees the worst possible outcome.

## MINIMUM VARIANCE HEDGE RATIO

When hedging, it is useful to choose a hedge that closely matches the item being hedged. The hedge and hedged asset need to be highly correlated and the same size. If a hedge is too small, there will be some residual risk that isn't removed. If a hedge is too large, hedging can end up adding risk to the portfolio. Since the ultimate goal of hedging is typically to minimize the changes in value (or cash flows) it is necessary to properly size the hedge to the hedged asset. The optimal point that minimizes as much risk as possible is called the *minimum variance hedge ratio.*

The effectiveness of a hedge is partially determined by the correlation between the hedge and the hedged item. The expected correlation between the hedge and hedged item is usually estimated by looking at the historical relationship between the two prices (this is described in more detail later in the chapter). If the items are not sufficiently correlated, just like getting the size wrong, hedging can again add risk to a portfolio. (See Figure 7.1, Correlation and Hedge Effectiveness.)

Mathematically, the volatility of the hedge needs to match the expected volatilities of the hedged asset. In addition, to be effective, the hedge and hedged item will need to be highly correlated, with one asset having a positive weight and the other asset having a negative weight. (See Equation 7.1, Portfolio Variance.)

The variance of the portfolio (the square of the volatility) is a function of the asset weights, the asset volatilities, and the correlation between the assets. A variation of this formula with more than two assets is described in Chapter 6, in the section on variance-covariance matrices.

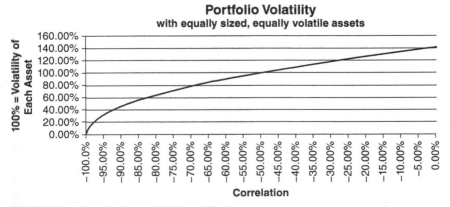

**FIGURE 7.1** Correlation and Hedge Effectiveness

$$\sigma^2_{Portfolio} = \frac{w_1^2\sigma_1^2 + w_2^2\sigma_2^2 + 2w_1w_x\rho\sigma_1\sigma_2}{(w_1 + w_2)^2} \tag{7.1}$$

where

$\sigma_x$     **Volatility.** The volatility of asset x

$w_x$     **Weight.** The weight of the asset x

$\rho$     **Correlation.** The correlation between asset 1 and asset 2

Of course, it is not always possible to find a hedge that is perfectly correlated with the hedged item. As a result, a second step in the hedging process is to determine the size of hedge that removes the most amount of risk. There are several factors that are involved in determining this relationship.

First, the prices of the two assets have to be considered in relation to their volatility. For example, if the hedge and the hedged item have different prices but the same percent volatility, it is necessary to adjust for the relative proportion of each item during creation of the hedge. For example, if jet fuel is $110/BBL and crude oil is $80/BBL, a 10 percent rise in prices is an $11 move for jet fuel and only an $8 move for crude. In other words, if the two products have the same volatility, it is necessary to hedge the same dollar amount of products (like a $1 million position) and not the same volume (1 million barrels).

Second, if the two assets have different volatilities, an adjustment will need to be made to ensure that the dollar size of the expected moves is the same. For example, if crude oil is expected to exhibit 30 percent volatility and jet fuel 15 percent volatility, then a crude oil hedge would need half the size of the jet fuel position. This allows the larger volatility to offset the smaller dollar size and ensure that the dollar volatility is the same between the hedge and hedged asset.

Finally, it is necessary to adjust for the correlation between the hedge and the hedge item. The hedge will need to be smaller for less correlated assets. Otherwise, the hedge will start to increase the risk of the portfolio. For example, if the hedge and hedged item have a correlation of 80 percent, a 1:1 ratio between the hedge and hedged item will add unnecessary risk. For an 80 percent correlation, the best hedge would be a 0.8:1 hedge ratio.

The optimal ratio of the hedge compared to hedged item is called the Minimum Variance Hedge Ratio. (See Equation 7.2, Minimum Variance Hedge Ratio.)

To maximize the effectiveness of the hedge, it is necessary to hedge the dollar amounts (or some other unit of currency). Then, the ratio can be calculated by looking at the correlation and volatility of the hedge and hedged asset.

$$h = \rho \frac{\sigma_a}{\sigma_b} \tag{7.2}$$

where

| | |
|---|---|
| h | **Minimum variance hedge ratio.** The ratio (in currency units) of the hedge to the hedged asset |
| ρ | **Correlation.** The expected forward correlation between the hedged asset and the hedge |
| $\sigma_a$ | **Volatility.** The volatility of the hedged asset |
| $\sigma_h$ | **Volatility.** The volatility of the hedge |

Properly choosing the hedge ratio substantially improves the quality of the hedge. For example, using a properly sized 90 percent correlated hedge, the total risk can be reduced to 19 percent of the risk of the hedged asset. However, if the hedge had been traded to be the same size as the hedged asset, the hedge would have only removed 56 percent of the risk (leaving 44 percent of the risk). In other words, properly sizing the hedge reduces the combined volatility from 44 percent to 19 percent. (See Figure 7.2, An Improved Hedge.)

A common error when doing hedge calculations is caused by unit conversions. This type of error can be minimized by converting everything into currency units (like dollars) prior to doing calculations. Then, the hedge ratio calculations can be done in terms of the dollar exposure, and then converted back into physical units. The reason that this simplifies most

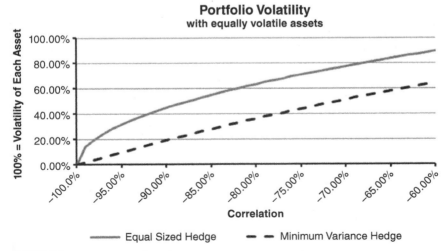

**FIGURE 7.2**  An Improved Hedge

calculations is that volatility and correlation are measured in terms of price movements. Converting everything into currency units avoids mixing and matching different units in one equation.

## Example: Natural Gas Hedging

A natural gas marketing company has agreed to sell 1,000,000 MMBTU of natural gas to customers in Chicago for a fixed price of $3.50/MMBTU in December. An MMBTU is a million British Thermal Units—a common unit used to trade natural gas. As a result of the transaction, the marketer will lose money if the price of gas rises, since the marketer will have to purchase gas at a higher price to sell at $3.50. A week later, December natural gas price rises to $4.00 MMBTU in Chicago. Scared of losing more money, the marketing company decides to eliminate the risk of further moves. To do this, the marketer decides to hedge this exposure by buying NYMEX Natural Gas Futures.

The Natural Gas Futures aren't identical to the marketing company's exposure. Chicago Natural Gas prices tend to be higher and more volatile than at the NYMEX Natural Gas Futures delivery location (Henry Hub) on the U.S. Gulf Coast. The Gulf Coast has warmer winters than Chicago. As a result, natural gas prices in that location are less volatile because there is less seasonal need for heating. (See Table 7.1, Natural Gas Price, Volatility, and Correlation.)

**TABLE 7.1**   Natural Gas Price, Volatility, and Correlation

| December Natural Gas | Chicago | NYMEX Futures |
|---|---|---|
| Price | $4.00/MMBTU | $3.85/MMBTU |
| Volatility | 32% | 30% |
| Correlation | 96% | |

Intuitively, since the NYMEX futures have lower volatility than Chicago natural gas, the NYMEX futures hedge need to have a slightly larger dollar exposure. This will be somewhat offset by the correlation being less than 100 percent. Using the minimum variance hedge formula to calculate the hedge ratio will calculate the relative dollar size of the positions.

- Hedge ratio = (correlation) × (volatility$_{hedge}$ / volatility$_{asset}$)
- h = .96 × (.32/.30) = 1.024

Based on this calculation, the best hedge will be $1.024 of hedge (NYMEX NG Futures) for each $1 of hedged item (Chicago NG). The size of the exposure being hedged (the hedged item) is $4,000,000.

- Exposure being hedged = (1,000,000 MMBTU) × ($4.00/MMBTU) = $4,000,000
- Minimum Variance Hedge Size = $4,000,000 × 1.024 = $4,096,000

The volume of the hedge can be found by dividing the size of the hedge by the price per unit of the futures contract.

- Volume of Hedge = $4,096,000 / ($3.85/MMBTU) = 1,063,896.10 MMBTUs

NYMEX Natural Gas futures are traded in 10,000 MMBTU lots. Dividing 1,063,896.10 by 10,000 can determine how many futures contracts need to be purchased. The best hedge would be 106.29 contracts—which would need to be rounded up or down. Rounded to the nearest contract, the best hedge for a 1 million MMBTU exposure of gas in Chicago is buying 106 NYMEX Natural Gas futures.

---

### KEY CONCEPT: HEDGING CALCULATIONS

When hedging, converting everything into a single type of unit, like an amount of currency exposure (a dollar, euro, or similar exposure), simplifies the work substantially compared to using mixed units.
Some common steps when performing hedge calculations are:

1. Calculate dollar size of exposure to hedged item.
2. Find a source for forward volatility and correlation estimates.
3. Use the hedge ratio equation to calculate the dollar size of the minimum variance hedge.
4. Convert the dollar size of this hedge into physical units.
5. Calculate the number of contracts needed to hedge by rounding physical units.

## MISMATCHED CASH FLOWS

Hedges and hedged items don't always have the same cash flows. They also might not qualify for the same accounting treatment. For example, a farmer planting soybeans might wish to hedge to lock in favorable prices when the crops are planted. This would eliminate much of the uncertainty in selling the soybeans at harvest. However, if a hedge would require the farmer to pay money prior to the sale of the crop, there would be a mismatch between the cash flows on the hedge and the hedged item.

In a typical hedge, the value of the hedge and the hedged item move in opposite directions. In the example of the soybean farm, if soybean prices started to appreciate, the value of the soybeans in the field would go up. However, assuming the position was perfectly hedged, the hedge would show an equal and offsetting loss. If neither the hedge or the hedged item created early cash flows and if both the crop and contracts were valued at the same dates, the farm would be unaffected by changing prices.

Unfortunately, hedges often create intermediate cash flows, and unless the hedge qualifies for special accounting treatment it is unlikely to be valued the same way as the hedged asset. In many cases, this creates a set of accounting problems that need to be considered. Typically, the instruments used to hedge are derivatives. This means that the hedges are subject to mark-to-market accounting. Many items being hedged do not require mark-to-market. This mismatch can create a substantial amount of risk to an individual or company interested in hedging a future exposure.

For example, futures are a popular financial contract used for hedging. These contracts are subject to both mark to market and daily margining. Daily margining is a daily transfer of profits and losses between traders based on the daily change in price of the contract. In other words, if soybean prices start to rise, the soybean farmer would need to settle the losses on the futures contract every day. However, the farmer would have no offsetting income from the soybeans until the crop was sold at harvest time.

Another problem is that the valuation date on a hedge and a hedged item may differ from one another. Most hedges are financial instruments whose values flow into corporate financial statements every day. In other words, futures contracts are typically marked to market every day. In contrast, the accounting value for a physical asset (like a field of half-grown soybeans) is not typically subject to daily mark to market. This can create a problem because the financial reporting obscures the reduced risk from hedging.

## KEY CONCEPT: HEDGING CAN CREATE VOLATILE EARNINGS

A hedge can introduce substantial volatility in reported earnings unless it qualifies for hedge accounting treatment. A hedge qualifies for hedge accounting by documentation created prior to entering the hedge (prospective testing) and justified by mathematical testing afterward (retrospective testing).

## HEDGE EFFECTIVENESS TESTING

To reflect the relationship between hedges and hedged items, there are exceptions to normal accounting rules specifically for hedges. Hedges qualify for this special accounting treatment if the hedge is considered a *highly effective hedge* and the proper documentation is put in place. This is a voluntary process. Hedges can always be valued using standard accounting rules.

The benefit of hedge accounting is that the hedging firm can match the timing of the gains and losses on the hedged item with the hedge. This will help a hedger avoid many of the problems associated with timing mismatches between the hedge and hedged item. Hedge accounting allows the gain or loss on the hedging derivative to be recorded concurrently with the gain or loss on the hedged item. For example, in a cash flow hedge, the effective portions of any change in the fair value are not recognized into earnings until the hedged item is recognized. This accounting treatment allows companies to hedge while minimizing the effect of mismatched valuations on earnings.

To test for effectiveness, the hedger must identify both the hedge and hedged item and develop a testing plan prior to entering the hedge. The hedge and the testing plan need to be documented in a *hedge designation memo*. The testing plan should state the objective of the hedge, the method of testing, the data and time period used to test the hedge, and an objective standard for determining if the hedge is *highly effective*. The hedge is also typically assessed for effectiveness over a historical period of time at this point. The initial testing plus the documentation is called *prospective testing*.

There is no accounting requirement for specific types of tests that must be performed. However, if the hedger has multiple hedges, all similar hedges must use the same methodology to test effectiveness and follow similar testing plans. In addition, all hedges should be consistent with the hedging firm's stated approach to risk management. This documentation should be updated on an ongoing basis.

It is also necessary to test whether the hedge has actually been effective at offsetting changes in fair value or cash flows. This type of testing is called *retrospective testing*. Like prospective testing, retrospective testing must be updated regularly. Retrospective and prospective tests are typically updated each quarter or whenever financial statements or earnings are reported.

It is possible for a hedge to fail a retrospective test while passing a prospective test. If that occurs, hedge accounting typically cannot be applied to the period covered by the retrospective test. However, it is generally acceptable for hedge accounting to be used in the future (assuming the retrospective tests pass at that point) without de-designating and re-designating the hedge.

For a perfectly effective hedge, the hedge will exactly offset changes in the hedged item. For example, if the value of the hedged item increases by $100,000 then a perfect value hedge would need to decline in value by $100,000. Any ineffectiveness (where the hedge does not perfectly balance

---

### KEY CONCEPT: HEDGE ACCOUNTING TERMINOLOGY

Some common terms related to hedge accounting are:

- **Hedge Accounting.** Hedge accounting is an accounting methodology where a hedge and hedged item are combined and treated as a single unit. Hedge accounting is used to reduce the volatility caused by daily mark to market of the hedge (which is typically a derivative and subject to mark-to-market accounting) when the hedged item is subject to a different type of accounting.
- **Mark-to-Market (MTM) Accounting.** An accounting methodology that determines the fair value of an asset or liability based on current market prices. This accounting is commonly applied to derivatives and other financial instruments.
- **Prospective Testing.** A test used in hedge accounting to support the premise that the hedge and hedged item will be closely related in the future. There are a variety of different types of prospective tests. This test must follow the methodology described in the hedge-designation memo.
- **Retrospective Testing.** A test used in hedge accounting to test the assertion that the hedge has been effective over some historical period. This test must follow the methodology described in the hedge-designation memo.

the hedged item) typically needs to be immediately reflected in financial statements.

Most hedges are not perfectly matched to the hedged item. However, a hedge may still be considered highly effective if it substantially offsets changes in the hedge item. The typical range accepted as a highly effective hedge is offsetting between 80 and 125 percent of the changes in the hedged item. For example, if the value of the hedged item increased $100,000, a fair value hedge would be considered highly effective if it declined in value between $80,000 and $125,000. If a hedge fails the highly effective test, the entire change in value of the hedge must be reported in the financial statements.

In practice, a hedged item can be any portion of the balance sheet of the hedging firm. This includes most financial commitments and expected future obligations. The hedge itself typically is a type of financial contract called a *derivative*. A derivative is any financial instrument that derives its value from an underlying commodity. Some derivatives commonly used for hedging are futures, forwards, and various types of commodity swaps.

To facilitate making a precise hedge, the hedger can generally exclude changes in value/cash flow unrelated to the item being hedged. This allows part of the derivative to act as a hedge while another part of the derivative is subject to mark-to-market accounting. If this is done, it must be documented prior to the hedge as part of the prospective testing. In addition, the hedger can generally determine what type of hedging test will need to be performed.

In practice, hedgers don't always have a lot of flexibility due to the need to follow a consistent approach for hedging similar items. Although hedgers have flexibility when designating their first hedge and determining which hedging test will be used for that test, those decisions will affect any similar hedges in the future. This works both ways, and choosing a different approach for a new hedge may cause any previous hedges to be restated or altered. In addition, the hedging plan will need to be approved by the hedger's auditor and conform to the latest accounting guidance.

## HEDGE-ACCOUNTING MEMO

To qualify for hedge accounting, the hedge relationship must be documented in a memo that is written prior to the inception of the hedge. This documentation must do several things:

1. Identify the hedged item.
2. Select the type of hedge accounting that will be applied.
3. Describe the hedge.

4. Document the risk management objectives and strategy.
5. Specify the hedge-effectiveness tests.

## Step 1. Identify the hedged item

The hedged item must be sufficiently detailed so that a third party (like an auditor or regulator) can identify what is being hedged. Since the hedged item may be almost any portion of the firm's balance sheet, the description has to be very clear. For example, the hedged item may be an entire asset or liability, a specific portion of those assets or liabilities, or a portfolio of several similar assets and liabilities.

## Step 2. Select the type of hedge accounting that will be applied

The three main types of hedges are (1) fair value hedges, (2) cash flow hedges, and (3) foreign currency hedges. The hedging documentation must explicitly state the type of the hedge.

## Step 3. Describe the hedge

The hedging instrument must be fully described. This description needs to clearly link the hedge and hedged item. This is fairly straight forward when the key terms of the hedge closely match the hedged item. However, this needs to be expanded when the relationship between the hedge and hedged item is not immediately obvious to a third party.

## Step 4. Document the risk management objectives and strategy

The senior management of the hedging firm and its board of trustees need to document policies and procedures which allow employees of the firm (like traders or risk managers) to create hedges. These policies should list the approved types of financial instruments to be used as hedges, allowed hedging strategies, and the approved methods for assessing hedge effectiveness.

## Step 5. Specify the hedge-effectiveness tests

Both at inception and on an ongoing basis, the hedging relationship must be regularly tested for effectiveness. The test methodology and passing results must be documented. In addition, the testing plan needs to include a schedule for when hedge-effectiveness testing will be performed. An assessment of hedge effectiveness is required whenever financial statements or earnings are reported and must be done at least every three months.

## REGRESSION TESTS

There are several types of tests performed for retrospective testing. Not all of these will be discussed in this book. However, one of the most common methods of retrospective test is called the *regression method* or the *variance reduction method*. The variance reduction method is a special case of the regression method where the derivative position is equal and opposite in size to the hedged item. In a regression test, a mathematical analysis is undertaken to examine the nature of the relationship between the hedge and the hedged item.

📖 Note: In this discussion, the terminology for fair value hedges will be used in the examples. Other types of hedges will work in a similar manner.

The regression method is based on the concept of mathematical regression. Mathematical regression examines linear relationships between two series. Typically, changes in the hedge are compared to changes in the hedged item. There are a variety of different ways that two data series can be related. For example, it's possible to have a seasonal cyclical relationship, a linear relationship, or some type of curved line relationship. Hedging tests typically look only for linear relationships. (See Figure 7.3, Types of Relationships.)

A common way to visualize the relationships between two data series is to use a scatter diagram. In a scatter diagram, the horizontal axis (X axis) represents values from one data series and the vertical axis (Y axis) represents values from the second data series. A line is fit to the data to describe the relationship. (See Figure 7.4, Regression Plot).

**Linear Relationship**
A straight line relationship

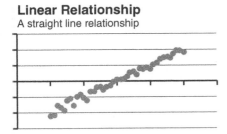

**Non-Linear Relationship**
A relationship that is not a straight line

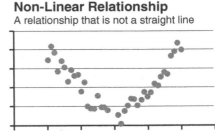

**FIGURE 7.3**  Types of Relationships

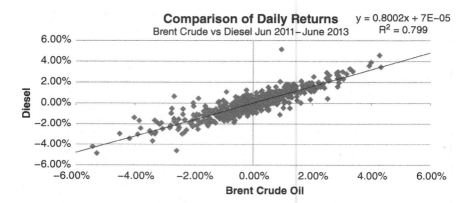

**FIGURE 7.4**   Regression Plot

The underlying assumption in a linear regression is that there is a straight line that best fits the data. (See Equation 7.3, Regression Equation.) To find the line

$$y_i = a + bx_i \pm e \qquad (7.3)$$

that best fits a set of paired data (x, y), the least-squares method is commonly used to find the parameters a and b.

$$b = \frac{\sum (x_i - \bar{x})(y_i - \bar{y})}{(x_i - \bar{x})^2}$$

$$a = \bar{y} - b\bar{x}$$

where

| | |
|---|---|
| b | **Slope.** The slope of the best fit line |
| a | **Y Intercept.** The point where the line crosses the Y (vertical) axis |
| e | **Residual Error.** The random variations around the line that cannot be explained by a linear relationship |
| i | **Element Identifier.** The subscript i indicates (x, y) pairs that are used to create the graph |
| $\bar{x}, \bar{y}$ | **Average.** The line above the name of the variable indicates the average of that series |

In this type of analysis, the two data series (x and y) represent *changes* in the hedge and the hedged item respectively. To be an effective hedge, if the value of the hedged item goes up in price by $1, the value of the hedge also needs to go up in price $1. As long as the hedge and hedged item have similar changes in value, the hedge is effective. The relative size of the value assigned to the hedge and hedged item do not affect hedge effectiveness.

A number of summary statistics are produced by a regression analysis. These statistics are commonly used to evaluate the effectiveness of the hedge. Two major statistics used for this purpose are the slope (abbreviated *b* above) and the correlation coefficient (usually squared and abbreviated as $R^2$ or R-squared). Secondary statistics include checking that there are enough observations to conduct a valid test, and that the slope and $R^2$ tests are sufficiently stable to trust the results.

For example, a hedge-accounting memo might define five tests to determine a highly effective hedge. Highly effective is commonly interpreted to mean that:

- **Test 1 (Slope).** The slope of the regression line is between 0.80 and 1.25. This test ensures that changes in the hedge and hedged item largely offset.
- **Test 2 (R-Squared).** An $R^2$ test indicates how well observations fit a line or curve. A common test is to ensure an $R^2$ greater than 0.80.
- **Test 3 (Slope Significance).** It is common to test that the slope test is mathematically significant. This can be done by checking that the p-value of the F-statistic is less than 0.05.
- **Test 4 ($R^2$ Significance).** It is common to test that the $R^2$ test is significant. This can be done by checking that the p-value of the t-statistic is less than 0.05.
- **Test 5 (Number of Samples).** A sufficient number of samples needs to be taken for a valid test. For most situations, this means 30 or more samples.

Generally, a statistical package in a spreadsheet is used to calculate effectiveness. To pass a hedge-effectiveness test, all of the tests defined in the

## KEY CONCEPT: EFFECTIVENESS DEPENDS ON CHANGES IN VALUE

A hedge is effective if the changes in the hedge match changes in the asset. As a result, hedging analysis examines *changes in price* rather than *prices*.

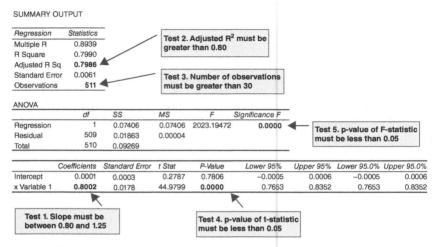

SUMMARY OUTPUT

| Regression | Statistics |
|---|---|
| Multiple R | 0.8939 |
| R Square | 0.7990 |
| Adjusted R Sq | **0.7986** |
| Standard Error | 0.0061 |
| Observations | 511 |

Test 2. Adjusted $R^2$ must be greater than 0.80

Test 3. Number of observations must be greater than 30

ANOVA

| | df | SS | MS | F | Significance F |
|---|---|---|---|---|---|
| Regression | 1 | 0.07406 | 0.07406 | 2023.19472 | 0.0000 |
| Residual | 509 | 0.01863 | 0.00004 | | |
| Total | 510 | 0.09269 | | | |

Test 5. p-value of F-statistic must be less than 0.05

| | Coefficients | Standard Error | t Stat | P-Value | Lower 95% | Upper 95% | Lower 95.0% | Upper 95.0% |
|---|---|---|---|---|---|---|---|---|
| Intercept | 0.0001 | 0.0003 | 0.2787 | 0.7806 | −0.0005 | 0.0006 | −0.0005 | 0.0006 |
| x Variable 1 | **0.8002** | 0.0178 | 44.9799 | **0.0000** | 0.7653 | 0.8352 | 0.7653 | 0.8352 |

Test 1. Slope must be between 0.80 and 1.25

Test 4. p-value of t-statistic must be less than 0.05

**FIGURE 7.5**   Regression Output

hedge documentation memo must pass the retrospective tests. In this example, five tests have been identified, and the hedge-effectiveness test would fail because the adjusted $R^2$ of 0.7986 is less than the 0.80 required for passing result. (See Figure 7.5, Regression Output.)

## LOGARITHMIC RETURNS

Hedge-effectiveness calculations need to be performed on changes in value. The underlying assumption is that if the asset loses money, then the hedge should make money. To make running calculations easier across a number of hedges, testing is often performed on a special type of percent change called *continuously compounded returns*. Other terms for continuously compounded returns are *logarithmic returns* or *log returns*.

A typical percent change is calculated over a finite step size (like the daily change in price). Continuous compounding can be thought of as making the compounding period infinitely small. This leads to a slightly different value for the rate of return. However, it allows different time periods to be compared to one another.

A continuously compounded return can be calculated with the following formula. (See Equation 7.4, Continuously Compounded Returns.)

$$r_t = \ln\left(\frac{p_t}{p_{t-1}}\right) \tag{7.4}$$

where

r_t     **Return at time t.** The continuously compounded return at time t

t       **Time.** When used as a subscript, t indicates an observation at a specific point in time

P_t     **Price at time t.** The price of the asset at time t

ln()    **Natural logarithm.** This is a standard mathematical function found on financial calculators and spreadsheets

## TEST YOUR KNOWLEDGE

1. Angela, a risk manager at a mining company, wants to hedge the output of copper ore using exchange traded copper futures. What is the minimum variance hedge ratio if both copper and copper ore have 17 percent volatility and are 85 percent correlated?
   A. 0.17
   B. 0.85
   C. 1.02
   D. 1.18
2. What is the primary effect that an effective hedge will have on a portfolio?
   A. It will increase profitability.
   B. It will make investors happier.
   C. It will help regulatory agencies approve the investment.
   D. It will reduce the uncertainty associated with an investment.
3. For the purposes of calculating hedge effectiveness, what is a prospective test?
   A. It is a stress test examining large potential future price movements.
   B. It is a regression test predicting how likely profits are to occur in the near future.
   C. It is documentation of a hedge prior to the hedge being transacted.
   D. It is a mathematical test done whenever financial reports are sent to investors to assess if the hedge has been effective.
4. What values for slope are commonly accepted as part of a hedge-effectiveness test?
   A. 0.75 to 1.20
   B. 0.75 to 1.25
   C. 0.80 to 1.20
   D. 0.80 to 1.25
5. If a hedge is 100 percent correlated with the hedged item but has greater volatility, how will this affect the minimum variance hedge ratio, h?
   A. h > 1

    **B.** h = 1

    **C.** h < 1

    **D.** Insufficient information is provided to answer the question.

6. Pick the sentence that best describes hedges.

    **A.** Hedging can reduce potential profits.

    **B.** Hedging can reduce potential losses.

    **C.** Hedges represent a large trading position that has the potential to introduce additional risks into a portfolio and not just mitigate risks.

    **D.** All of the above.

7. For the purpose of testing hedge effectiveness, what is most commonly accepted minimum value for an R-squared test?

    **A.** 0.6

    **B.** 0.8

    **C.** 0.9

    **D.** 0.95

8. Dan, a risk manager, is constructing a hedge-effectiveness test. He knows he wants to do a regression test. What two data series does he need to use as inputs into the regression calculation?

    **A.** The prices of the hedge and hedged item.

    **B.** The log-returns of the hedge and hedged item.

    **C.** The rolling implied volatility and correlation of the hedge.

    **D.** The price of the hedge and the volatility of the hedged item.

9. Ken, the chief risk officer of an oil exploration company, is examining two possible hedging opportunities. Both will economically hedge the firm's positions. However, one of the hedges is unlikely to qualify for hedge accounting treatment. Assuming that the hedges are otherwise identical, what are the risks of using a hedge that doesn't qualify for hedge accounting?

    **A.** There might be a timing mismatch between the hedge and hedged items that leads to more volatile earnings.

    **B.** The hedge that doesn't qualify for hedge accounting will draw more regulatory scrutiny.

    **C.** The hedge that doesn't qualify for hedge accounting will have greater market risk.

    **D.** The hedge that doesn't qualify for hedge accounting will have greater credit risk.

10. MegaBank has purchased several power-generation units. It has hedged the expected changes in value. However, during its hedge-effectiveness testing for its latest quarterly earnings report, the hedges failed the retrospective tests. The prospective tests had previously passed. What is likely to occur?

    **I.** The change in value of the hedges is reflected in earnings.

    **II.** The change in value does not have to be reflected in earnings.

**III.** The hedge becomes de-designated and a new hedge designation memo is required if these assets are hedged in any future periods.

**IV.** The existing hedge designation memo stays in effect.

    **A.** I and III

    **B.** II and III

    **C.** I and IV

    **D.** II and IV

## CHAPTER 8

# Options, Greeks, and Non-Linear Risks

This chapter discusses how the risks of complex financial instruments are modeled. Certain types of financial instruments, like options, present much more complicated risk management challenges than simpler financial instruments like stocks and bonds. Risk managers have developed a variety of techniques to model this risk and fit it into the position limit (value-at-risk) framework used for other financial instruments. The most common technique used to monitor option risk is to break the option into several risk factors. These risk factors are named after Greek letters (and collectively called *Greeks*).

The option pricing formulas and Greeks described in this chapter are used by traders to control risk. By reducing complex financial instruments to a handful of exposures, options portfolios can be concisely described to senior management. This also allows position limits, like value-at-risk, to be applied to options. In practice, option portfolios often have a value-at-risk limit as well as a limit on each of their Greeks.

## OPTIONS

Options are financial derivatives that give their owner the right, but not the obligation, to take some action at a predetermined point in the future. The ability to make a decision complicates the valuation of options. However, this also makes option pricing a flexible way to look at a wide variety of financial contracts. As a result, options can be both traded and found embedded in larger contracts. An introduction to options can be found near the end of Chapter 2.

As a quick refresher, an option will allow the owner of the option to buy (if it is a *call option*) or sell (if it is a *put option*) a financial instrument (the *underlying asset*) at a fixed price (the *strike price*) at a specific point in the future (the *expiration date*). The price that the buyer pays to acquire the option is the *premium*. Prior to expiration, the owner of a call option benefits when the price of the underlying asset rises. In a similar manner, the owner of a put option benefits when prices decline.

Some options can be exercised early (these are called *American options*) while others can only be exercised on the expiration date (these are called *European options*). Regardless of whether an option can actually be exercised on the current day, the terms *in-the-money, at-the-money*, and *out-of-the-money* are used to describe whether exercise would be profitable. Terms that describe the *moneyness* of an option are descriptive. These terms don't imply a contractual obligation.

When options can be immediately exercised for a profit, they are described as *in-the-money*. When options are sufficiently *in-the-money*, they act just like their underlying asset. For example, an option to buy a $100 stock for $0 is worth $100 dollars because the stock could be purchased and then immediately resold. If the price on the stock drops to $50, the price of the option drops $50 too. There is relatively little trading in in-the-money options.

When an option cannot be immediately exercised at a profit, it is described as *out-of-the-money*. When options are sufficiently far *out-of-the-money*, they are almost worthless. An option to buy a stock for one trillion dollars is essentially worthless if the stock has no chance of ever getting to that price. When traded, out-of-the-money options are used to speculate on extreme volatility or large moves in the price of the underlying.

An option's *at-the-money* point divides the in-the-money and out-of-the-money ranges. This occurs when the price of the underlying asset is exactly equal to the strike price. Options are most commonly traded when they are at-the-money. After they are first purchased, they will drift either in-the-money or out-of-the-money as the price of the underlying asset changes over time.

Options are different than most other financial instruments in this regard. For many financial instruments the value will go up and down proportionally with prices. However, with options, the amount that an option's value goes up or down changes whether the underlying asset is in or out of the money.

Because of this complexity, describing what will happen to the combination of several thousand option trades has required risk managers to develop ways to summarize option exposures. Typically, this is done by describing certain risk factors (like prices, volatility, and interest rates) that affect the value of options. Some common risk factors described in this manner are changes in prices, time, volatility, and interest rates.

## GREEKS

To combine a portfolio of options into a single risk report, it is fairly common to break individual options into pieces that can then be aggregated into a summary. Typically, this works by examining the sensitivity of the option price to various risk factors like movements in the underlying price, market volatility, and interest rates.

The four factors most commonly examined for option pricing are:

- **Price of Underlying Asset.** The value of the underlying asset ultimately determines the value of the option at the expiration date.
- **Volatility.** Part of the value of an option comes from the fact that changes in the price of the underlying asset affect the option holder asymmetrically. For example, the owner of call options benefits when prices rise, but has limited losses if prices decline. The more that the price of the underlying can change prior to expiration, the more valuable the option.
- **Time until Expiration.** Similar to volatility, a longer time before expiration allows the option more time to become valuable. This benefits the owner of an option because their potential losses are limited.
- **Interest Rates.** Rising interest rates can affect the value of assets in the future. Since the strike price of an option is fixed, rising interest rates tend to benefit call options and hurt put options. For interest rate options, this is a key factor that is closely related to the price of the underlying asset. It is less important for most other options.

Risk factors are typically used to estimate changes in the value of the option if something were to occur. For example, for a stock option, one risk factor is the price of the stock on which the option is written. This might be described *"for every $1 the stock price goes up, the option price goes up $0.50."* In other words, the sensitivity of the option price to stock prices is 50 percent.

Once sensitivities are calculated per option, they can be aggregated together for use in a risk management report. For example, if a trading desk is long an option to buy 100 shares of stock, and the sensitivity of the option prices to stock prices is 50 percent, then the trading desk stands to make $50 for every $1 increase in the stock price. The exposure can be calculated by multiplying the volume (100) by the sensitivity (50 percent) and the size of the move (a $1 increase in stock prices).

The most common risk factors have specific names. These names are based on the Greek letters that are commonly used to abbreviate these terms in equations. These risk factors are introduced here but will be

**KEY CONCEPT: VOLUME NOTATION**

Options, particularly puts, can be confusing for people new to the financial market. Buying a put option gives the buyer the right to sell at a fixed price. Buying a put option involves buying a piece of paper (the option contract). That paper happens to give the owner the right to sell at a fixed price. The act of purchasing a contract, and the rights assigned by the contract, are two different concepts.

The convention for volumes is that positive volume indicates a long position in an asset (the option buyer will benefit when the price of that asset rises) and a negative volume indicates a short position in an asset (the option buyer will lose money if the asset drops in price). Exposures use the same notation. A positive risk factor indicates that the option will benefit from an increase in the value of that risk factor.

- A positive sensitivity indicates that the option buyer benefits when the risk factor rises. This is often described as being *long* the factor.
- A negative sensitivity indicates that the option buyer benefits when the risk factor falls. This is often described as being *short* the factor.

examined in more detail later in the chapter. The most important *Greeks* are:

- **Delta.** Delta is a linear approximation that describes how the value of the option will change with respect to price. In calculus terminology, this is the first derivative of option value with respect to changes in the price of the underlying. Delta measures the *velocity* of the option price (how quickly the option price moves given a change in the underlying price.)
- **Gamma.** Gamma describes the curvature in the option value with respect to changes in the price of the underlying. Gamma measures how much delta changes with respect to changes in the underlying prices. Alternately, to use other terminology, Gamma is the second derivative of value with respect to changes in the underlying price. Gamma measures the *acceleration* of the option price.
- **Theta.** Theta is an estimate of how much the value of the option will decline over time. All things being equal, options lose value as they get closer to expiration. To use calculus terminology, theta is the first derivative of the option value with respect to time.

- **Vega.** Vega is an estimate of how the option's value will change with respect to changes in volatility. Higher volatility makes options more valuable. This effect is most pronounced when underlying prices are close to the strike price. Vega is relatively less important when the option is extremely far in or out of the money. Mathematically, Vega is the first derivative of the option value with respect to volatility.
- **Rho.** Rho is an estimate of how the option value will change when interest rates change. This is very important for interest rate-sensitive options, like bond or foreign exchange options, and much less significant to other options, like stock or commodity options. Rho is the first derivative of the option value with respect to interest rates.
- **Phi.** Phi is an estimate of how the option value will change when cash flows that reduce the value of the underlying are paid to the owners of the underlying asset. Dividends on stock options are an example of this type of cash flow. When a stock pays a dividend, the owners of the stock will get the cash. However, the owners of stock options will not receive this money.

## KEY CONCEPT: GREEKS ARE CALCULUS DERIVATIVES

In finance, the "Greeks" are (calculus) derivatives of option price with respect to various other items. For example, the first derivative of option price with respect to time is typically called *delta*. The second derivative of option price with respect to time is called *gamma*. For options, price, delta, and gamma are related to one another in the same way that distance, velocity, and acceleration are related for a car trip. Using delta to approximate how much the price will change is a lot like using the speed of the car to estimate how much distance will be traversed in a given amount of time. It works great when the car doesn't accelerate or decelerate.

### TAYLOR EXPANSION

The mathematics behind combining option risk factors into an estimate of prices uses a methodology called a Taylor Series Expansion. Mathematically, a Taylor Series Expansion is a way of calculating how much the value of a function changes given known changes in the derivatives. The reason that Taylor Series are used is that they allow each option to be characterized as the sum of separate risk factors (the Greeks) and then reassembled on a portfolio level.

A Taylor Series works by calculating the change in value (abbreviated here as dC) that will occur if certain risk factors

*(Continued)*

**KEY CONCEPT: (*Continued*)**

(S = underlying price, T = time to expiration, σ = volatility, r = interest rates) change.

$$dC = \frac{\partial C}{\partial S}\,dS + \frac{1}{2}\frac{\partial^2 C}{\partial S^2}\,dS^2 + \frac{\partial C}{\partial T}\,dT + \frac{\partial C}{\partial \sigma}\,d\sigma + \frac{\partial C}{\partial r}\,dr + \dots \qquad (8.A)$$

| Delta | Gamma | Theta | Vega | Rho |

Mathematically, the Greeks are partial derivatives of the option price (option price is abbreviated C) with respect to each factor. Each Greek gets multiplied by a change in a risk factor to estimate how far the option price will move. For example, Delta is similar to velocity. If a car is currently moving at speed of 60 miles per hour, after one minute the car will have traveled approximately 1 mile. The longer the time period, the less accurate the estimate because the car has more time to speed up or slow down.

## THE VALUE OF OPTIONS

An option gives its owner the right, but not the obligation, to take some pre-determined action at some point in the future. Options are modeled assuming that the option owner attempts to maximize his/her profit. Because of that, options have a non-linear payoff—they are worth nothing any time there would be a negative value. The two main types of options are Call and Put options. Call options are valuable when the price of the underlying, abbreviated S, is above the strike price, abbreviated X. The other type of option, a Put option, is valuable when the price of the underlying is below the strike price. (See Equation 8.1, Option Payoff Formulas.)

The two main types of options are *call* and *put* options. At expiration:

$$C = \text{Max}(0, S - X)$$
$$P = \text{Max}(0, X - S) \qquad (8.1)$$

## KEY CONCEPT: NON-LINEAR RISK

Option risk is called non-linear because the payoff is not a straight line. It has a discontinuity at the strike price. On one side of the strike price, the option has value. On the other side of the strike price, the option wouldn't be exercised and would expire worthless.

where

| | | |
|---|---|---|
| C | **Call.** The theoretical fair value (price) of a call option |
| P | **Put.** The theoretical fair value (price) of a put option |
| X | **Strike.** The price which the option owner can buy (with a call option) or sell (with a put option) |
| S | **Underlying Price.** The price of the underlying asset |

The right to eliminateing the negative payoffs results in a non-linear payoff for options. This allows options to be exercised when they are worth something and allowed to expire when they are worthless. If graphed, the payoff of an option looks like a hockey stick. (See Figure 8.1, Option Payoffs.)

Prior to expiration, the division between valuable and worthless isn't as clear as at expiration. For an option that still has some time prior to expiration, there is a possibility that prices will move so that the option is worth something. However, the closer that options get to expiration, the less that they are worth since there is less time remaining for price movements. The magnitude of how much the option is worth depends on a large number of factors including price of the underlying and the time before expiration. (See Figure 8.2, Option Prices Changing over Time.)

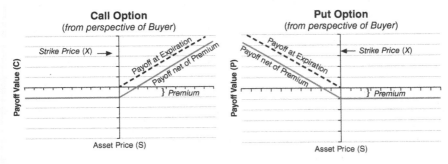

**FIGURE 8.1**  Option Payoffs

**FIGURE 8.2**    Option Prices Changing over Time

When options are very far in the money, they behave almost like the underlying. This is because volatility has an almost equal chance to cause the option to lose money as it does to help it make money. On the other extreme, options that are very far out-of-the-money are essentially worthless. Out-of-the-money options are unlikely to move enough to be in-the-money. The area where volatility and time have the greatest effect is when the option is at-the-money where the strike price is close to the price of the underlying.

This relationship is typically explained using calculus terminology. Calculus is a branch of mathematics that looks at how changes in values in independent variables (things like price of the underlying, time to expiration, and volatility) affect a dependent variable (the value of the option).

One measure of risk, value-at-risk (VAR), examines linear changes in value. This is only somewhat useful for options because linear approximations of curved lines break down if prices move too far. However, linear approximations are a useful starting point for examining option risk. On the graph, the solid curved line is the price of the option for various prices of the underlying. The dashed straight line is the estimated value of the option using a linear approximation at three different points. (See Figure 8.3, Linear Approximations of Option Value.)

The linear approximation of an option is sometimes called a *delta approximation*. Using calculus terminology, the *delta* of an option is the first derivative of the value—the straight line tangent to the curve at a specific point.

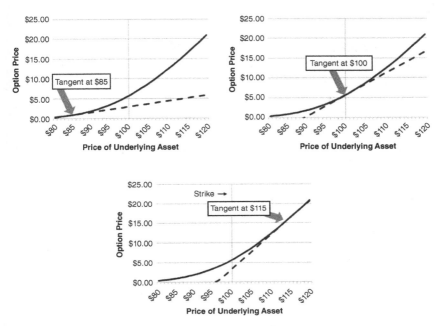

**FIGURE 8.3**  Linear Approximations of Option Value

## BLACK SCHOLES FORMULA

A tremendous amount of academic thought has gone into how to correctly price various types of options. Even so, most of that research focuses on unusual or exotic options—exceptional options that are rarely traded. A large majority of options can be valued with a variant of a single formula, called the *Black Scholes Formula*. Even in cases where Black Scholes can't appropriately price an option, the intuition behind Black Scholes is often still useful from a risk management perspective.

The original Black Scholes model was published in 1973 for non-dividend paying stocks. A variety of extensions to the original Black Scholes model have been developed. Collectively, these are referred to as *Black Scholes genre* option models. The extensions to the Black Scholes formula allow the same mathematical framework to value other financial instruments like dividend paying stocks, commodity futures, and foreign exchange (FX) forwards. The primary difference between these models is how the underlying asset is present valued.

Black Scholes genre option models make a number of simplifying assumptions about how financial markets operate. These assumptions are made in order to enable an easy-to-use framework suitable for pricing a wide variety of options. The key assumptions made by Black Scholes models:

1. **Arbitrage-Free Markets.** Most option models, including Black Scholes, assume that traders try to maximize their personal profits and don't allow arbitrage opportunities (riskless opportunities to make a profit) to persist. An implication of this assumption is no one can predict the future. Anyone who can predict the future would already have made trades, and kept borrowing money to make trades, until prices change enough to remove the potential for profit. This makes future price movements a random walk where prices are equally likely to move up or down around a time-value of money adjusted for fair value.

2. **Frictionless, Continuous Markets.** Option models generally assume the ability to buy and sell any amount of the underlying at any time without transaction costs. This assumption simplifies the creation of the models because it allows for a continuous process rather than one that starts and stops at irregular intervals.

3. **Risk-Free Rates.** Option models assume that it is possible to borrow and lend money at a risk-free interest rate. Commonly, risk-free rates are assumed to be at the London Inter-Bank Offer Rate, called LIBOR, which is the rate at which large banks borrow and lend money to one another.

4. **Normally Distributed Returns/Log-normally Distributed Price.** Option models typically assume that returns are normally distributed. Since continuously compounded returns are based on the log of prices, this means that prices are log-normally distributed. If percentage changes (returns) are normally distributed, then prices can approach zero (perhaps by cutting the price in half), but can never go negative. Using the same assumption, price can get infinitely large (it is always possible to double the price).

5. **Constant Volatility.** The Black Scholes genre options formulas assume that volatility is constant across the life of the option contract. This is another assumption to simplify the creation of the model.

Some of the more common variations of the Black Scholes Formula are:

1. **Black Scholes (Stocks without dividends).** In the original Black Scholes model, the underlying asset is a common stock that doesn't pay dividends. Stock is an instrument that is traded at its present value. For an option model, the stock price starts at its present value (a *spot price*) and its end point is randomly distributed around the present value inflated at the risk-free rate.

2. **Merton (Stocks with continuous dividend yield).** The Merton model extends the Black Scholes model by assuming that a dividend is continuously paid to shareholders. Dividends reduce the value of the option because before the

## KEY CONCEPT: IS THE DESTINATION MORE IMPORTANT THAN THE JOURNEY?

In a Black Scholes framework, the destination is often more important than the journey. The reason for this is due to the fact that it is extremely rare for options to be exercised early. Exercising options prior to the expiration date will lock in prices. This is usually financially a bad decision for the option buyer because the risk of owning an option is limited. Exercising early gives up that protection. It is usually better just to sell the option. The primary time that early exercise is worthwhile is when the underlying asset gives its owner a benefit that doesn't get paid to the option holder. If that benefit is greater than the benefit of downside protection, then it makes sense to exercise early.

The implication of selling options rather than exercising early is that only the endpoint is important. As long as simplifying assumptions like continuous trading and constant volatility allow the potential payoffs at expiration to be reasonably described, what happens at intermediate points is of relatively little importance (since the option won't be exercised there).

There are some options where this doesn't occur. These are called *path-dependent options* and are much more complicated to value than standard options. On a trading desk, understanding whether options are standard options or path-dependent options is an important early step in the risk management process.

option is exercised, it is the shareholder rather than the option owner who owns the rights to the dividends. As long as dividends are relatively small (won't be large enough to make someone exercise the option early), this variation is a reasonable approximation for any dividend-paying stock.

3. **Black 76 (Commodity Forwards).** The Black 76 model replaces the underlying commodity in a Black Scholes model with a forward contract. The price of a forward is the quantity of cash that needs to be paid on delivery of the commodity at some point in the future. As a result, instead of dealing with a spot price that drifts upward at the risk-free rate, an option on a futures contract deals with a forward price that needs to be present valued.

4. **Asay (Exchange Traded Futures).** The Asay model is similar to the Black 76 model except that there is no need to present value prices since daily margining creates daily cash flows rather than having a large cash flow upon delivery.

5. **Garman-Kohlhagen (FX Futures).** The Garman Kohlhagen model is based on a foreign exchange (FX) transaction where one currency is exchanged for another at some point in the future. Interest rates are different for each currency. As a result, for FX options, each currency in the currency pair is discounted based on its own interest rate.

Black Scholes genre option formulas have one important feature that makes them extremely popular—they can be represented as an equation. (See Equation 8.2, Generalized Black Scholes Formula.)

$$\textbf{Call Option} \quad C = Se^{(b-r)T}N(d_1) - Xe^{-rT}N(d_2)$$
$$\textbf{Put Option} \quad P = Xe^{-rT}N(-d_2) - Se^{(b-r)T}N(-d_1)$$

(8.2)

where

$$d_1 = \frac{\ln\left(\dfrac{S}{X}\right) + \left(b + \dfrac{\sigma^2}{2}\right)T}{\sigma\sqrt{T}}$$

$$d_2 = \frac{\ln\left(\dfrac{S}{X}\right) + \left(b - \dfrac{\sigma^2}{2}\right)T}{\sigma\sqrt{T}} = d_1 - \sigma\sqrt{T}$$

This generalized formula will need to be modified for the specific type of underlying by using an adjustment factor, b, that is specific to each model. (See Table 8.1, Black Scholes Adjustments). The definition of each variable in the Black Scholes equation follow. (See Table 8.2, Black Scholes Inputs.)

**TABLE 8.1**   Black Scholes Adjustments

| Model | Underlying | Cost of Carry Formula |
|---|---|---|
| Black Scholes | Non-dividend paying common stocks | $b = r$ |
| Merton | Continuous dividend paying common stock and stock indices | $b = r - q$ |
| Black (1976) | Forwards and Commodity Swaps | $b = 0$ |
| Asay | Exchange Traded Futures (Daily Margining) | $b = 0, r = 0$ |
| Garman and Kohlhagen | Foreign Exchange | $b = r - r_f$ |

**TABLE 8.2**  Black Scholes Inputs

| Symbol | Meaning |
| --- | --- |
| S | **Underlying Price.** The price of the underlying asset on the valuation date $t_o$. |
| X | **Strike Price.** The strike, or exercise, price of the option. |
| T | **Time to expiration.** The time to expiration in years. This can be calculated by comparing the time between the expiration date and the valuation date. $T = (t_1 - t_0)/365$ |
| $t_0$ | **Valuation Date.** The date on which the option is being valued. For example, it might be today's date if the option were being valued today. |
| $t_1$ | **Expiration Date.** The date on which the option must be exercised. |
| σ | **Volatility.** The volatility of the underlying security. This factor usually cannot be directly observed in the market. It is most often calculated by looking at the prices for recent option transactions and back-solving a Black Scholes-style equation to find the volatility that would result in the observed price. |
| q | **Continuous Yield.** Used in the Merton model, this is the continuous yield of the underlying security. Option holders are typically not paid dividends or other payments until they exercise the option. As a result, this factor decreases the value of an option. |
| $r_f$ | **Foreign Risk-Free Rate.** Used in the Garman Kohlhagen model, this is the risk-free rate of the foreign currency. Each currency will have a risk-free rate. |
| N(x) | **Cumulative Normal Distribution Function.** This is a common mathematical formula describing the probability of some event within a standard normal distribution. A standard normal distribution is a normal distribution with mean = 0 and standard deviation = 1. This is the cumulative version of the function. $$N(x) = \frac{1}{\sqrt{2\pi}} \int_{-\infty}^{X} e^{\left(\frac{x^2}{2}\right)} dx$$ Spreadsheets will usually have this as part of their standard spreadsheet library. For example, Excel will use *Norm.S.Dist(x, true)* to find N(x). |

Although this formula looks complicated, it is an extension of the option payoff formula. The call option formula is modified. (See Equation 8.3, Call Option Payoff.)

$$C = Max(0, S - X) \qquad (8.3)$$

First, both the strike price and the underlying price have to be present valued. The steps needed to present value the option will vary depending on the type of instrument. For example, a stock price is already present valued and will need no more adjustment. However, a forward price will need adjustment. The strike price will almost always need to be present valued. (See Equation 8.4, Present Valuing in Black Scholes.)

The formula for present valuing is

$$PV = e^{-rT} FV \qquad (8.4)$$

where

$$PV = \text{present value}$$
$$FV = \text{future value}$$
$$r = \text{interest rate}$$
$$T = \text{time}$$

In a Black Scholes equation, both the price of the underlying and the strike price get present valued.

$$C = Se^{(b-r)T} N(d_1) - Xe^{-rT} N(d_2)$$

The adjustments made to the Black Scholes formula to allow different underlying instruments primarily affect present valuing. For example, with common stock, which is already at present value, the conversion is to set b equal to r. This forces the present value term to be $e^0$ which simplifies to multiplying by 1.

The second complexity in the Black Scholes formula are the $N(d_1)$ and $N(d_2)$. These pieces of the equation calculate the likelihood that the option is greater than the strike price. This factor is discussed in more detail in the discussion on Delta.

## DELTA

Delta, abbreviated by the capital Greek letter $\Delta$, measures the sensitivity of an option's value to changes in the price of the underlying asset. It is a way to estimate how much the option will go up or down in value. Because price

## KEY CONCEPT: ARE YOUR OPTIONS AMERICAN OR EUROPEAN?

Some options can be exercised at any point in time, others only on a specific date. The terms *American* and *European* describe when options can be exercised. In most cases, it is always more profitable to sell the option than exercise it early. As a result, usually they are valued exactly the same way—with the Black Scholes formula.

- **American.** The option can be exercised at any time.
- **European.** The option can only be exercised at a specific time (the expiration date).

An example of an option that is useful to exercise early is a stock option that is undergoing an especially large dividend payment to shareholders. Owners of the stock will get paid the dividend, but not owners of the option. However, these cases are pretty rare. In almost all cases, it is better to sell the option rather than exercise early.

risk is usually the most important risk facing option traders, delta is the most important of the option Greeks.

Mathematically, delta is a linear approximation of how an option will change in value. If the value of the option relative to the price of the underlying is graphed, the delta will be the slope of the tangent line at the current price. When the option is out-of-the-money, this slope will typically be close to zero. An at-the-money option will have a slope close to one half (+/–0.5). An in-the-money option will have a slope close to +/–1. (See Figure 8.4, Delta Approximations.)

A delta of zero indicates that the option value will change very little when the price of the underlying changes. A delta of +/–0.5 will indicate that the option will go up or down half as much as the underlying. For example, a call option with a delta of 0.5 would fall $1 in value if the underlying drops $2. Finally, a delta of 1 indicates that changes in the option price will exactly mirror changes in the underlying price.

## KEY CONCEPT: DELTA APPROXIMATES OPTION PAYOFFS

Delta allows options to be combined with other instruments to calculate profit and loss. It also is the approximation used to estimate the size of the option exposure.

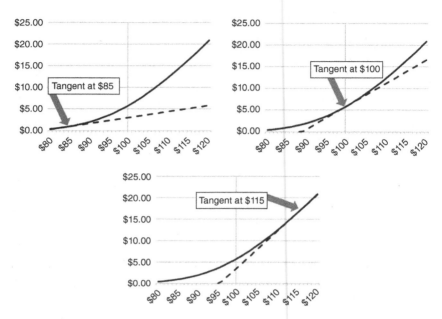

**FIGURE 8.4** Delta Approximations

For relatively small moves in underlying prices, options can be approximated by using delta. Delta indicates how much of the underlying is needed to offset changes in option prices. This isn't a perfect approximation because the option's value does not change linearly with the price of the underlying (it is a curved rather than straight line). However, frequent updating of the hedge can reduce some of this exposure. This is called *delta hedging*. Two major uses of delta calculations are:

- **Hedging.** Delta can be used to determine how much underlying needs to be purchased or sold to offset price moves in the option due to price moves in the underlying.
- **VAR.** Delta is commonly used to approximate the size of the option for use in a VAR calculation.

In the mathematical sense, Delta is the derivative of option value with respect to price. Using standard notation, Delta is also the first term in a Taylor Series expansion of the option. (See Equation 8.5, Delta Approximation.)

$$dC = Delta * dS \tag{8.5}$$

where

$$dC = \text{Change in the option price C}$$
$$dS = \text{Change in the price of the underlying price S}$$

**Note:** The calculation for this comes from a Taylor Series approxima-tion of option price and is an approximation of the real value. This estimate can typically be improved by including addition factors as described in the gamma discussion. Mathematically, this formula comes from the first ele-ment in a Taylor Series Expansion (a way to approximate a function with a finite number of terms).

$$dC = \frac{\partial C}{\partial S} dS \qquad \boxed{\text{(1st Order Taylor Series Expansion)}}$$

For options that can be priced with the Black Scholes formula, there are well-known formulas to calculate delta. The delta is the part of the Black

## KEY CONCEPT: DELTA

The magnitude (absolute value) of delta will always be between 0 and 1. However, the sign of delta will depend on the type of option and whether the option is long or short.

- **Long Call = Positive Delta.** The buyer of a call option has the op-tion to buy at a fixed price. The buyer benefits when the price of the underlying goes up. As a result the buyer of a call has a positive delta—the option increases in value when underlying prices go up and loses money when underlying prices go down.
- **Long Put = Negative Delta.** The buyer of a put option has the op-tion to sell at a fixed price. The owner of a put benefits when prices of the underlying go down. As a result the buyer of a put has a negative delta. The value of the put increases when prices go down and decreases when prices go up.
- **Short Options.** The seller of an option (someone who is short an option) will have the opposite sign on the delta compared to a buyer. Options are a zero sum financial instrument—every gain by the buyer is a loss to the seller and vice versa.

Scholes equation that gets multiplied by the price of the underlying. (See Equation 8.6, Delta.)

Delta is the first derivative of value with respect to price.

| Name | Abbreviation | Calculus Formula | Formula |
|------|-------------|------------------|---------|
| Delta for a Call | $\Delta_C$ | $\dfrac{\partial C}{\partial S}$ | $e^{(b-r)T}N(d_1)$ |
| Delta for a Put | $\Delta_P$ | $\dfrac{\partial P}{\partial S}$ | $e^{(b-r)T}[N(d_1)-1]$ |

$$(8.6)$$

where

C or P **Option Price.** The theoretical fair value of the option

$\Delta_{C \text{ or }} \Delta_P$ **Delta.** The delta of the option. In some cases, this will be subscripted for clarity. In this case $\Delta_C$ would refer to the delta of a Call option and $\Delta_P$ would refer to the delta of a put option

$\dfrac{\partial C}{\partial S}$ or $\dfrac{\partial P}{\partial S}$ **Partial Derivative.** The delta is sometime represented in mathematical terms as a partial derivative. For example, $\frac{\partial C}{\partial S}$ is the partial derivative of a call option value with respect to the price of the underlying S. In plain English, this is a shorthand method of describing the how much C or P (the value of the option) goes up or down when S (the underlying financial instrument) changes in price.

$d_1$ **$d_1$.** This is used as shorthand to simplify the Black Scholes equation

$$d_1 = \frac{\ln\left(\dfrac{S}{X}\right)+\left(b+\dfrac{\sigma^2}{2}\right)T}{\sigma\sqrt{T}}$$

*other variables* Shared with other Black Scholes equations

## KEY CONCEPT: EXCEPTIONS TO DELTA CALCULATIONS

The delta, $\Delta$, for most non-option positions is either +/–1. For example, long positions have $\Delta = +1$, and short positions have $\Delta = -1$.

The primary exception to this rule occurs on forward contracts where the underlying asset pays percent dividends to the owner of the asset but not the holder of the forward contract. For example, if an asset is worth $100 today and will pay 10 percent in dividends over the next year, the expected value of the asset when delivered in a year is approximately $90 ($100 less the $10 paid to the original owner). This would imply that the delta is approximately 0.9 since for every dollar the asset gains today, the owner of the forward would keep 90 percent

This does not happen very often in real life. For example, an asset paying a fixed dividend (a $100 asset paying $10 a year) would have a delta of 1. The reason is that even though the asset is worth less in the future, the size of the dividend is unaffected by the price. In other words, for every dollar it goes up today, the value to the owner of the forward contract also goes up $1.

Delta is a number whose magnitude is between zero and one. It is smallest in magnitude (closest to zero) when the option is far out-of-the-money and close to +/–1 when the option is far into the money. When an option is at-the-money, the delta is approximately +/–0.5. (See Figure 8.5, Delta Values.)

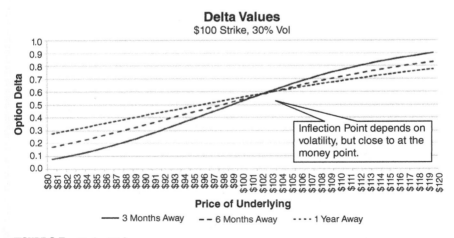

**FIGURE 8.5** Delta Values

## KEY CONCEPT: DELTA AND MONEYNESS

Delta goes between 0 and +/−1. The sign of the delta depends on the type of option and whether it is long or short.

- **Out-of-the-Money** (likely to expire worthless), $\Delta = 0$
- **At-the-Money**(at the border of worthless/worth something), $\Delta = +/-0.5$
- **In-the-Money** (likely to expire with some value), $\Delta = +/-1$

**NOTE**
These are only approximations. At-the-money delta is not exactly +/−0.5, although it is often very close to that value. Delta will depend on volatility and the time remaining before expiration. As time or volatility gets sufficiently large (goes to infinity), delta approaches +/−1.0 for any combination of underlying price and strike price.

## GAMMA

Gamma, abbreviated with the Greek capital letter $\Gamma$, quantifies the curvature (convexity) of an option payoff. Mathematically, gamma describes how delta changes with respect to changes in the price of the underlying asset. In a calculus sense, Gamma is also the second derivative of option price with respect to the price of the underlying. (See Figure 8.6, Gamma Measures Curvature.)

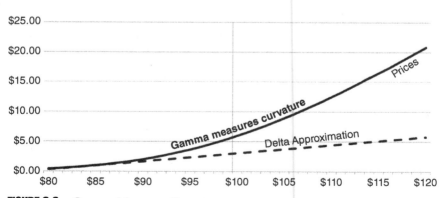

**FIGURE 8.6** Gamma Measures Curvature

From a risk management perspective, gamma is used to describe the overall optionality in a portfolio. This is useful because extreme events tend to occur all at the same time (for example, during a financial crisis) and options provide protection from extreme events. More importantly, gamma from individual options can be combined into a gamma for an entire portfolio. This provides a way to estimate the expected impact of large moves. It also provides a way to limit the exposure of an option portfolio. For example, it provides an objective measure to say "You can take this much option risk but no more."

An important feature of option prices is that they are convex. The actual price of the option is always at or above the price estimated by a delta approximation. In other words, option buyers (the traders that benefit from higher option prices) will never get an unpleasant surprise using a delta approximation. On the other hand, option sellers can get nothing but unpleasant surprises. (See Figure 8.7, Gamma Always Benefits Option Buyers.)

For options that can be priced with the Black Scholes formula, there are well-known formulas to calculate gamma. Puts and calls both use the same formula to calculate gamma. (See Equation 8.7, Gamma.)

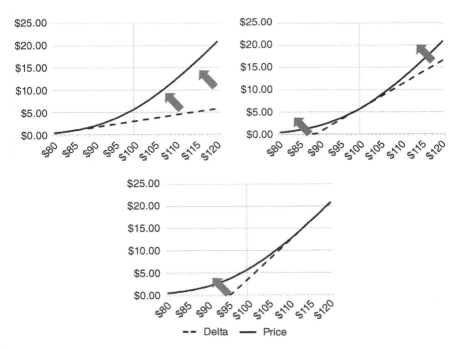

**FIGURE 8.7** Gamma Always Benefits Option Buyers

## KEY CONCEPT: GOT GAMMA?

Gamma describes how much optionality (protection from adverse price moves) exists in a single option. However, it is also possible to combine gamma from multiple option calculations to describe the overall risk of a trading portfolio.

**Gamma provides a way to describe the combined optionality from a large number of option trades.**

A trading book might be described as *long gamma* or *short gamma* to describe if unusual events are likely to help or hurt the trading book. Because gamma is convex, the only way to get gamma is to purchase options. As a result, gamma is also a way to approximate the overall optionality in a trading book.

- **Long Gamma.** More options have been purchased than sold. Lower risk since results will always be better than the delta approximation.
- **Short Gamma.** More options have been sold than purchased. Higher risk since results will always be worse than the delta approximation.

If an option trading book is looking to protect itself from unusual moves, it will generally need to buy enough options that it is long gamma. The primary way to be long gamma is to buy more options than have been sold. There is generally a cost to purchasing options.

Intuitively, this is logical. An option buyer is paying up-front money for protection from unusual events. The more likely those events are to occur, the more valuable the option. On the other hand, an option seller has the opposite risk profile.

Gamma is the second derivative of value with respect to the price of the underlying asset.

| Name | Abbreviation | Calculus Formula | Formula | |
|------|--------------|------------------|---------|---|
| Gamma | $\Gamma$ | $\dfrac{\partial^2 C}{\partial S^2}\ or\ \dfrac{\partial^2 P}{\partial S^2}$ | $\dfrac{e^{(b-r)T}n(d_1)}{S\sigma\sqrt{T}}$ | (8.7) |

where

n(x)   **Standard Normal Distribution Function.** This is a common mathematical formula describing the probability of some event within a standard normal distribution. A standard normal distribution is a normal distribution that has mean = 0 and standard deviation = 1. This is different than the other formulas that use a cumulative version which is abbreviated by a capital N(x). The lower case name indicates the non-cumulative version of the function:

$$n(x) = \frac{1}{\sqrt{2\pi}} e^{\left(\frac{x^2}{2}\right)}$$

Spreadsheets will usually have this as part of their standard spreadsheet library. For example, Excel will use *Norm.S.Dist(x, false)* to find n(x).

When gamma is graphed, gamma is typically higher when the prices are close to at-the-money than when prices are either far in- or out-of-the-money. This approximation is most accurate when prices can't change very much (close to expiration or volatility close to zero). The overall level of gamma also tends to rise as prices get closer to expiration. This is because a small change at expiration (particularly when prices are close to at-the-money) will be enough to go from zero value to some value. (See Figure 8.8, Gamma Compared to Price.)

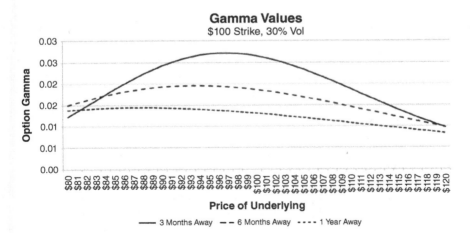

**FIGURE 8.8**   Gamma Compared to Price

## KEY CONCEPT: GAMMA

Gamma is highest for at-the-money options close to expiration. In addition, gamma is always a positive quantity—it always helps option buyers and hurts option sellers.

Gamma is also important to value-at-risk (VAR) calculations. VAR estimates can incorporate both delta and gamma approximations to better predict how a portfolio will move with respect to a risk factor. In the case of delta and gamma, the risk factor will usually be the price of the underlying asset or something highly correlated to the price of the underlying asset. (See Equation 8.8, A Delta/Gamma Approximation.)

$$dC = Delta * dS + \frac{Gamma}{2}(dS)^2 \tag{8.8}$$

where

$$dC = \text{change in the option price C}$$

$$dS = \text{change in the price of the underlying price S}$$

**Note:** The calculation for this comes from a Taylor Series approximation of option price and is an approximation of the real value. This estimate can typically be improved by including addition factors as described in the gamma discussion. Mathematically, adding a second term into the expansion creates a more complicated, but substantially more accurate, approximation of the actual behavior.

$$dC = \frac{\partial C}{\partial S} dS + \frac{1}{2} \frac{\partial^2 C}{\partial S^2} dS^2 \qquad \boxed{\text{(2nd Order Taylor Series Expansion)}}$$

Incorporating gamma into the estimate of how far option prices will move relative to movements in the underlying price will improve the accuracy of VAR models. Since gamma varies with price, the quality of the approximation is better for small moves than large moves. An example of limited improvement for this type of approximation is for a far in-the-money or far out-of-the-money option to cross the strike price in a single day. (See Figure 8.9, Out-of-the-Money Delta/Gamma Approximation.)

The delta/gamma approximation has substantially improved the estimate. The reason why the approximation didn't fully correct the difference

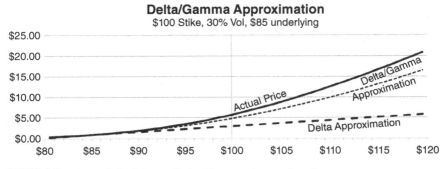

**FIGURE 8.9** Out-of-the-Money Delta/Gamma Approximation

is that gamma is also a variable. Gamma is highest around the strike price and lower further to either side. Delta/gamma approximations on options that are relatively close to at the money are generally much more accurate. (See Figure 8.10, At-the-Money Delta/Gamma Approximation.)

A delta approximation is called a *first-order* approximation or a *linear approximation*. It is called a first-order approximation because only first

## KEY CONCEPT: DELTA/GAMMA APPROXIMATIONS FOR VAR

Including gamma in a VAR calculation can improve predictive ability of VAR. Because of convexity, gamma will improve the profits of option buyers under extreme moves and hurt the profitability of sellers. This decreases the risk to option buyers and increases the risk to option sellers. In other words, positive gamma will reduce VAR, and negative gamma (which comes from selling options) will increase VAR.

$$VAR_{DeltaGamma} = |Delta| VAR_{Factor} - \frac{Gamma}{2}(VAR_{Factor})^2$$

where

$VAR_{Factor}$        VAR for the underlying risk factor

**NOTES:**

The VAR calculation is based on a Taylor Series approximation with two changes. First, since VAR is always positive, it is necessary to take the absolute value of delta. Second, since positive gamma reduces risk and negative gamma increases risk, the sign on the gamma term is reversed.

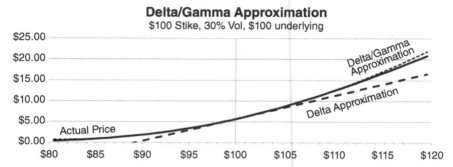

**FIGURE 8.10**   At-the-Money Delta/Gamma Approximation

derivative (delta) is used in the approximation. It is called a linear approximation because it forms a straight line. In a similar manner, a delta/gamma approximation is a second-order approximation since it includes both the first derivative (delta) and the second derivative (gamma). A delta/gamma approximation is not a linear approximation.

When applied to VAR calculations, positive gamma will reduce the risk of the portfolio and negative gamma will increase risk. Buying options of

---

### KEY CONCEPT: LIMITATIONS OF APPROXIMATIONS

Managing the risk of options is based on aggregating risk factors among options. Mathematically, each option Greek is a factor in a Taylor Expansion. Typically, these approximations use a Taylor Expansion to estimate specific values for each exposure. Taylor Expansions provide less accurate approximations when there are:

- **Large Movements in Underlying.** Approximations are more accurate with smaller movements in the underlying risk factors.
- **Options with Discontinuities.** Approximations work best when the series being modeled has a smooth progression of values. An at-the-money option right at expiration or exotic options that pay off when a certain boundary is hit are examples of series with discontinuities.
- **Correlation between Risk Factors.** While a Taylor Expansion can be expanded to account for correlation between risk factors, the most common assumption is that the factors are uncorrelated. If that assumption is incorrect, the expansion will be less accurate.

any type reduces risk. In other words, buying options adds positive gamma. Selling options does just the opposite. Selling options increases risk and decreases gamma.

## RELATIONSHIP BETWEEN PUT/CALL PARITY AND GAMMA

There are two main ways to look at options—payoff diagrams and their Greeks. Sometimes, it is easier to think about payoff diagrams and Greeks as two sides of the same coin rather than two different concepts. The basic put/call parity relationship is often described with the following formula:

$$Call = Forward + Put \qquad (Put/Call\ Parity)$$

The relationship can be observed from payoff diagrams of puts and calls. For example, the payoff of a long call and a short put combine to equal the payoff of a forward. (See Figure 8.11, Put/Call Parity.)

In this formulation, a call option is being replicated by a forward and a put option. Buying either a put or a call will give the purchaser a long gamma position. The only way to get gamma exposure is to buy an option. In other words, the only way to replicate the long call option position on the left side of the equation is to have a long option position on the right side of the equation. Otherwise, the gamma will never match.

This can be used to help remember put/call parity. In a practical situation, trying to draw option-payoff diagrams can be a bit difficult. However, it may be easier to remember that if you are trying to replicate a long call option, the Greeks (including gamma) of the replicating portfolio need to match.

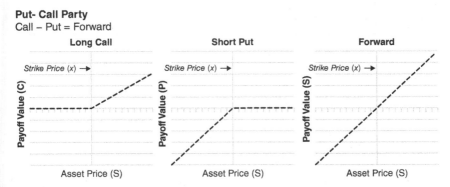

**Put- Call Party**
Call – Put = Forward

**FIGURE 8.11**  Put/Call Parity

Some option features that should be memorized:

- **Long Call.** Positive delta, positive gamma
- **Long Put.** Negative delta, positive gamma
- **Long Forward.** Positive delta (exactly 100 percent), no gamma
- **At-the-Money Options.** The delta of an at-the-money call or put is approximately 50 percent

The sign of the forward in a put/call parity formula can be estimated using deltas. A delta approximation of an option is essentially a replication of an option with only a single asset (the forward). The delta of an at-the money option is approximately 50 percent. The delta of a long forward is 100 percent. To get a 50 percent delta (delta of an at-the-money call), from the starting point of a −50 percent delta (the delta of an at-the-money put), it is necessary to add 100 percent delta (the delta of a forward).

## THETA

Options have a limited lifespan and lose value every day. Theta is a measure of how quickly an option value will decay over time. As options approach their maturity dates, the expected value of the options becomes more certain and therefore less valuable. For example, a 50/50 chance of making between $1 and $100 is more valuable than a 50/50 chance of making $1. This is because losses on options are limited and options with a long time to expiration have more time for something unusual to occur.

### KEY CONCEPT: THETA

The passage of time hurts option buyers and helps option sellers.

- Theta is negative for buyers.
- Theta is positive for sellers.

Note: Theta is typically reported as a negative number. This will be multiplied by the number of options held by the trader. This is done, because by convention, positive volume indicates a buyer and negative volume indicates a seller.

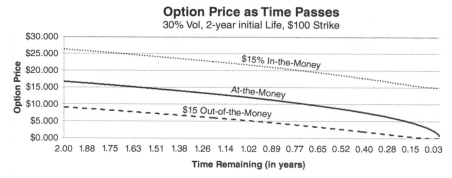

**FIGURE 8.12** At-the-Money Option Prices as Time Passes

Theta is closely related to gamma, but works in the opposite direction. For an option to be fairly priced, buyers and sellers need to have the same expected average profit. As a result, to counterbalance the benefit that an option buyer gets from extreme price moves (gamma), buyers lose money when large moves fail to occur (theta). In other words, there is a fairly good chance that an option buyer will have spent money to get an option that is worthless at expiration. (See Figure 8.12, At-the-Money Option Prices as Time Passes.)

For at-the-money options, theta causes options to decay fastest close to expiration. That is because all of the benefit of the option disappears at that point. However, for options that are deep in-the-money or deep out-of-the-money, theta ceases to have much effect. The reason is because once options are very far in-the-money or out-of-the-money, delta hits an extreme value (zero or one), and the extrinsic value disappears. (See Figure 8.13, Option Prices at Expiration.)

In general, theta has the largest magnitude (is the most negative for option buyers) for at-the-money options close to expiration. Theta decreases the extrinsic value of options. Every day it makes the extrinsic value move closer toward the intrinsic value. This naturally has the biggest effect where options have a lot of extrinsic value relative to the intrinsic value. (See Figure 8.14, Theta Values.)

Like delta and gamma, the formulas to find theta for Black Scholes style options are well known. Compared to other Greeks, the sign on the theta formulas are negative. This is because T (the time to expiration) gets smaller as time passes. However, in case of doubt, theta is always negative for an option buyer and positive for a seller. (See Equation 8.9, Theta.)

Theta is the first derivative of value with respect to the passage of time. It describes how much value the option loses every day.

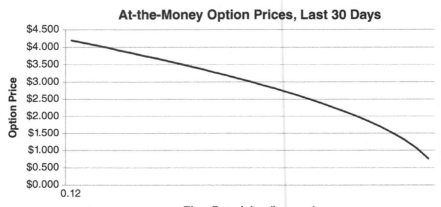

**FIGURE 8.13** Option Prices at Expiration

| Name | Abbrev | Calculus Formula | Formula |
|------|--------|------------------|---------|
| Theta$_{\text{Call}}$ | $\theta_C$ | $-\dfrac{\partial C}{\partial T}$ | $-\dfrac{Se^{(b-r)T}n(d_1)\sigma}{2\sqrt{T}} - (b-r)Se^{(b-r)T}N(d_1) - rXe^{-rT}N(d_2)$ |
| Theta$_{\text{Put}}$ | $\theta_P$ | $-\dfrac{\partial P}{\partial T}$ | $-\dfrac{Se^{(b-r)T}n(d_1)\sigma}{2\sqrt{T}} + (b-r)Se^{(b-r)T}N(-d_1) + rXe^{-rT}N(-d_2)$ |

$$(8.9)$$

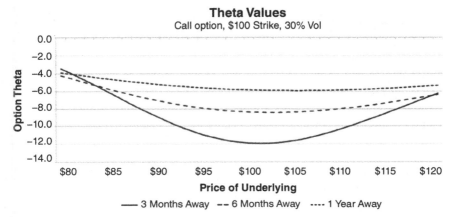

**FIGURE 8.14** Theta Values

## KEY CONCEPT: THERE IS NO FREE LUNCH

There is a cost associated with eliminating risk and buying options. Buying options removes some risk of extreme events. However, it comes at a high price. All other things being the same, options will lose money every day. For relatively quiet days in the market, options buyers typically lose money (and option sellers make money) on their option investments.

In a mathematical sense, gamma (protection from extreme events) and theta (daily loss of money) are closely related concepts. With a high gamma position, an option trader can make a lot of money when prices move substantially. However, the downside of a high gamma position is a large theta position. In other words, for every day that a substantial price move does not occur, the option buyer loses money. If enough days go past without a large price move, the option buy might end up losing a lot of money.

Studying risk management, it is easy to focus on the benefits of removing risk without considering the cost of doing so. Theta quantifies the cost of trading options. In other words, eliminating risk is an easy way to go bankrupt due to the costs associated with eliminating risk. Another way to think about this is that an uncertain profit, even though it contains an element of risk, is generally preferable to a certain loss.

*(Continued)*

## KEY CONCEPT: (*Continued*)

A fair price means that the seller and buyer will, on average, make the same profit (zero profit). The implication of this is that if the buyer has the potential to make an extremely large profit under some situations (like a stock market crash), the buyer will need to consistently lose money under more normal circumstances. As a result, a position that benefits from extreme events is going to steadily lose money on any days without an extreme event.

## VEGA

Vega indicates the sensitivity of an option price to changes in volatility. Unlike linear financial instruments (investments like stocks, bonds, and futures), options are affected by both prices and volatility. Options, because

## KEY CONCEPT: VEGA

Unlike prices, forward volatility cannot be directly observed in the market. Volatility is a measure of the market's perception on how uncertain prices will be in the future. It is possible to make some guesses on volatility, but no one knows for certain what will happen in the future.

Part of the issue with estimating volatility is that, in many cases, volatility is a catch all to explain price movements that are not due to any other factor. For example, it is common for option trading desks to calculate a market's implied volatility from trades that have been observed in the market. This creates a chicken and egg problem going back to prices from implied volatility.

Even so, it is generally useful for risk managers to track forward-implied volatility against historical comparisons like previously observed forward volatility and historical spot market price volatility. By breaking volatility into its own risk factor, it is possible for risk managers to create stress scenarios that get a feeling for how much option books can change in price.

they provide protection from adverse price moves, get more valuable when the probability of large price moves increase.

Vega is commonly abbreviated with the upper case Greek Lambda, $\Lambda$, or spelled out. Vega is actually the name of a constellation rather than a Greek letter. The formula for vega is similar to the formula for gamma, except that the square root of time appears in the numerator. As a result, vega is typically large when options are a long way from expiration and falls as the expiration date approaches. (See Equation 8.10, Vega.)

Vega measures the sensitivity of the option's price to changes in market volatility.

| Name | Abbreviation | Calculus Formula | Formula | |
|------|-------------|-----------------|---------|---|
| Vega | $\Lambda$ | $\dfrac{\partial C}{\partial \sigma}$ or $\dfrac{\partial P}{\partial \sigma}$ | $Se^{(b-r)T}n(d_1)\sqrt{T}$ | **(8.10)** |

Vega tends to decline over time and will eventually approach zero just prior to the expiration of the option. Vega is always a positive number since rising volatility always helps options buyers and hurts option sellers. (See Figure 8.15, Vega Compared to Underlying Price.)

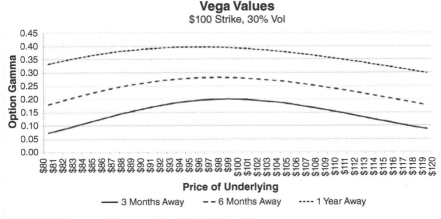

**Vega Values**
$100 Strike, 30% Vol

— 3 Months Away    – – 6 Months Away    ···· 1 Year Away

**FIGURE 8.15**  Vega Compared to Underlying Price

### KEY CONCEPT: VEGA DECLINES WITH TIME

Option buyers benefit from the possibility of a large dispersion of prices at expiration. As a result, vega is highest when the expiration date is far in the future because this gives more opportunity for prices to disperse.

- Vega is always positive (option buyers always benefit from increasing volatility).
- Vega is highest for long-term at-the-money options.
- Vega is lowest for in-the-money and out-of-the-money options close to expiration.
- At expiration, vega is zero—the time over which prices can change runs out.

## RHO AND PHI

Rho indicates the sensitivity of an option to changes in the risk-free interest rate. An increase in interest rates increases the value of call options, and decreases the value of put options. This is because future prices of the

### KEY CONCEPT: RHO AND THE TIME VALUE OF MONEY

Higher interest rates push the future price of the underlying upward. This benefits options that benefit from higher prices in the underlying asset (call options) and has the opposite effect on options that benefit from lower prices (put options). Rho is also proportional to time—the less time that rates can push prices up, the lower the effect.

- Rho will have the same sign as delta.
- Rho will be positive for call options and negative for put options.
- The magnitude of rho will be largest for in-of-the-money call options and out-of-the-money put options.
- The magnitude of rho will get smaller over time (rho will approach zero close to expiration).

underlying asset are expected to increase with higher interest rates (the time value of money effect) but the strike price is fixed.

Rho measures the sensitivity of the option's price to change in interest rates. The mathematical formula for rho can be found below. (See Equation 8.11, Rho.)

| Name | Abbreviation | Calculus Formula | Formula | |
|------|-------------|------------------|---------|--|
| Rho$_{Call}$ | $\rho_{call}$ | $\dfrac{\partial C}{\partial r}$ | $TXe^{-rT}N(d_2)$ | (8.11) |
| Rho$_{Put}$ | $\rho_{Put}$ | $\dfrac{\partial P}{\partial r}$ | $-TXe^{-rT}N(-d_2)$ | |

For call options, rho is highest for in-the-money options and lowest for out of the money options (vice versa for put options). Rho also declines over time. (See Figure 8.16, Rho Compared to the Price of the Underlying Asset.)

Dividends and other cash flows that decrease the value of the underlying prior to delivery will have an opposite effect compared to an increase in interest rates. This Greek doesn't have a standard name—it is sometimes called *rho*, *rho-2*, or *phi*. (See Equation 8.12, Phi.)

Phi measures the sensitivity of the option's price to changes in the dividend rate (or other cash flows paid to the owner of the asset but not the option holder).

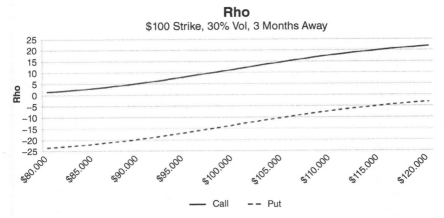

**Rho**
$100 Strike, 30% Vol, 3 Months Away

— Call  - - Put

**FIGURE 8.16**  Rho Compared to the Price of the Underlying Asset

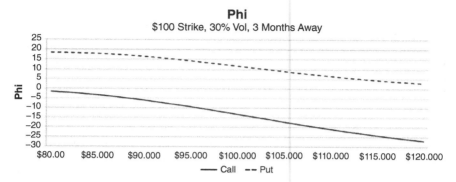

**FIGURE 8.17** Phi Compared to the Price of the Underlying Asset

| Name | Abbreviation | Calculus Formula | Formula | |
|------|--------------|------------------|---------|---|
| Phi$_{Call}$ | $\Phi_{call}$ | $\dfrac{\partial C}{\partial b}$ | $-TSe^{(b-r)T}N(d_1)$ | |
| Phi$_{Put}$ | $\Phi_{Put}$ | $\dfrac{\partial P}{\partial b}$ | $TSe^{(b-r)T}N(-d_1)$ | (8.12) |

For call options, Phi values are highest for out-of-the-money options and lowest for in-the-money options (vice-versa for put options). Like rho, the magnitude of phi will decline over time. Close to expiration phi will be close to zero. (See Figure 8.17, Phi Compared to the Price of the Underlying Asset.)

---

### KEY CONCEPT: CARRYING COSTS

Changes in dividends, foreign interest rates, and similar items which reduce the value of the underlying will affect the price of options. This sensitivity to these values (phi) will have the opposite sign from rho.

- Like rho, the magnitude of phi will be largest for in-the-money call options and out-of-the-money put options. However, compared to rho, the sign of the exposure is flipped.
- Like rho, the magnitude of rho will get smaller over time (rho will approach zero close to expiration).

## TEST YOUR KNOWLEDGE

1. Tom, the head trader at an oil drilling company, is worried that a potential decline in prices would affect his company. He has decided to buy an at-the-money put option on crude oil futures on $10 million worth of crude oil. If the 99 percent five-day VAR of crude oil is 10 percent, what is the approximate VAR of the put option using a linear (delta) approximation?
   A. −$1 Million
   B. $500,000
   C. $2.5 Million
   D. $5 Million
2. Flora, a senior risk manager, is looking over a VAR analysis prepared by the trading group for a portfolio of options. The book is net long gamma. The VAR analysis uses a first-order delta approximation of option risk. What happens to the VAR calculation if a second-order (delta/gamma) approximation is used in place of a linear (delta) approximation?
   A. VAR will be larger.
   B. VAR will be smaller.
   C. VAR will stay the same.
   D. Insufficient information is provided to answer the question.
3. Spencer, a trader at a hedge fund has sold a short put on ABCD stock. The time to maturity is 1 year, the strike price is $25, the stock pays no dividends, and the risk-free rate is 3.2 percent. The underlying is currently $25. What is the approximate delta of the option?
   A. −1.0
   B. −0.5
   C. +0.5
   D. +1.0
4. Barbara, a litigant in a lawsuit, was recently awarded a call option to get EFG stock for a $0 strike. There is no dividend. What is the approximate delta and gamma of the call option?
   A. delta = +0.5, significant positive gamma
   B. delta = +1.0, significant positive gamma
   C. delta = +0.5, gamma = 0
   D. delta = +1.0, gamma = 0
5. Richard, a risk manager at a bank, wants to estimate the loss caused by owning a long put option given a $2 per unit rise in price of the underlying. The option is for 100,000 units, the delta is −0.6, gamma is 0.1, and interest rates are zero. Using a second-order approximation (a delta/gamma approximation) what is the expected profit or loss?
   A. +$120,000 (profit)
   B. −$100,000 (loss)

**C.** –$120,000 (loss)

**D.** –$140,000 (loss)

6. Angela, a trader at a bank, has a large option portfolio on crude oil. The portfolio has delta = 0 but a large negative gamma. To reduce the gamma exposure to zero, what does she need to do?

   **A.** Buy options.

   **B.** Sell options.

   **C.** Take a position in the underlying asset.

   **D.** Insufficient information is provided to answer the question.

7. Jennifer, a private investor, wants to buy options because they have no risk. What should be one of her primary concerns when buying options?

   **A.** She will benefit from an increase in market volatility.

   **B.** She will have a positive gamma position.

   **C.** She will have a negative theta position.

   **D.** The cost of the option will outweigh any possible benefits.

8. Sabina, a junior trader at a hedge fund, owns a portfolio of options. She wants to estimate how much the option value will change every day if prices, volatility, and interest rates stay constant. What calculation should she perform?

   **A.** Sum the delta for every option in the portfolio.

   **B.** Sum the gamma for every option in the portfolio.

   **C.** Sum the theta for every option in the portfolio.

   **D.** Sum the rho for every option in the portfolio.

9. Roger, a risk manager at a hedge fund, is at a meeting with the firm's chief risk officer. He is asked whether a rise in volatility will help or hurt profitability of the option trading desk. Roger only has the following Greeks in front of him:

   Delta:            0

   Gamma:         +$1.5MM

   What should he say?

   **A.** A rise in volatility will help profits.

   **B.** A rise in volatility will hurt profits.

   **C.** The portfolio will not change in value.

   **D.** Insufficient information is provided to make an estimate.

10. Jean, the head trader at a hedge fund, has a long call position that she would like to liquidate. What combination of trades would remove that exposure?

    **A.** Buy a put option.

    **B.** Sell a put option.

    **C.** Sell a put option and sell a forward.

    **D.** Buy a put option and buy a forward.

## CHAPTER 9

# Credit Value Adjustments (CVA)

Counterparty credit risk is a specific type of credit risk related to the probability that a counterparty to a financial contract will fail to meet its obligations. This type of credit risk is commonly obtained by signing contracts with other companies or entering into trading agreements. Counterparty credit risk differs from other types of credit risks, like a loan or a lease, because it is bilateral (both sides to the contract depend on the counterparty to meet its obligations) and occurs as a part of doing business.

This chapter discusses techniques that traders use to manage counterparty credit risk. The basic cause of counterparty risk is that trading can't be done in isolation. Every time someone wants to buy an asset, someone else needs to sell. When trades involve obligations that are not immediately resolved, traders are exposed to the risk that their counterparty will not meet its part of the bargain. As a result, traders depend on their trading partners to meet their trading obligations, and are exposed to the risk that their trading partners will default on their obligations.

In addition to managing risk, financial regulations require traders to calculate expected losses from credit events and adjust the value of their positions accordingly. The adjustments are called *credit value adjustments* or *CVA*.

From the perspective of making trading and risk management decisions, credit value adjustments allow traders to control risk associated with trading with a particular counterparty. This can be done by placing limits on the amount of business that can be done with any single counterparty, using collateral to ensure counterparty performance, or by using legal agreements that limit counterparty risk.

## TRADING IS A SOCIAL ACTIVITY

Trading cannot be done in isolation. Buyers need to trade with sellers and vice versa. Traders depend upon those trading partners to meet the obligations that were agreed upon during the trade.

Counterparty credit risk is the risk that a trading partner will fail to meet an obligation. For example, a trading partner not paying for something that was delivered is an example of counterparty credit risk. Companies often put in place procedures to limit or control the credit risk they take on when they sign contracts with other companies. Some of these procedures encompass the rule of thumb, "know your customer". In other cases, credit risk can be mitigated by trading through an exchange or requiring a good faith deposit, called *margin*.

For example, two traders might enter into a trade, each with the hope of making a profit. As the market moves, the trade will change in value and sometimes favor one trader or the other. The traders both want the prices to move in their favor. However, until the trade is settled, the trader with the favorable position is at risk that he won't actually get paid by the other trader. The more profitable the trade, the more money the counterparty will owe and the greater the risk of non-payment.

It is not always desirable to completely eliminate credit risk. It is better to end up having the counterparty owe money rather than vice versa. As a result, credit risk is often monitored and controlled rather than avoided.

From a reporting perspective, credit risk is important because companies are often required to consider counterparty risks when they report the value of their investments in their financial statements. The process of adjusting the value of their investments is called *credit value adjustment* or *CVA*. A credit value adjustment is a discount applied to the value of an investment. The purpose of this type of adjustment is to incorporate expected credit losses into financial statements.

## CREDIT RISK

*Credit risk* is the risk that a creditor will not repay or perform on its obligations. Credit risk commonly occurs when a lender, like a bank or credit card company, loans money to a borrower. *Counterparty Credit Risk* is a specific type of credit risk related to obligations that result from transactions or contracts. In these circumstances, obligations typically result from price changes in the market. As a result, unlike a loan, the potential credit risk associated with trading is often hard to predict ahead of time. In addition, both sides of most trades have the possibility of being exposed to credit risk. In a loan situation, only the lender is exposed to credit risk.

Some common terms related to credit risk are:

- **Obligor.** A person who is obligated to do something required by law.
- **Default.** A failure to do something required by law.
- **Credit Value Adjustment (CVA).** An adjustment in value to an asset reflecting the potential effect of counterparty default.
- **Debit Value Adjustment (DVA).** An adjustment to a liability, similar to CVA, reflecting your own potential for default.
- **Cross-Default Clause.** A cross default clause is a contractual clause that prevents a trader from selectively defaulting on an obligation. These clauses, which are standard in most trading contracts, create a default event on every obligation if the obligor defaults on any obligation.
- **Master Netting Agreement.** A clause in many over-the-counter financial contracts that combines all transactions into a single agreement. This forces a bankruptcy court to combine the exposures from various trades. Without this agreement, a bankruptcy court will selectively invalidate the parts of trades owed by the bankrupt party.

The need to include credit adjustments into valuations of positions and financial statements is driven by accounting requirements. For example, in 2006, the requirement for accounting for counterparty risk was specifically mentioned by the Financial Accounting Standards Board (the organization responsible for U.S. accounting standards) in FASB *Financial Accounting Standards 157—Fair Value Measurements* (FAS 157) guidance in Paragraph 5 of Appendix B:

> *B5. Risk-averse market participants generally seek compensation for bearing the uncertainty inherent in the cash flows of an asset or liability (risk premium). A fair value measurement should include a risk premium reflecting the amount market participants would demand because of the risk (uncertainty) in the cash flows. (FASB, 2006)*

This guidance has been strengthened in later FASB Guidance. For example, in the *FASB Accounting Standards Convergence Topic 820* (ASC 820), which superseded FAS 157, the relationship between fair value and credit adjustments is discussed in Subtopic 10, Section 55, Paragraph 55:

> *55-8. A fair value measurement should include a risk premium reflecting the amount market participants would demand because of the risk (uncertainty) in the cash flows. Otherwise, the measurement*

*would not faithfully represent fair value. In some cases, determining the appropriate risk premium might be difficult. However, the degree of difficulty alone is not a sufficient basis on which to exclude a risk adjustment. (FASB, 2009)*

In simpler language, this guidance states that credit value adjustments need to be included in financial statements. This creates a regulatory need for these adjustments in addition to voluntary risk management that might be done by each firm. As a result of this guidance, risk managers are asked to directly contribute to the valuation process by estimating the effect of non-performance risk. This needs to be done for both assets and liabilities.

Some other common terminology related to credit risk:

- **PD (Probability of Default).** The likelihood that the obligor or borrower will fail to meet its financial obligations within a specified timeframe.
- **LGD (Loss Given Default).** The amount of loss, usually expressed as a percentage of total exposure, which will result from a default.
- **EAD (Exposure at Default).** The expected magnitude of the exposure at the time of the default.
- **EL (Expected Loss).** The average credit loss that is expected to occur within the specified timeframe.
- **UL (Unexpected Loss).** A loss amount in excess of the Expected Loss.

These factors are designed to work together. For example, expected loss (EL) can be calculated using the probability of default (PD), the loss given default (LGD), and the exposure at default (EAD). (See Equation 9.1, Expected Loss.)

## KEY CONCEPT: CREDIT RISK IS IMPORTANT TO EVERYONE—NOT JUST BANKS!

Credit risk is the single largest risk that faces owners of large loan portfolios—like the portfolios commonly held by banks. As a result, credit risk is often focused on the need of banks to manage these portfolios. However, credit risk doesn't just affect banks—accounting regulations require every publicly owned company to consider credit risk.

## KEY CONCEPT: COMMON ABBREVIATIONS

The abbreviations for expected loss (EL), unexpected loss (UL), probability of default (PD), loss given default (LGD), and exposure at default (EAD) are common industry abbreviations and should be memorized. These abbreviations are commonly used with little or no description as to their meaning.

The expected loss at the time of the default is the weighted average of the two possibilities. There either is a default event or there is not a default event.

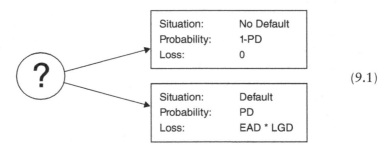

(9.1)

The expected loss is the weighted average of the two results:

$$EL = (1\text{-PD}) * 0 + (PD) * (EAD * LGD)$$

or (simplifying since the first term has a zero in it)

$$EL = PD * EAD * LGD$$

The credit loss is called *expected* because the actual probability of default, loss given default, and exposure at the time of default is not known ahead of time. These are only known for sure after bankruptcy proceedings are concluded. Mathematically, later in the chapter, all of these values will be described as statistical distributions and their value is actually the central tendency (mean value) in the distribution.

While expected loss describes the typical loss, another term is used to describe the actual losses. For a single exposure, *unexpected losses* (UL) are losses in excess of the expected loss (EL). For example, if a trading partner were to owe one million dollars on an obligation, it might have a 10% chance of not paying. The probability of default would be 10%. Assuming a total loss if a default occurred, the expected loss would $100,000 (10% of the exposure).

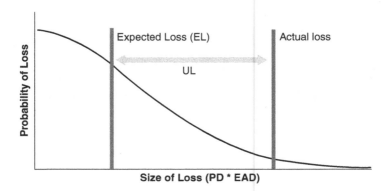

**FIGURE 9.1**   Unexpected Loss

However, if a loss actually occurred, it would be for the full amount. The difference between the actual loss and the expected loss (EL) is called the unexpected loss (UL). Expected Loss works best in a situation where a company has a lot of small debtors (like a credit card company) so that when some default, the losses will average out over time. It works less well in cases of a single large trading partner who has a very low probability of default. (See Figure 9.1, Unexpected Loss.)

## KEY CONCEPT: CREDIT DEFAULT SWAPS (CDS)

Credit Default Swaps (CDSs) are financial instruments that are closely associated with credit markets. Hedge funds and trading desks can use these instruments to either speculate on the possibility of corporate default or to protect themselves from defaults.

Credit default swaps are derivatives whose value is based on corporate bonds issued by some corporation. In event of a default, the CDS issuer (the CDS seller) will take possession of the corporate bond and give a payoff to the buyer. In compensation for taking on this risk, the CDS seller will receive a series of payments from the CDS buyer. The issuer of the bond (the *reference entity* or *reference obligor*) is not a party to the transaction. In addition, the CDS buyer does not have to own the bond at the time the CDS is purchased, nor is there any limit to the number of CDS contracts that can be issued. For example, there may be more CDS contracts issued for a corporation's debt than actual debt.

The price at which CDS products are traded is called the *CDS spread*. The term relates to the difference between the credit adjusted interest rate and risk-free rates. These spreads are often described in terms of *basis points*. A basis point is one hundredth of a percentage point (0.01 percent). For example, 30 basis points would be equal to 0.3 percent.

EL and UL can change over time. For example, in the case of a mortgage, a homeowner may continue to make monthly payments for some time before running into financial difficulties and defaulting. As a result, the size of the mortgage at the time of the default, and any losses due to default, will generally decline over time. In other cases, like a commodity swap, the value of the swap (and the expected loss on the position) will depend on market prices.

## EXPOSURE AT DEFAULT (EAD)

Exposure at default is a term that describes the magnitude of the potential loss at the time of a bankruptcy. The commonly accepted way to estimate exposure is the cost of replacing the same exposure with a different counterparty. For example, if a default occurs on a trading obligation, the exposure will be the cost to close out the contract and replace it with an identical trade with a different counterparty. This will ensure that the non-bankrupt party will have the same exposure before and after the default. In other words, the replacement cost of the contract is the exposure at default.

The nature of the financial instrument will determine whether credit risk can occur to either party or just to one party. For example, with a commodity

### Example

Angela, a trader at a refinery, has agreed to purchase 1000 barrels of crude oil for $100/barrel to be delivered in 6 months. At the time of the trade, this contract was at fair value. In the months following the trade, crude oil prices rose and Angela was pleased to lock in the purchase at a favorable price. However, at the end of the fourth month, the oil driller from whom Angela had purchased the contract went bankrupt and Angela had to replace the contract.

After four months, the price to buy oil for delivery in two months is $125/BBL. To replace the purchase contract, Angela had to enter

*(Continued)*

into a contract to buy at $125/BBL. As a result, she lost the $25 per barrel benefit from the original contract and had a $25,000 total loss (some of which might be recovered in the bankruptcy proceedings). (See Figure 9.2, Forward Prices.)

|  | Price of Oil ($/BBL) | Exposure ($/BBL) |
|---|---|---|
| After 1 Month | $105 | $5 |
| After 2 Months | $95 | $0 |
| After 3 Months | $110 | $10 |
| After 4 Months | $125 | $25 |

**FIGURE 9.2**   Forward Prices

swap either side of the transaction can end up owing the other party money, depending on how prices move prior to expiration. However, with an option, the buyer pays a set fee (the premium) to the seller when the contract is purchased. Once that premium is paid, the option seller is responsible for the remaining obligation—to pay the buyer money if something happens. Loans are another example of a one-sided exposure. The lender is exposed to the credit risk of the borrower. However, once the borrower has the loan, all of the remaining obligations (repaying the loan) are the responsibility of the borrower.

To calculate the amount of loss due to a default, it is necessary to look at the cost of closing out the transaction with the defaulted counterparty and entering a new transaction with someone else. The mechanism of closing the contract can vary slightly by financial instrument. However, the same general pattern applies to most instruments.

If the position is currently at a loss:

- Close out the position with the counterparty by paying the counterparty the market value of the position
- Enter into a similar contract and receive the market value of the contract from the new counterparty
- Have zero net profit since the value received from the new counterparty offsets the value paid to the defaulted counterparty

If the position is currently at a profit:

- Close out the position, receiving no immediate payment, and seek recovery value as part of the bankruptcy process

## KEY CONCEPT: EXPOSURE AT DEFAULT

For contracts, exposure at default (EAD) is equal to the replacement cost of the contract. Contracts that have negative value (where money is owed to the defaulting company) don't have any credit exposure. This will typically affect the reserves needed for potential credit losses. From a valuation perspective, contracts with a debit exposure would still need to calculate a debit value adjustment.

For calculating reserves:

$$EAD = Max[0, V(t)]$$

For calculating CVA or DVA

$$EAD = V(t)$$

where

$$V(t) = \text{Value of the contract on the default date}$$
$$t = \text{date of the default}$$

■ Enter into a similar contract and pay the new counterparty the market value of the contract
■ Have a net loss equal to the market value of the contract paid to the new counterparty

For a single simple exposure, like a loan, it is possible to calculate EAD by estimating the nominal amount of exposure expected on potential default dates. This will not take into account collateral or the potential advantage of netting exposures (when a master netting agreement is in place between traders). For more complicated situations, firms might consider a wider set of transaction characteristics. These might include the type of transaction, the counterparty type, and various credit mitigation tools like master-netting agreements and collateral.

## LOSS GIVEN DEFAULT (LGD)

In a bankruptcy, there is a priority order that determines the order in which debts of the bankrupt company get paid. Unpaid wages and taxes are paid first. Then, the senior debt holders (bond holders) get paid. After that, the

**Bankruptcy Priority**

1. Unpaid wages
2. Unpaid taxes
3. Secured bonds (collateralized bonds)
4. Unsecured debt (trading obligations, general creditors, debentures)
5. Preferred stock
6. Common stock

**FIGURE 9.3** Bankruptcy Priority

unsecured debts of the company are paid. Unsecured debts include monies owed to trading partners. Finally, the owners receive anything that is left over. (See Figure 9.3, Bankruptcy Priority.)

On average, since 1970 about 40 percent of obligations have been recovered through bankruptcy proceedings. However, this is a bit misleading since the results don't converge on the average. The lower range of recovery rates is often in the range of 15 to 30 percent recovery. The average is brought up by a large number of recoveries in the 60 to 100 percent range. (See Figure 9.4, Annual Average Sr. Unsecured Recovery Rates, 1982–2005.)

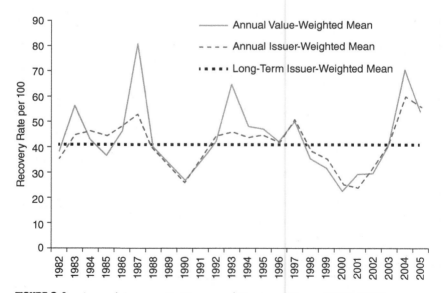

**FIGURE 9.4** Annual Average Sr. Unsecured Recovery Rates, 1982–2005
*Source:* Moody's Investment Services, Defaults and Recovery Rates of Corporate Bond Issuers 1920–2005.

## KEY CONCEPT: LGD MODELS

Models for LGD can run from simplistic to fairly complicated. For example, once a company is in default, LGD can generally be estimated by observing trades in the bond market. Bonds are quoted based on par value, where 100 = 100 cents on the dollar. A bond that is trading at 25 is expected by the market to pay 25 cents on the dollar (a 25 percent recovery rate or a 75 percent loss given default).

However, before a default, the recovery rate is much harder to observe. For portfolios with a relatively large number of defaults (like a credit card or consumer loan portfolio), statistical sampling might be used to estimate typical losses.

However, for portfolios with a relatively low number of defaults, it is common to use a market-based approach that examines prices of credit-related instruments to estimate LGD. The spread at which various corporate bonds trade over risk-free rates, the interest rate charged on loans, and prices of credit default swaps (CDS) can all be used to estimate expected losses (EL). For these models, an estimate is made for either the loss given default (LGD) or probability of default (PD) and then the price is used to solve for the value of the other variable.

Recovery rates and loss given default (LGD) are related. LGD equals 100 percent minus the recovery rate. For example, if 25 percent of the money is recovered, the trader has suffered a 75 percent loss. (See Equation 9.2, LGD and Recovery Rate.)

$$LGD = 100\% - RecoveryRate \tag{9.2}$$

Recovery of unsecured debts also depends on where the debts fall in the bankruptcy priority and how many debts are in line ahead of the trading obligation. Most trading obligations are fairly low in priority and are grouped in with the rest of the bankrupt firm's unsecured debts. Higher-priority debts have a much higher chance of being repaid than lower-priority debts.

## PROBABILITY OF DEFAULT (PD)

Probability of default, commonly abbreviated PD, indicates the likelihood that an obligor will be unable to make scheduled repayments or similar obligations. When an obligor is unable to pay their debts, the obligor is said to be in default of the debt. Typically, this will lead to bankruptcy or similar proceedings where the creditors will seek partial repayment.

There are a number of ways to estimate probabilities of default. Trading portfolios typically have low default probabilities, and one way to estimate default probabilities is to use credit ratings. Probabilities of default are also commonly estimated using data from either the credit default swap (CDS) market or bond markets. The rationales for using market-based default probabilities are similar to the arguments for using implied volatility in the option markets. They give a continuously updated view on risk because, in an efficient market, traded instruments should reach an equilibrium price that is fair to the buyer and seller.

### Credit Rating Model

With a credit rating model, credit ratings are used to estimate default probabilities. Credit ratings are published by a variety of ratings companies to make it easier for investors to understand the risks of buying certain bonds. Not every bond has a credit rating. To get a credit rating, the bond issuer needs to pay the rating agency a fee to get a rating. Bond issuers voluntarily pay for credit ratings to establish the issuer's creditworthiness and willingness to protect the interests of bondholders.

Credit ratings are typically an alphanumeric code ranging from extremely high credit quality (typically AAA or Aaa) to already in default (D). The two major grades of bonds are *investment grade* and *high yield*. Investment grade bonds are generally low risk and suitable for investors who are not going to spend much time looking into the risks of their investments (like widows, orphans, and retirement accounts). High-yield bonds are typically much riskier than investment grade bonds. However, they generally pay much higher coupon rates to investors. (See Figure 9.5, Bond Ratings.)

These ratings can be converted into default probabilities using transition rates published by bond ratings agencies. Transition rates indicate the likelihood that bonds at one credit rating will migrate to another credit rating over some timeframe. Typically, these transitions are based on historical studies, but newer models can include data updated to include recent economic events and the likelihood that a cluster of defaults occurs simultaneously. (See Figure 9.6, Average One-Year Corporate Whole Letter Rating Migration Rates, 1970–2005.)

### Cumulative PD

The calculations shown in Figure 9.6 provide a way to estimate the probability of default in a given year. If the exposure is over a longer (or shorter) period, this calculation will need to be adjusted. Assuming that defaults occur once per year,

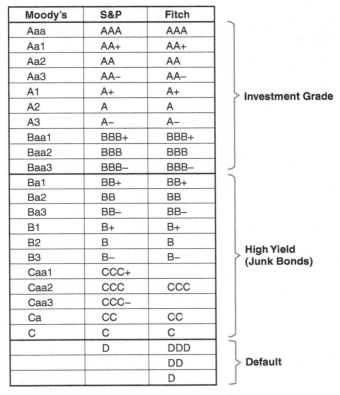

| Moody's | S&P | Fitch | |
|---------|------|-------|---|
| Aaa | AAA | AAA | |
| Aa1 | AA+ | AA+ | |
| Aa2 | AA | AA | |
| Aa3 | AA– | AA– | |
| A1 | A+ | A+ | Investment Grade |
| A2 | A | A | |
| A3 | A– | A– | |
| Baa1 | BBB+ | BBB+ | |
| Baa2 | BBB | BBB | |
| Baa3 | BBB– | BBB– | |
| Ba1 | BB+ | BB+ | |
| Ba2 | BB | BB | |
| Ba3 | BB– | BB– | |
| B1 | B+ | B+ | |
| B2 | B | B | High Yield |
| B3 | B– | B– | (Junk Bonds) |
| Caa1 | CCC+ | | |
| Caa2 | CCC | CCC | |
| Caa3 | CCC– | | |
| Ca | CC | CC | |
| C | C | C | |
| | D | DDD | |
| | | DD | Default |
| | | D | |

**FIGURE 9.5** Bond Ratings

| Beginning of Year Rating | End of Year Rating | | | | | | | | |
|---|---|---|---|---|---|---|---|---|---|
| | Aaa | Aa | A | Baa | Ba | B | Caa-C | Default | WR |
| Aaa | 89.899 | 6.724 | 0.54 | 0.191 | 0.013 | 0.002 | 0 | 0 | 2.632 |
| Aa | 1.036 | 87.885 | 6.918 | 0.269 | 0.053 | 0.017 | 0 | 0.008 | 3.814 |
| A | 0.055 | 2.573 | 88.124 | 4.946 | 0.516 | 0.102 | 0.022 | 0.021 | 3.641 |
| Baa | 0.045 | 0.208 | 4.92 | 84.716 | 4.436 | 0.793 | 0.246 | 0.177 | 4.461 |
| Ba | 0.009 | 0.056 | 0.483 | 5.652 | 76.678 | 7.605 | 0.623 | 1.178 | 7.715 |
| B | 0.009 | 0.049 | 0.169 | 0.412 | 5.549 | 74.539 | 5.442 | 5.367 | 8.463 |
| Caa-C | 0 | 0.036 | 0.036 | 0196 | 0.738 | 7.166 | 60.648 | 19.523 | 11.659 |

**FIGURE 9.6** Average One-Year Corporate Whole Letter Rating Migration Rates, 1970–2005
*Source:* Moody's Investment Services, Defaults and Recovery Rates of Corporate Bond Issuers 1920–2005.

## KEY CONCEPT: CRITICISM OF CREDIT RATING MODELS

The largest criticism of using credit ratings models for CVA work is that they are based on historical studies and don't react as quickly as bond markets or credit derivatives markets to rumors of trouble.

if a company has a 2 percent chance of going bankrupt in the first year then it has a 98 percent chance of surviving to year two. The second year, assuming the company still has the same probability of default, 98 percent of the time it will survive. The cumulative probability that it survives two years is 96.04 percent (this is $.98^2$). This is calculated by multiplying the survival probability in the first year by the survival probability in the second year.

Consideration has to be given to how often the compounding effect occurs. This should match the frequency that the interest rate (or spread) used to estimate the PD is compounded. Since bond coupons are typically paid twice a year (semiannually), PD calculations based on bond rates should also have semiannual compounding. This tends to match the intuition that bankruptcies are often triggered by a missed bond payment. (See Equation 9.3, Cumulative Default Probability.)

The probability of default occurring by time t can be calculated:

$$PD_t = [1 - \left(1 - \frac{PD}{m}\right)^{mt}]$$  (9.3)

where

PD$_t$     **Cumulative Probability of a Default occurring by time t.** The probability that a default has occurred will increase over time

PD     **Probability of Default (per year).** The annual survival probability calculated from either bond or CDS calculations

t     **The number of years.** The number of years in the future that is being estimated

m     **The number of times compounding occurs per year.** For example, spreads based of bond markets might assume that default events occur twice a year (when bond payments are due). This would correspond to m = 2

## Building PD Forward Curves

A slightly more advanced approach to calculating PD is to use a forward rate curve. It is common for interest rates to vary with time. For example, the interest rate on a 10-year loan might be than higher than interest rate needed for a 3-year loan. In the same way, a BAA-rated bond might have an interest rate that is 1 percent over the one-year risk-free rate, 2 percent over the five year risk-free rate, and 3 percent over the 10-year rate. Using these points, it is possible to construct a forward curve by using an iterative process—first calculating the default rates associated with the soonest-to-mature bonds and then calculating the later rates.

When interest rates are calculated using interest rates or CDS spreads, they will be calculated from the valuation date to some point in the future. To construct a forward curve, it is necessary to use the probability of default between the valuation date $(t_0)$ and the dates in the future $(t_1, t_2)$ to calculate the probability of default between $t_1$ and $t_2$. This process is commonly called _bootstrapping_ and is similar to the bond math calculation of the same name. (See Figure 9.7, Bootstrapping a PD Curve, and Equation 9.4, Forward PD Curves).

If the probability of default between $t_0$ and $t_1$ (PD$_1$) and the probability of default between $t_0$ and $t_2$ (PD$_2$) are known, the easiest way to calculate the probability of default between $t_1$ and $t_2$ (PD$_{1-2}$) is to examine survival probabilities.

$$PS_t = \left(1 - \frac{PD}{m}\right)^{mt} \tag{9.4}$$

once the PS$_1$ and PS$_2$ values are calculated

$$PD_{t1-t2} = 1 - \left(\frac{PS_{t2}}{PS_{t1}}\right)^{\left(\frac{1/m}{t2-t1}\right)}$$

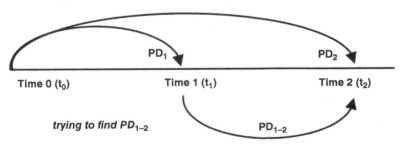

_Having already calculated PD$_1$ and PD$_2$_

**FIGURE 9.7** Bootstrapping a PD Curve

where

$PS_t$      **Cumulative Probability of Survival at time t.** The probability that a default has not occurred is $1 - PD_t$

PD      **Probability of Default (per year).** The annual survival probability calculated from either bond or CDS calculations

t      **The number of years.** The number of years in the future that is being estimated

t1, t2      **Time 1 and Time 2.** When used as a subscript, this indicates a value at t1 or t2 respectively. If used alone, the number of years at t1 and t2

m      **The number of times compounding occurs per year.** For example, spreads based of bond markets might assume that default events occur twice a year (when bond payments are due). This would correspond to $m = 2$

### Market-Based

A second way to estimate default probabilities is to look directly at the prices of credit default swaps (CDS) or corporate bonds. It is possible to calculate the survival assumption embedded in the market prices of bonds and credit default swaps assuming that the risk of default is the only reason that a corporate bond will sell for less than a similar risk-free bond. The logic behind this assumption is that a rational investor should be indifferent between the two investments as long as the present value of the cash flow incorporates the possibility of loss. This leads to the relationship between risk adjusted discount rates and risk-free rates. (See Equation 9.5, CDS-Based Default Probability.)

A Credit Default Swap (CDS) is a financial derivative where the issuer of the swap will compensate the CDS buyer in the event of a default.

$$PD = (1 - CDSSpread) / LGD \qquad (9.5)$$

where

PD            **Probability of Default**

CDS Spread     **CDS Spread.** The price of the Credit Default Swap

LGD          **Loss Given Default**

A similar calculation can be performed on bond prices. When this is done, the bond rate (a credit adjusted rate) is compared to risk-free rates. The spread between the bond rate and the risk-free rate is due to two factors—the risk of default and a liquidity premium—since the corporate bond will be more difficult to trade than the risk-free bond. (See Equation 9.6, Corporate Bond Spreads.)

The interest rate at which a corporation can borrow money is approximated by the following formula.

$$r_c = r_f + PD * LGD + S \tag{9.6}$$

where

$r_c$      **Credit Adjusted Interest Rate.** The interest rate paid by the borrower

$r_f$      **Risk Free Interest Rate.** The risk free interest rates at time the bond was issued. LIBOR rates and US Treasury Rates are the most common choices for risk free rates

PD      **Probability of Default**

LGD      **Loss Given Default.** The amount of the exposure which will be lost in event of a default

S      **Spread.** The spread on the issuance. This is typically related to liquidity risk since the corporate bond may be harder to trade than the risk-free bonds. This can also include bank-specific costs like issuance costs

Solving for the probability of default with these formulas allows the probability of default to be calculated as a function of interest rates. (See Equation 9.7, Bond-Based Default Probability.)

The probability of default for a corporation can be estimated by the following formula:

$$PD = (r_c - r_f - S) / LGD \tag{9.7}$$

or approximated by an even simpler formula assuming that $S = 0$

$$PD = (r_c - r_f) / LGD$$

where

$r_c$      **Credit Adjusted Interest Rate.** The interest rate paid by the borrower.

$r_f$      **Risk Free Interest Rate.** The risk-free interest rates at time the bond was issued. LIBOR rates and U.S. Treasury Rates are the most common choices for risk free rates

PD      **Probability of Default**

LGD      **Loss Given Default.** The amount of the exposure which will be lost in event of a default

S      **Spread.** The spread on the issuance. This is typically related to liquidity risk since the corporate bond may be harder to trade than the risk-free bonds. This can also include bank-specific costs like issuance costs

## KEY CONCEPT: CRITICISM OF MARKET-BASED MODELS

The largest criticism of using market-based models is that market prices are not just set by expectations of defaults. Market prices are also heavily influenced by liquidity—typically short-term supply and demand. In periods of limited liquidity (like a market panic or late in the afternoon before a three-day weekend), prices may not accurately reflect market views on default probability.

## CORRELATION BETWEEN PD AND LGD

Both the counterparty's probability of default and the loss given default are heavily dependent on business cycles. Because of this shared factor, there is a correlation between the probability of default and the recovery rate achieved during bankruptcy.

In periods with few bankruptcies (like an economic expansion) the recovery rate is higher than in periods with a lot of bankruptcies (like a recession). One reason may be that in an expansion, firms will pay a premium to acquire the assets of bankrupt firms. When there are few firms in bankruptcy, and acquiring the assets of an existing firm may provide a cheaper way to achieve growth targets, then the recovery rate during bankruptcy improves. However, in recessions, when there are more bankrupt firms and the remaining firms have fewer resources with which to acquire the assets of bankrupt firms, recovery rates decline. (See Figure 9.8, Correlation between Defaults and Recoveries, 1983–2005.)

A simple way to account for this correlation is to assume a lower recovery rate. Another way to address the correlation is to create a credit model that explicitly models this relationship. Either way, credit losses during a stressed market situation can be worse than what would occur during more stable periods.

## KEY CONCEPT: RIGHT- AND WRONG-WAY RISK

The assumption in most CVA models is that counterparty exposure and probability of default are not correlated. Risks where the size of exposure and default are not correlated are called *right-way* risks. Risks where probability of loss and potential exposure are correlated are called *wrong-way* risks.

The definitions for right-way and wrong-way risk are:

- **Right-Way Risk.** The exposure and probability of loss are not particularly correlated.
- **Wrong-Way Risk.** The exposure and probability of loss are highly correlated.

An example of a company typically exposed to wrong-way risk is a single-strategy hedge fund. The more money the investment strategy loses, the greater the amount it owes and the greater the probability of bankruptcy. Another common example of wrong-way risk is insurance companies that make a business of selling credit-based derivatives (like credit default swaps). In this case, companies that sell CDS contracts are very likely to have a cash shortage (that makes their own default more likely) due to paying on the credit derivatives caused by other bankruptcies. The most effective ways to identify right-way and wrong-way risk is often to understand the counterparty and the business that they are in.

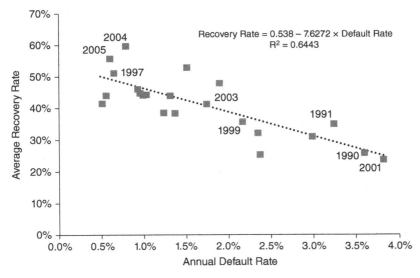

**FIGURE 9.8**  Correlation between Defaults and Recoveries, 1983–2005
*Source:* Moody's Investment Services, Defaults and Recovery Rates of Corporate Bond Issuers 1920–2005.

## CREDIT LIMITS AND COUNTERPARTY EXPOSURE

Most contracts have a cross-default clause. This means that defaults don't occur on the level of individual contracts—they occur on a counterparty level. In other words, if a company defaults on any contract, they default on all of their contracts. As a result, it is necessary to look at the aggregate exposure to that counterparty. The easiest way is to look at the gross risk from all contracts associated with that counterparty. However, this approach does not incorporate two common ways that companies mitigate credit risks.

- **Netting Agreements.** Netting agreements are legal contracts between the two counterparties that aggregate all transactions between two parties into a single exposure.
- **Collateral.** Collateral is a pledge of specific property used to secure repayment of an obligation. Collateral agreements are sometimes called *margin* agreements.

## KEY CONCEPT: MASTER NETTING REDUCES CREDIT RISK

A master netting agreement makes all transactions between two counterparties into a single contract. This reduces credit risk by allowing trades with a negative value to cancel out trades with a positive value. Otherwise, the bankruptcy court will enforce the bankruptcy priority on each contract separately. Master netting agreements have become standard in many over-the-counter derivative and commodity markets.

**Example:**
Austin, a trader, has entered into two trades with MegaCorp. First, on July 1, he agreed to buy 1 million bushels of corn for December delivery for $15 per bushel. A week later, on July 9, prices rose to $20 per bushel and Austin entered into a second contract—also with MegaCorp—to sell 1 million bushels of corn for $20 per bushel to lock in his $5 per bushel profit.

In October, MegaCorp goes bankrupt and the price of corn has risen to $50 per bushel. The bankruptcy court enforces all contracts where MegaCorp is owed money and places all payments owed to other parties in priority order for repayment. Expected recovery is 20 percent.

**With Master Netting:**
With master netting, the two trades are considered a single contract. The volumes offset one another, and Austin gets to keep his $5 million profit.

**Without Master Netting:**
Without master netting, the court will decide to enforce the contract where Austin has agreed to sell 1 million bushels at $20 per bushel. With prices at $50 per bushel, this will require Austin to pay $30 million to MegaCorp to close the trade. When the bankruptcy court completes its work, he can expect to get $7 million back in the recovery. $7MM is 20 percent of the $35 million contract value on the default date.

Netting turns a gross exposure into a net exposure. Without master netting agreements, the total exposure to the defaulting counterparty depends on any contract that has been previously traded. (See Equation 9.8, Aggregate Exposure without Netting.)

Without netting, the exposure at default (EAD) is calculated by summing all of the positive exposures.

$$EAD_{Counterparty} = \sum{}^{E} AD_{Conract} = \sum{}^{M} ax(0, V(t)_{Contract}) \tag{9.8}$$

where

$V(t)_{Contract}$     **Value.** The expected value of the contract at a default date

$t$     **Default date.** The date on which a default might occur

With netting agreements, the counterparty exposure is reduced to a net exposure. This can be very important to companies that execute a large number of trades. Trading positions are typically closed by entering into an offsetting transaction rather than cancelling the original contract. As a result, netting can dramatically reduce exposures for traders active in over-the-counter trading. (See Equation 9.9, Aggregate Exposure with Netting.)

Netting will allow the positive and negative exposure to cancel prior to calculating the exposure. This will result in a much smaller exposure.

$$EAD_{Counterparty} = Max(0, \sum V(t)_{Conract}) \tag{9.9}$$

where

$V(t)_{Contract}$     **Value.** The expected value of the contract at a default date

$t$     **Default date.** The date on which a default might occur

Another way to reduce credit risk is through the use of collateral. Collateral is a pledge of specific assets to secure trading positions. It is typically applied in conjunction with netting agreements. A typical collateralization clause will specify that any trades between the two counterparties must be marked to market periodically, and if the net value is above a certain threshold, then one of the counterparties has the ability to ask the other counterparty for collateral. (See Equation 9.10, Aggregate Netting with Netting and Collateral.)

Collateral will further reduce the net exposure obtained by netting positions.

$$EAD_{Counterparty} = Max\left[0, -C(t) + \sum{}^{V}(t)_{Conract}\right] \qquad (9.10)$$

where

$V(t)_{Contract}$     **Value.** The expected value of the contract at a default date

$C(t)$     **Collateral.** The expected value of the collateral at a default date

t     **Default date.** The date on which a default might occur

In practice, there are several different types of collateral. For example, it is possible to supply cash or physical assets to meet a collateral obligation. However, it is more common for the counterparty needing collateral to get a guaranteed line of credit from a bank and to use that line of credit as collateral. This transfers the credit risk from the trading partner to the bank. Banks will typically need to meet some credit standards, but as long as the

## KEY CONCEPT: CREDIT MITIGATION

Risk managers should make sure that netting is included as a standard part of any trading agreements. In addition, they will typically want to examine the size of potential exposure to determine if collateral might be required. For example, a risk manager might ask for a trading agreement to include a clause that requires collateral to be posted whenever the current exposure exceeds some level.

- Netting is a standard part of many derivatives contracts. For example, the standard ISDA (International Swap Dealers Association) contract includes a master netting clause.
- Netting is subject to local jurisdiction. Particularly in emerging markets, some jurisdictions may not allow netting or netting clauses may not be tested in court.

counterparty and the bank don't go bankrupt at the same time, the credit risk due to trading will be eliminated or substantially reduced.

Collateral is related to the concept of credit limits for a counterparty. Credit limits are typically implemented by limiting how much exposure is allowed per counterparty before new trades are prohibited or collateral is required. The decision as to where credit limits are to be set is usually a discussion that involves both the business and risk management teams.

It should be noted that even in cases where collateral exists there is execution risk. For example, in the period after the default has been identified but before the position can be fully closed out, prices may continue to move. This is typically called a *gap* risk.

---

### KEY CONCEPT: IMPLEMENTING CREDIT LIMITS REQUIRES THOUGHT

A one-size–fits-all mentality to credit risk is usually very destructive to a trading organization. Understanding the counterparty is a key part of the credit risk process.

For example, a large commodity trading desk might be considering how to set credit limits for two potential clients.

- **Client A.** Client A is a new manufacturing company with limited liquid assets. The assets consist mostly of physical property and manufacturing equipment. It has recently signed an agreement with a large retailer to produce widgets to be sold across the United States and is looking for a single financial services firm to help hedge its raw materials purchases.
- **Client B.** Client B is a hedge fund specializing is high-speed financial transactions. It is known as a cut-throat competitor that is focused on making daring market bets. It is looking to line up trading agreements with a large number of commodity trading desks to take advantage of price differences between their trading partners.

Even if the two companies had exactly the same probability of default and recovery rates, they have very different business plans. Client A is looking for a single provider of financial services. As a result, restrictive credit limits might impair one of Client A's major goals—to have a single trading partner. Client A has a high likelihood of being a profitable client since they are likely to delegate trading

*(Continued)*

### KEY CONCEPT: *(Continued)*

responsibility and value financial advice and trading assistance even if they had to pay slightly higher prices.

In contrast, Client B presents a much weaker case as a trading counterparty. Client B is probably not interested in higher-margin services. Client B is interested primarily in getting the best possible prices. In addition, it may be very risky to facilitate their trades—the company specializes in making risky bets—bets where your company would be taking the opposite position.

## CURRENT EXPOSURE AND POTENTIAL FUTURE EXPOSURE

When calculating the exposure at default for CVA purposes, the expected timing on the default will have a major effect on the calculation. For example, it is relatively straightforward to calculate how much is lost on each contract if a default occurs immediately. Both the EAD and fair value under mark-to-market accounting depend on the concept of liquidation value. The current fair value of the contract (the mark-to-market value) is today's exposure at default (EAD). However, if a default were to occur at some point in the future, the contract might have changed in value. The longer the time between the present and the default, the more the value can change. This has led to two common measurements—*current exposure* and *potential future exposure.*

*Current exposure* (CE) estimates the replacement costs of the contracts if the counterparty defaults immediately. If the value of the contract is positive, a credit value adjustment (CVA) is calculated based on the counterparty's credit rating. If the value is negative, a debit value adjustment (DVA) is calculated using your own credit rating. The *potential future exposure* (PFE) calculates the expected replacement cost of the contract if a default occurs at some pre-specified point in the future (like a year). This calculation tends to work very much like a value-at-risk (VAR) calculation and is commonly used in risk management.

## CALCULATING A CREDIT VALUE ADJUSTMENT

A CVA calculation has two main steps. First, it is necessary to calculate each of the factors (PD, LGD, EAD) needed for an expected loss calculation. Then, it is necessary to calculate the present valuing of the expected loss. (See Equation 9.11, Credit Value Adjustment.)

A credit value adjustment is the present value of the expected loss due to default.

$$CVA = (e^{-rt}) * LGD * PD * EAD \qquad (9.11)$$

where

| | |
|---|---|
| LGD, PD, EAD | **Expected Loss.** These factors are the expected loss formula defined previously |
| $e^{-rt}$ | **Present Value.** This term is the continuous compounding calculation. In this equation, "e" is a constant – it is the base of the natural logarithm |
| r | **Risk-Free Rate.** The risk-free interest rate. This is typically based on LIBOR or high quality government bond rates |
| t | **Time.** The time until expiration (by convention, 1.0 = 1 year) |
| LGD | **Loss Given Default.** The percentage of exposure that is expected to be lost after a defaults. |
| PD | **Probability of Default.** The probability of a default |
| EAD | **Exposure at Default.** The exposure expected at default. This can either be the exposure under current market conditions (Current Exposure) or the potential exposure under expected future market conditions (Potential Future Exposure) |

For example, a trader wants to calculate the CVA needed for a $1000 payment payable to you in 6 months using a current exposure methodology. He has calculated that the counterparty's default probability over this period is 0.7 percent and the expected recovery rate in event of a default is 40 percent. The risk-free rate for six months is 1 percent.

The problem defines the following variables:

- PD = 0.7 percent
- LGD = 60 percent (found by 1 – recovery rate)
- EAD is $1000
- t = 0.5
- r = 1 percent

The expected loss can be found by the formula:

$CVA = e^{-rt} \times PD \times EAD \times LGD$
$CVA = e^{-(.01 * 0.5)} \times (.007) \times (1000) \times (.60)$
$CVA = \$4.179052$

**TABLE 9.1** Multi-Period CVA

| Time (t) | EAD | PV (EAD) | PD | CVA |
|---|---|---|---|---|
| 1 | $1,000.00 | $951.23 | 0.30% | −$1.71 |
| 2 | $1,000.00 | $904.84 | 0.60% | −$3.26 |
| 3 | $1,000.00 | $860.71 | 0.80% | −$4.13 |
| 4 | $1,000.00 | $818.73 | 1.00% | −$4.91 |
| 5 | $1,000.00 | $778.80 | 1.20% | −$5.61 |
| Total | | $4,314.31 | | −$19.62 |

## MULTI-PERIOD CVA CALCULATION

When an instrument has cash flows paid out over multiple periods and the probability of default changes over time, it is necessary to calculate the exposure at various points in time. This is done in a very similar manner to a single-period CVA calculation.

For example, a $1000 payment is made each year for 5 years. The discount rate is a constant 5 percent, and the loss given default is 60 percent. (See Table 9.1, Multi-Period CVA.)

In this example, a $1000 payment is made each year for 5 years. Each payment is treated as its own exposure and calculated individually. The CVA is the sum of those individual exposures.

The columns in the table are:

- The EAD column shows the exposure at each period.
- The PV (EAD) column shows the present value of the exposure remaining at each payment date.
- The PD column indicates the probability of default at each date.
- The CVA column shows the present value of the expected loss. CVA = PV (EAD) × PD × (60 percent LGD).

## SETTLEMENT RISK

Credit risks can also occur at the settlement of a trade. Particularly in cases where each party has to deliver something to the other, the transfer might not be done simultaneously. For example, an FX swap might involve a transfer of two currencies and occur at the close of business in each country. An exchange of Euros (perhaps from France) might be exchanged for U.S. dollars. Since French markets close before the U.S. markets, there might

## KEY CONCEPT: CVA/DVA CAN CREATE UNEXPECTED RISKS

CVA has the potential to create volatility in earnings. For example, a company might be fully hedged with respect to market risks. However, if one of the counterparties with whom it has traded announces negative news, this might cause a mark-to-market loss (if the counterparty's probability of default goes up). Of course, this might work the other way too—the trade might become more profitable (if the company announces good earnings and it is perceived to be less risky).

Even more counterintuitive is what happens when the company with liabilities on which it is calculating a DVA reports good news. With DVA, liabilities are discounted at the company's own credit rate. If that credit rating improves, a smaller discount will be applied to the liabilities. This will increase the size of the liability and lead to a mark-to-market loss.

In other words, CVA/DVA adjustments have introduced another source of earnings volatility that is very difficult to hedge. Unexpected profits and losses can occur at any time. The credit derivatives markets can help in some cases. For example, for large well-known counterparties, it is often possible to buy a credit default swap (CDS). Buying a CDS will transfer the risk from the counterparty to the seller of the credit default swap. This is much like buying insurance, although CDS contracts receive different accounting treatment.

However, this won't work for all counterparties. Only the largest counterparties will have traded CDS instruments. In addition, buying a CDS exposes the buyer to the risk that the CDS seller will default. This can be quite substantial, since this typically involves a lot of wrong-way risk—a CDS seller will be at highest risk of default when they have to pay out on a lot of CDS contracts.

be a short period where one party has paid, but not the other. Generally, the time frames are of short duration. However, since the gross transaction rather than the net size is at risk, the amounts involved can be large.

## TEST YOUR KNOWLEDGE

1. As used in credit risk calculation, what does PD mean?
   A. Probability Density
   B. Population Density

    C. Probability of Default

    D. Potential Difference

2. What is wrong-way risk?

    A. Wrong-way risk is a term that means that default probabilities are highly correlated with exposure.

    B. Wrong-way risk describes the fact that a debit value adjustment leads to increased profits when your own credit rating worsens.

    C. Wrong-way risk uses a skewed payoff distribution rather than a normal distribution.

    D. Wrong-way risk describes risk at settlement, when one party has delivered their final payment, but the other has not.

3. What is the credit adjusted fair value if the risk-free fair value is $100, PD is 2.0 percent, and LGD is 50 percent?

    A. $99

    B. $100

    C. $101

    D. Insufficient information is provided to answer the question.

4. In a credit risk sense, why are master netting agreements important?

    A. Netting provides a way to trade out of a position without exposing oneself to a large amount of credit risk.

    B. Netting reduces the size of credit exposures.

    C. Netting can reduce the size, frequency, and need for collateral payments.

    D. All of the above.

5. What happens if a trading counterparty to which you owe $1.2MM goes bankrupt? Assume that netting applies and there is no collateral.

    A. You still owe $1.2MM.

    B. You will owe the bankrupt company (1 - LGD) × 1.2MM.

    C. You will owe the bankrupt company (1- PD × LGD) × 1.2MM.

    D. Insufficient information is provided to answer the question.

6. What is a situation where settlement risk is important?

    A. Credit Default Swap settlement.

    B. Financial trades that are net settled.

    C. Payoff on options contracts.

    D. Physical commodity swaps.

7. Benjamin, a credit analyst at a hedge fund, is trying to calculate the default probability of a company that doesn't have traded CDS spreads. The company issued bonds at 6 percent. At the time of issuance, risk-free rates were 3.5 percent and the spread for liquidity risk was 50 basis points. The estimated recovery rate in event of a default is 40 percent.

    A. 2.00 percent

    B. 3.33 percent

    **C.** 5.00 percent

    **D.** 6.25 percent

8. A large hedge fund has agreed to sell an asset worth $1MM to a company in exchange for a payment due in one year. An analyst at the hedge fund needs to calculate the size of the repayment to incorporate default risk. Ignoring liquidity risks, if continuously compounded risk-free rates are 4 percent, the probability of default is 5 percent, and the LGD is 60 percent, what should be the size of the final payment?

    **A.** $932,000

    **B.** $1,000,000

    **C.** $1,040,000

    **D.** $1,072,000

9. What kinds of companies have published credit ratings?

    **A.** All companies will have credit ratings published by major ratings agencies.

    **B.** Only publicly owned corporations that have issued common stock have credit ratings.

    **C.** Only publicly owned companies that are listed on the New York Stock Exchange or Nasdaq have published credit ratings.

    **D.** Only companies that have issued publicly traded debt and requested that their bonds be rated by a rating agency have published credit ratings.

10. When performing a credit value adjustment on a trade where you owe the counterparty money, what will happen?

    **A.** The size of the loss will be increased since risk adjustment will never decrease the size of losses.

    **B.** A debit value adjustment (DVA) will be performed on losing positions which will reduce the size of the loss.

    **C.** The counterparty will make an adjustment to their trading positions to estimate the decreased loss, but no adjustment will be made to your own books and records.

    **D.** Insufficient information is provided to answer the question.

# Afterword

*If you only have a hammer, you tend to see every problem as a nail.*
—Abraham Maslow

**R**isk management is a tool. Like all tools, it is better suited for some jobs than other jobs. At the end of the day, whether risk management helps or hurts an organization depends on how it is used. Some firms use risk management techniques as a core part of their business and find great benefit from it. For others, it is a waste of time and resources that creates as many problems as it prevents.

Risk management is most effective when decisions that might be made differently are altered as a result of analysis. If decisions or behavior won't change, the analysis is largely wasted. Because of that, one of the ways to effectively use risk management is to focus on the decisions that might be affected. Some of those decisions include:

- **Avoidance.** For some risks, deciding to stay away is the best possible outcome. Companies often fall into the trap of trying to do everything. It is often better for them to focus on the areas where they have a competitive advantage.
- **Control.** Risk can come from unpredictable markets or unpredictable employees. A comprehensive plan to proactively identify and manage risks can help. However, it only helps if the monitoring is used.
- **Transfer.** Transferring risk can substantially improve a firm's risk profile. Unfortunately, if done poorly, this can lead to worse results or substitute a guaranteed loss for an uncertain profit.
- **Acceptance.** Some risks are not worth eliminating. There is a relationship between risk and reward. Risky investments often have potentially higher payouts than safe investments. That doesn't mean that all

risky investments are good. They are called risky for a reason. But, that doesn't mean that all risky activity is bad either.

Although the relationship between risk and reward tends to get the headlines on a trading desk, another relationship—the one between details and summarized data—is equally important. The details that differentiate one risk from another are often lost in the process of summarizing risk. On one hand, summarized data is needed to make decisions. On the other hand, ignoring details can lead to bad decisions. Either extreme is bad.

Finally, risk management is not always complicated. While the amount of math in risk management can make it seem complicated, the analysis all comes down to a couple of key decisions around whether to avoid, control, transfer, or accept risk. Even so, some of the math is complicated and the implications of risk management policies are not always obvious. I hope that this book has helped provide a context to understand how those complicated pieces fit into the big picture of trading risk management.

# Answer Key

## CHAPTER 1

1. What is market risk?
   A. The risk that causes the reputation of the firm to be adversely affected.
   B. The risk that activities internal to an organization (like properly scheduling a commodity delivery) will cause a loss.
   C. The risk that a trading partner will default on its obligations
   D. The risk of losses arising from adverse price moves in market prices.

Correct Answer: D

Explanation: Answer D describes market risk. The other answers describe reputational risk, operational risk, and credit risk.

2. Choose the best answer. Can you buy a contract to sell an asset?
   A. Yes. However, the purchase and sale offset, so there won't be any purpose in making this trade.
   B. No. It is not possible to purchase a contract to sell an asset.
   C. Yes. A contract is a piece of paper, which can have value, and be bought and sold like any other asset.
   D. No. Financial contracts cannot be transferred.

Correct Answer: C

Explanation: A contract to sell something can be a very valuable asset. For example, a contract to sell electricity to the U.S. government at $90/MWH is very valuable if the prevailing price of electricity is $30/MWH. In general, contracts can be bought and sold like any other asset. In some cases, this requires amending or replacing the contract in a process called *novation*.

3. If an investor is long a gasoline/crude oil spread, what will happen?
   A. The investor will benefit if the spread gets larger.
   B. The investor will benefit if the spread gets smaller.
   C. The investor will benefit if gasoline and crude oil both rise in price equally.

**D.** The investor will benefit if both gasoline and crude oil drop in price equally.

Correct Answer: A

**Explanation:** If an investor is long a spread, the investor benefits when the spread gets larger. There is insufficient information to know whether answer C or D is correct.

4. Which group is typically responsible for the filing of financial statements?
   **A.** Risk Management
   **B.** Trading Desk
   **C.** Financial Control
   **D.** Middle Office

Correct Answer: C

**Explanation:** The Financial Control (Controllers) group is responsible for accounting and P&L reporting.

5. Hedge funds are typically organized in what type of structure?
   **A.** Corporation
   **B.** Limited Liability Company (LLC)
   **C.** Limited Partnership
   **D.** Sole Proprietorship

Correct Answer: C

**Explanation:** Hedge funds are typically organized as limited partnerships. The general partners manage the company and are personally liable for losses. The limited partners are investors whose risk is limited to their investment.

6. Who can invest in hedge funds?
   **A.** Anyone.
   **B.** Only accredited investors or officers of the hedge fund.
   **C.** Only citizens of the United States.
   **D.** Only employee of the hedge fund.

Correct Answer: B

**Explanation:** Hedge funds typically limit themselves to only accepting accredited investors, who are limited partners. This eliminates many of the requirements placed on investment firms designed to protect individual investors and gives the hedge funds operating flexibility.

7. What kinds of investments are made by a global macro hedge fund?
   **A.** Directional bets on major economic events.
   **B.** Spread positions in closely related assets.

C. Positions in stocks of companies undergoing corporate actions like mergers or restructuring.

D. Investments in other hedge funds.

Correct Answer: A

**Explanation:** Answer A describes a trade that might be made by a global macro hedge fund. Answer B describes a relative value hedge fund, answer C describes an event-driven hedge fund, and answer D describes a fund of funds.

8. Which answer correctly defines a *short sale* in the financial markets?

A. A sale that has to be executed quickly, that is, "on short notice."

B. A sale made under distressed conditions.

C. An asset sale at a price that falls short of repaying the borrowing that was originally used to purchase the asset.

D. A sale of a borrowed asset.

Correct Answer: D

**Explanation:** In the financial markets, a short sale is the sale of a borrowed asset which must be repaid when the original owner needs it back. This is done to speculate that the price of the asset will fall and can be purchased back at a cheaper price. Answer C describes a real estate short sale—a different concept altogether.

9. Lynne is a trader at a hedge fund. She has a flat position in gold. What happens to the position if the price of gold rises?

A. The position makes money.

B. Nothing.

C. The position loses money.

D. Insufficient information is provided to answer the question.

Correct Answer: B

**Explanation:** A flat position is closed—it neither makes nor loses money.

10. What kinds of fees are typically charged by hedge funds?

A. Hedge funds will charge investors a percentage of net assets invested.

B. Hedge funds will charge investors a percentage of any net profits.

C. Hedge funds will charge investors a fixed fee regardless of the size of their assets.

D. Hedge funds will charge investors both a percentage of net assets and a percentage of net profits.

Correct Answer: D

**Explanation:** Hedge funds typically charge investors fees of 1 to 2 percent of net assets and 10 to 20 percent of net profits each year.

## CHAPTER 2

1. What is the difference between a broker and a dealer?
   A. A broker is a person, while a dealer is a firm.
   B. A broker deals with individual investors (retail market) while a dealer trades with institutions (wholesale market).
   C. A broker is limited to introducing traders and executes trades on the behalf of others while a dealer can make trades on its own behalf.
   D. There is no difference.

Correct Answer: C

Explanation: A broker acts as an agent for another party—introducing traders and arranging executions for other people. A dealer can execute trades on their own behalf. In some markets, broker/dealers will do both jobs.

2. What is not an example of a derivative?
   A. Shares of common stock.
   B. A call option on a bond.
   C. A forward contract to sell crude oil.
   D. A fixed/float interest rate swap.

Correct Answer: A

Explanation: Shares in common stock are a financial asset—they grant an equity (ownership) position in the underlying asset. Derivatives are typically contracts that obligate the counterparties to do something in the future.

3. Tom owns a portfolio of bonds. If interest rates rise, what will happen?
   A. Tom will make money.
   B. Tom will lose money.
   C. Tom's risk will increase.
   D. Tom's risk will decrease.

Correct Answer: B

Explanation: Bonds will go down in price if interest rates rise. As a result, Tom will lose money.

4. If a financial asset is described as *fungible*, what does that mean?
   A. The position has been sold short and is in danger of being recalled by its original owner. This will force the short seller to rebuy it immediately.
   B. The trader who owns the asset is being investigated by a regulatory agency.

C. The asset is distressed and there are no buyers for it.

D. The asset is interchangeable with like assets.

Correct Answer: D

**Explanation:** A fungible asset is interchangeable with like assets and can be traded or substituted for them. Most financial assets are fungible.

5. What is an underlying asset?
   A. A benchmark asset which is widely used by market participants to track fundamental changes in the economy.
   B. An asset that is less profitable than another asset.
   C. An asset whose value determines that value of another, derivative, asset.
   D. An asset that provides an ownership interest in a corporation.

Correct Answer: C

**Explanation:** An underlying asset determines the value of a derivative.

6. If a hedge fund wishes to take an ownership position in a corporation, what kind of asset should it purchase?
   A. Common Stock
   B. Interest Rate Swap
   C. Commodity Swap
   D. Real Assets

Correct Answer: A

**Explanation:** Common stock grants an ownership share in a corporation.

7. What kind of position does the owner of a put option have in the underlying asset?
   A. Long position
   B. Flat position
   C. Short position
   D. Insufficient information is provided to answer the question.

Correct Answer: C

**Explanation:** A put option gives its owner the right to sell at a fixed price. This becomes more valuable as the underlying asset declines in price. The definition of a short position is one that becomes more valuable as the price declines.

8. A bond is an example of what type of security?
   A. Real Asset
   B. Financial Asset

C. Derivative

D. Insufficient information is provided to answer the question.

Correct Answer: B

**Explanation:** A bond is a financial asset. Bonds are created when companies issue them to raise money.

9. What is a liquid market?
    A. A physical commodity market where crude oil is traded.
    B. A market where there are a large number of buyers and sellers willing to transact.
    C. An inter-bank market for transacting interest rate swaps.
    D. A derivatives market where traders can buy both put and call options.

Correct Answer: B

**Explanation:** A liquid market is one where trades are relatively easy to make because there are a large number of traders willing to both buy and sell.

10. What is an example of a primary market for financial assets?
    A. Brokers
    B. Inter-bank trading desks
    C. Stock Exchanges
    D. A market where new assets are issued to investors

Correct Answer: D

**Explanation:** Financial assets are issued in the primary market and traded in the secondary market.

## CHAPTER 3

1. What description best describes what the formula shown below is demonstrating?

$$df = \frac{df}{dx}\Delta x + \frac{1}{2}\frac{d^2 f}{dx^2}(\Delta x)^2$$

    A. Stochastic Process
    B. Taylor Series
    C. Integration
    D. Probability Density Function

Correct Answer: B

**Explanation:** The formula is a second-order Taylor Series expansion. Taylor Series expansions are extensively used in financial mathematics and the general form of the expansion should be memorized.

2. In a normal distribution, approximately what percentage of samples is within two standard deviations of the mean?
   A. 50.0 percent
   B. 68.3 percent
   C. 95.5 percent
   D. 99.7 percent

Correct Answer: C

**Explanation:** In a normal distribution, approximately 95.5 percent of samples are within the area covered by +/–2 standard deviations.

3. How are variance and volatility related to one another?
   A. volatility = square root of variance
   B. volatility = square of variance
   C. $\Delta$ volatility = ($\Delta$ variance) + (1/2) ($\Delta$ variance)$^2$
   D. Insufficient information is provided to determine a relationship

Correct Answer: A

**Explanation:** Volatility (the standard deviation) is the square root of the variance.

4. How are the median and mean related for a log-normally (right-skewed) distribution?
   A. median = mean
   B. median < mean
   C. median > mean
   D. Insufficient information is provided to answer the question.

Correct Answer: B

**Explanation:** In a right-skewed distribution, extreme events are more likely on the right (positive) side of the distribution than on the left side of the distribution. As a result of including those extreme events into the mean, the mean is skewed to the right.

5. What is the excess kurtosis of a normal distribution?
   A. 0
   B. 1
   C. 2
   D. 3

Correct Answer: A

**Explanation:** Kurtosis is a measure that describes how sharply a distribution is peaked. Excess kurtosis is the amount of kurtosis in excess of that shown by a normal distribution. As a result, a normal distribution has zero excess kurtosis. A variant of this question might ask "what is the Kurtosis of a normal distribution?"—the answer is three.

6. With positive interest rates, what is the relationship between the value of a dollar today and the value of a dollar delivered in one year?
   A. dollar today > dollar future
   B. dollar today < dollar future
   C. dollar today = dollar future
   D. Insufficient information is provided to answer the question.

Correct Answer: A

**Explanation:** Using time value of money, any time there are positive interest rates, a dollar today is worth more than a dollar in the future.

7. A trader might calculate the first derivative of a function at a specific point for what purpose?
   A. To determine the cumulative probability that the value is less than the point.
   B. To calculate the correlation of the function to a random variable.
   C. To determine the probability that the function will equal that point.
   D. To develop a linear estimate of the function at the point.

Correct Answer: D

**Explanation:** Differentiation (the process of taking a derivative) is often used to approximate the sensitivity of the function to some variable at that point. Sensitivity is typically measured by the slope of the straight line tangent to the curve at the point being examined.

8. What does the formula below mean?

$$? = \frac{1}{n} \sum_{1}^{n} x$$

   A. Determine the cumulative probability that the value is less than point n.
   B. Take an $n^{th}$ order Taylor series expansion of x.
   C. Find the natural log of x/n.
   D. Take the sum of all values of series x and divide them by the number of samples.

Correct Answer: D

**Explanation:** This is a mathematical notation indicating to take the sum of the series (which has n elements) and divide by the number of elements. While it is not part of the question, this is a way to calculate the mean (or average) of x.

9. What does stochastic mean?
   A. Exhibiting random behavior
   B. Involving more than one variable
   C. A series of functions that has a well-defined mathematical derivative
   D. A series having zero variance

Correct Answer: A

**Explanation:***Stochastic* is a synonym for *random*. In finance, it is often used to describe a type of process that evolves over time due to a random factor.

10. What is a characteristic of a mean reverting series?
    A. It will be log-normally distributed.
    B. It will be normally distributed.
    C. It will get pulled back to a long-term average value.
    D. It will always have a positive first derivative.

Correct Answer: C

**Explanation:** A mean-reverting series will tend to come back to its long-term average value.

## CHAPTER 4

1. Sharpe Ratios and Information Ratios both measure what?
   A. The ease of liquidating trades.
   B. Expected excess returns divided by volatility (standard deviation of returns).
   C. The theoretical price of the asset if held to maturity based on commonly accepted financial assumptions like non-existence of arbitrage and time value of money.
   D. The maximum expected drawdown of a trading strategy.

Correct Answer: B

**Explanation:** Sharpe Ratios and Information Ratios are similar—both examine expected excess returns (the average return) divided by volatility (standard deviation of returns).

2. What is the primary benefit of out-of-sample backtesting?
   **A.** It allows the strategy to be modeled with normally distributed returns.
   **B.** It decreases volatility of the strategy.
   **C.** It increases the expected returns of the strategy.
   **D.** It reduces the likelihood of over-fitting a model.

Correct Answer: D

**Explanation:** The primary benefit of out-of-sample modeling is that it reduces the likelihood of over-fitting. However, out-of-sample testing still does not completely eliminate the possibility of over-fitting.

3. Richard, the head of a trading desk, is examining the possibility of incorporating a new trading strategy into the trading desk operations. He has four possible strategies for which he calculated Sharpe Ratios and correlation with existing strategies. Which is the best strategy for Richard?
   **A.** Sharpe Ratio −0.5, correlation = 0
   **B.** Sharpe Ratio −0.5, correlation = 1.0
   **C.** Sharpe Ratio = +0.5, correlation = 0
   **D.** Sharpe Ratio = +0.5, correlation = 1.0

Correct Answer: C

**Explanation:** Since volatility can't be negative, a negative Sharpe Ratio indicates a negative expected return. As a result, a strategy with a negative Sharpe Ratio is expected to lose money, and unless it offers a very high diversification benefit, would generally not merit investment. Of the two remaining strategies, the strategy with the lowest correlation is preferable. A strategy with a 1.0 correlation adds no diversification benefit.

4. Chang, a trader at a hedge fund, is examining two trading strategies. Strategy A has a 2.0 Sharpe ratio, Strategy B has a −0.1 Sharpe Ratio, and the strategies have a −1.0 correlation. What is the best combination of strategies?
   **A.** Only Strategy A
   **B.** Only Strategy B
   **C.** An equal weight combination of Strategy A + Strategy B
   **D.** A combination of Strategy A and B, with a larger investment in Strategy A than Strategy B

Correct Answer: C

**Explanation:** This is a trick question. In general, a strategy with a negative Sharpe Ratio is expected to lose money. However, since Strategy A and

B are anti-correlated (correlation = −1.0), the volatility will exactly off-set. In other words, an equally weighted combination of Strategy A and Strategy B will have a positive return with no volatility.

5. What is a way to reduce trading risk?
   A. Require all trades to be recorded with a trading repository that en-sures that trades are accurately recorded on the day of entry.
   B. A system to prevent unusually large computerized trades without approval by a human.
   C. Perform suitability checks on trades, like credit risk approval and restricted lists, to ensure that approved instruments are being traded in approved sizes.
   D. All are ways to reduce risk.

Correct Answer: D

**Explanation:** All are examples of ways that computer systems can reduce the risk of trading.

6. Which answer best describes the term *slippage* in the context of a trad-ing strategy?
   A. The risk that the price obtained from trading will be different than the price expected when the order was sent to the market.
   B. The risk that the strategy works less well over time due to copycat trading.
   C. The risk that the order won't be transmitted quickly and that an-other trader will get the best transaction.
   D. The risk that risk management systems won't get updated reports to decision makers in a timely manner.

Correct Answer: A

**Explanation:** The best answer is A. Slippage is defined as the difference be-tween actual execution price and the price that was expected prior to trading. There are many factors that can contribute to slippage. Answer D (slow trading) is one factor that can contribute to bad executions. However, limited liquidity (not enough people wanting to make the op-posite trade) is usually a much bigger factor in slippage, which is why Answer D is not the best answer.

7. What is rogue trading?
   A. A trader that is making trades with someone else's money that he/she is unauthorized to make and makes money.
   B. A trader that is making trades with someone else's money that he/she is unauthorized to make and loses money.

    C. A trader that is making trades that he/she is authorized to make but has not reported the trades to the teams responsible for trading oversight.

    D. All of the above.

Correct Answer: D

**Explanation:** Rogue trading is generally defined as trading that is unauthorized or made without supervision.

8. What is an example of pre-trade monitoring?

    A. Checking a restricted list to determine if the trader is allowed to make a trade in the asset.

    B. Checking a counterparty credit report to make sure that additional trading is allowed with the counterparty.

    C. Checking that the size of the transaction is reasonable—allowable under current position limits and at a size that can be transacted in the market without moving prices too much.

    D. All of the above.

Correct Answer: D

**Explanation:** All of these items might be identified as part of a pre-trade screening.

9. What is model risk?

    A. The potential volatility in Sharpe Ratio calculations due to asymptomatic approximations of variance.

    B. The risk that a model has not been properly reviewed.

    C. The risk that a model fails to perform as expected.

    D. All of the above

Correct Answer: C

**Explanation:** Model risk refers to the risk that the model will not perform as expected. This is commonly a result of an assumption turning out to be invalid.

10. What is a likely repercussion of using data in a model that was assumed to be available at 8 a.m. on the day of the transaction but was actually available at 6 p.m.?

    A. There is no major difference as long as it is available the same day.

    B. Actual trading results are likely to under-perform the simulation.

    C. Actual trading results are likely to out-perform the simulation.

    D. Insufficient information is provided to answer the question.

Correct Answer: B

**Explanation:** Since the data is arriving later, the trading decision would have to be delayed until the data is available. This would lead to slower trades and give more opportunity for prices to move unfavorably. All of the expected profits made in the first trading day would be lost.

## CHAPTER 5

1. Under mark-to-market accounting, how is a fair value market price defined?
   A. The price that would be received to take on a liability or price paid to acquire an asset.
   B. The price that would be received to sell an asset or paid to transfer a liability to another market participant.
   C. The theoretical price of the asset if held to maturity based on commonly accepted financial assumptions like non-existence of arbitrage and time value of money.
   D. The expected price of the asset if sold under normal market conditions.

Correct Answer: B

**Explanation:** Mark-to-market accounting is based on the exit price under current market conditions. Answer A is incorrect because it defines an entry price. Answer C is incorrect because it describes a hold-to-maturity price. Answer D is incorrect because it is based on normal market conditions rather than current market conditions.

2. Andrew, an energy market analyst, is helping the Financial Control/Accounting team on the natural gas trading desk determine the proper level for natural gas trades in the fair value hierarchy. The trades are located 50 miles from the futures settlement point. This distance adds a fixed $0.01 spread to the cost of the natural gas. The price is set at the futures price plus $0.01.
   A. Level 1 Asset
   B. Level 2 Asset
   C. Level 3 Asset
   D. Insufficient information is provided to answer the question.

Correct Answer: B

**Explanation:** Unless a contract has identical specifications to the exchange-settled contract, the asset is fair value hierarchy Level 2. The spread to the index could be zero, but since the terms are not identical (delivery is not at the same location) this moves the trades from being a Level 1 to being a Level 2.

3. Brianna, a junior trader at MegaHedgeFund, needs to mark some bonds to market. They are 10-year risk-free bonds paying a 15 percent coupon every month (a 60 percent annual interest rate!). For the last two weeks, multiple transactions have been made pricing the bonds at 2 cents on the dollar ($20 per $1000 of face value). Not only is this an extremely low price for a risk-free high coupon bond, the observed market price is a fraction of the next coupon payment. With risk free rates at 3 percent, Brianna calculates that the fair-value should be $3,773 per $1,000 of face value. How should these bonds be marked to market?
   A. $20
   B. $1000
   C. $1600
   D. $3773

Correct Answer: A

Explanation: Mark to market requires that the bonds be priced according to current market conditions ($20) and not at the value of the bonds if held to maturity. However, given the disparity, Brianna should also double check the market data provider to make sure the price is correct and not the result of an error or computer glitch.

4. What is NOT true about mark-to-market accounting?
   A. It is commonly used to value derivatives.
   B. It is based on the concept of an exit price under current conditions.
   C. It is used only to price assets traded on the primary exchange (or the most advantageous venue if the asset is traded on multiple exchanges).
   D. A major goal of mark-to-market accounting is to protect shareholders from fraud related to earnings announcements.

Correct Answer: C

Explanation: Answer C is incorrect. Mark to market is commonly used for any security, not just those traded on primary exchanges. For example, mark-to-market accounting is commonly required to value any derivative (like a swap, forward, or option) based on a marked-to-market security.

5. What is a feature of illiquid markets?
   A. Market participants use limit orders more than market orders.
   B. Credit risks are much higher than normal.
   C. It is difficult for a trading desk to raise money.
   D. It is difficult to find trading partners and make trades.

Correct Answer: D

**Explanation:** Answer D is correct. Liquidity describes the ability to find trading partners. There is insufficient information to determine whether answers A, B, or C are correct.

## CHAPTER 6

1. With a 95 percent one-day VAR, approximately how often would a risk manager expect that a loss greater than the VAR be observed?
   A. Once a day
   B. Once a week
   C. Once a month
   D. Once a year

Correct Answer: C

**Explanation:** With a 95 percent VAR, 5 percent of the time losses will be greater than the VAR number. Since there are 21 trading days in a month for most financial instruments, this is approximately once a month. In practice, there might be several months without an outlier loss followed by several in close succession.

2. Colin, a risk manager needs to convert a 99 percent one-day VAR into a 95 percent one-day VAR. The 95 percent one-day VAR is $5MM. What is the 99 percent one-day VAR?
   A. $3.5MM
   B. $4.2MM
   C. $4.7MM
   D. $7.0MM

Correct Answer: A

**Explanation:** This requires that the following relationships have been memorized. 95 percent VAR = 1.645 standard deviations, 99 percent VAR = 2.326 standard deviations. If that hasn't been memorized, knowing that a 95 percent VAR is approximately 70 percent of a 99 percent VAR can help eliminate a couple of the answers.

| | | |
|---|---|---|
| Standard Deviation = $5MM / 2.326 | | = $2.150MM |
| 95 percent one-day VAR = $2.150MM × 1.645 | | = $3.536MM |

3. If two assets are combined, asset A has a 95 percent one-day VAR of $1MM, and asset B has a 95 percent one-day VAR of $2MM, the sum of the VAR numbers will be:
   A. less than zero.
   B. between zero and $1MM.

    C. between $1MM and $3MM.

    D. greater than $3MM.

Correct Answer: C

**Explanation:** If the assets are 100 percent correlated, the VAR will be $3MM (additive). If the assets are −100 percent correlated (exactly opposite), VAR will be the larger VAR minus the smaller VAR ($1MM). As a result, VAR will be somewhere between these two points. When subtracting VAR, it helps to remember that VAR can never be negative.

  4. What are criticisms of the historical VAR approach?

    A. Many return series are not normally distributed.

    B. The timeframe is arbitrary.

    C. Equal weight is given to each return and extreme returns cause large changes to VAR when they enter and exit the sample.

    D. All of the above.

Correct Answer: D

**Explanation:** All are reasons why historical VAR is criticized.

  5. Why is VAR used as a measure of portfolio size rather than the cash spent to enter the investment?

    A. Many financial instruments (like FX swaps and commodity forwards) commonly have zero fair value and large risks associated with them.

    B. The value of an investment doesn't measure the leverage inherent in that investment.

    C. Similar investments with the same price might have very different volatility and risks associated with them.

    D. All of the above.

Correct Answer: D

**Explanation:** VAR was created to make financial instruments more comparable. All of the answers describe problems comparing the size of two investments.

  6. Emily, a portfolio manager, is comparing two trading strategies with the same VAR. How do the risks of the portfolio compare to one another?

    A. The two strategies are likely to be equally profitable.

    B. The daily returns from each trading strategy should be of similar magnitude.

C. The traders who manage each portfolio have a similar outlook on the market.

D. All of the above.

Correct Answer: B

**Explanation:** VAR is a measure of size. It does not indicate which strategy is likely to be more profitable over the long term or that the traders have similar views on the market. Although there is a general relationship between risk (as measured by VAR) and return, strategies with the same amount of money invested in them are generally not equally profitable.

7. Keith, a risk manager, has calculated the standard deviation of expected daily returns for an investment. He used one year of data. How does he create an estimate of annual volatility assuming lognormal prices, 12 months a year and 21 trading days a month?

A. Do nothing—he already has the annualized volatility

B. Multiply the standard deviation of daily returns by the square root of 12.

C. Multiply the standard deviation of daily returns by the square root of 252

D. Insufficient information is provided to calculate an answer.

Correct Answer: C

**Explanation:** Volatility will scale with the square root of time. The standard deviation that Keith calculated is the daily volatility. He needs to scale this to an annual volatility by multiplying by the square root of the number of trading days in the year. 12 months $\times$ 21 days/month = 252 trading days per year.

8. Anna, a risk manager at a hedge fund, wants to estimate the worst-case move for the portfolio. Which measure of VAR is best suited to calculating an extreme result?

A. A 95 percent one-day VAR

B. A 99 percent one-day VAR

C. A 99 percent one-day VAR

D. These measures all contain the same information scaled differently

Correct Answer: D

**Explanation:** VAR typically does not do a good job estimating extreme moves. Most VAR methods assume normally distributed returns. This is a good approximation of typical price movements, but doesn't do a good job estimating the frequency or magnitude of rarely observed price moves.

9. What type of VAR model is well suited to a GARCH approach?
   A. A VAR calculation that needs to rapidly react to short-term changes in market volatility.
   B. A VAR calculation that needs to filter out the effect of recent market volatility to focus on long-term trends.
   C. A VAR calculation that uses forward implied volatility estimated from recent option transactions.
   D. GARCH is not useful for VAR modeling.

Correct Answer: A

Explanation: GARCH is an exponential weighting scheme that places more weight on recent observations. It is suitable for a VAR calculation that needs to react quickly to changes in observed market volatility.

10. What are the implications of an exponentially weighted VAR calculation?
   A. VAR limits on trading books will change rapidly and potentially lead to a costly cycle of forced liquidations and repurchasing of assets.
   B. VAR will react quickly to recent market behavior.
   C. Both A and B.
   D. Neither A nor B.

Correct Answer: C

Explanation: Exponentially weighted VAR will be heavily impacted by recently observed price movements. This can provide a better indication of likely moves within the next day. However, it can also lead to a series of forced liquidations and difficult to predict capital requirements if VAR is used to calculate regulatory asset requirements.

11. What information does VAR convey?
   A. The worst-case loss for a trading strategy.
   B. Whether a trading position is a good or bad investment.
   C. The exposure of the trading position to changes in implied volatility.
   D. The size of an investment.

Correct Answer: D

Explanation: VAR is primarily a measure of position size as estimated by average daily percent movements. It does a much better job of describing typical movements than worst-case losses. Like any other measure of size, VAR would need to be combined with expected profitability to determine how an investment compares to other trading opportunities.

12. Steve is a programmer working at a hedge fund. He is reading a technical documentation manual describing how a certain calculation was calculated. He wants to check the output from the calculation on a spreadsheet.
    Calculation Description:    daily_return = $\ln(\text{price}_t / \text{price}_{t-1})$
    What does the "ln" mean?
    A. It is a variable that is probably defined somewhere else in documentation.
    B. It is the inverse normal distribution function.
    C. It is a variable that means "last night's price."
    D. It is the natural logarithm function.

Correct Answer: D

**Explanation:** Answer D is correct; ln is a common abbreviation for natural logarithm. This function is commonly used to calculate continuous compounding and other time-value-of-money calculations.

## CHAPTER 7

1. Angela, a risk manager at a mining company, wants to hedge the output of copper ore using exchange traded copper futures. What is the minimum variance hedge ratio if both copper and copper ore have 17 percent volatility and are 85 percent correlated?
   A. 0.17
   B. 0.85
   C. 1.02
   D. 1.18

Correct Answer: B

**Explanation:** The minimum variance hedge ratio is (correlation) (volatility of hedged item/volatility of the hedge). In this case, .85 × (.17/.17) = 0.85.

2. What is the primary effect that an effective hedge will have on a portfolio?
   A. It will increase profitability.
   B. It will make investors happier.
   C. It will help regulatory agencies approve the investment.
   D. It will reduce the uncertainty associated with an investment.

Correct Answer: D

**Explanation:** Hedging will reduce the uncertainty associated with the investment. It is unlikely to improve profitability since the hedge costs money and future changes in value will be largely offset. Hedging might be done to make investors or regulators happy, but that is not the primary effect of a hedge in most cases.

3. For the purposes of calculating hedge effectiveness, what is a prospective test?
   A. It is a stress test examining large potential future price movements.
   B. It is a regression test predicting how likely profits are to occur in the near future.
   C. It is documentation of a hedge prior to the hedge being transacted.
   D. It is a mathematical test done whenever financial reports are sent to investors to assess if the hedge has been effective.

Correct Answer: C

Explanation: Prospective testing is the accounting documentation designating the hedge and hedge item supporting the premise that they are likely to reduce risk in the future.

4. What values for slope are commonly accepted as part of a hedge-effectiveness test?
   A. 0.75 to 1.20
   B. 0.75 to 1.25
   C. 0.80 to 1.20
   D. 0.80 to 1.25

Correct Answer: D

Explanation: Commonly accepted ranges for slope are between 0.80 and 1.25.

5. If a hedge is 100 percent correlated with the hedged item but has greater volatility, how will this affect the minimum variance hedge ratio, h?
   A. $h > 1$
   B. $h = 1$
   C. $h < 1$
   D. Insufficient information is provided to answer the question.

Correct Answer: C

Explanation: The minimum variance hedge ratio is (correlation) (volatility of hedged item/volatility of the hedge). If correlation is 1.0, and volatility of the hedge is greater than the volatility of the hedged item, the hedge ratio will be less than 1.

6. Pick the sentence that best describes hedges.
   A. Hedging can reduce potential profits.

    **B.** Hedging can reduce potential losses.

    **C.** Hedges represent a large trading position that has the potential to introduce additional risks into a portfolio and not just mitigate risks.

    **D.** All of the above.

Correct Answer: D

**Explanation:** All of these statements describe hedges. When working correctly, hedges limit both profits and losses. In addition, hedges can add risk to a portfolio if they are sized improperly, invested in a poorly chosen asset, or have some other unexpected problem.

7. For the purpose of testing hedge effectiveness, what is the most commonly accepted minimum value for an R-squared test?

    **A.** 0.6

    **B.** 0.8

    **C.** 0.9

    **D.** 0.95

Correct Answer: B

**Explanation:** An $R^2$ of greater than 0.8 is commonly accepted as the minimum value for a successful test.

8. Dan, a risk manager, is constructing a hedge-effectiveness test. He knows he wants to do a regression test. What two data series does he need to use as inputs into the regression calculation?

    **A.** The prices of the hedge and hedged item

    **B.** The log-returns of the hedge and hedged item

    **C.** The rolling implied volatility and correlation of the hedge

    **D.** The price of the hedge and the volatility of the hedged item.

Correct Answer: B

**Explanation:** Regression tests need to be based on changes in value. The only answer that is based on a change in value is B.

9. Ken, the chief risk officer of an oil exploration company, is examining two possible hedging opportunities. Both will economically hedge the firm's positions. However, one of the hedges is unlikely to qualify for hedge accounting treatment. Assuming that the hedges are otherwise identical, what are the risks of using a hedge that doesn't qualify for hedge accounting?

    **A.** There might be a timing mismatch between the hedge and hedged items that leads to more volatile earnings.

    **B.** The hedge that doesn't qualify for hedge accounting will draw more regulatory scrutiny.

    **C.** The hedge that doesn't qualify for hedge accounting will have greater market risk.

    **D.** The hedge that doesn't qualify for hedge accounting will have greater credit risk.

Correct Answer: A

**Explanation:** There might be a mismatch between when the hedge creates cash flows or is marked to market and the hedged item. Companies are always free to use standard accounting for hedges—designating an item for hedged accounting typically draws more scrutiny than the other way around.

10. MegaBank has purchased several power-generation units. It has hedged the expected changes in value. However, during its hedge-effectiveness testing for its latest quarterly earnings report, the hedges failed the retrospective tests. The prospective tests had previously passed. What is likely to occur?

    I.    The change in value of the hedges is reflected in earnings.

    II.   The change in value does not have to be reflected in earnings.

    III. The hedge becomes de-designated and a new hedge designation memo is required if these assets are hedged in any future periods.

    IV. The existing hedge designation memo stays in effect.

       **A.** I and III

       **B.** II and III

       **C.** I and IV

       **D.** II and IV

Correct Answer: C

**Explanation:** The hedges will not qualify for hedge accounting in periods when they fail retrospective testing. Failed tests do not require the hedge to be re-designated to meet hedge accounting requirements in the future. If the hedges pass retrospective tests in the future, the changes in value will be considered subject to hedge accounting.

# CHAPTER 8

1. Tom, the head trader at an oil drilling company, is worried that a potential decline in prices would affect his company. He has decided to buy an at-the-money put option on crude oil futures on $10 million worth of crude oil. If the 99 percent five-day VAR of crude oil is 10 percent, what is the approximate VAR of the put option using a linear (delta) approximation?

    **A.** –$1 Million

    **B.** $500,000

**C.** $2.5 Million
**D.** $5 Million

Correct Answer: B

**Explanation:** Since the delta for an at-the-money option is approximately 0.5, the linear VAR approximation will be $10MM $\times$ 0.5 $\times$ 10 percent = $500,000. Answer A is incorrect since VAR is always a positive number.

2. Flora, a senior risk manager, is looking over a VAR analysis prepared by the trading group for a portfolio of options. The book is net long gamma. The VAR analysis uses a first-order delta approximation of option risk. What happens to the VAR calculation if a second-order (delta/gamma) approximation is used in place of a linear (delta) approximation?
   **A.** VAR will be larger.
   **B.** VAR will be smaller.
   **C.** VAR will stay the same.
   **D.** Insufficient information is provided to answer the question.

Correct Answer: B

**Explanation:** From a P&L perspective, gamma (convexity of the option payoff) will always help option buyers and hurt sellers. Gamma decreases the risk to the buyer and increases the risk of the seller. Since Flora is a buyer, a second-order approximation (also called a delta/gamma approximation) will lower the VAR.

3. Spencer, a trader at a hedge fund has sold a short put on ABCD stock. The time to maturity is 1 year, the strike price is $25, the stock pays no dividends, and the risk-free rate is 3.2 percent. The underlying is currently $25. What is the approximate delta of the option?
   **A.** −1.0
   **B.** −0.5
   **C.** +0.5
   **D.** +1.0

Correct Answer: C

**Explanation:** There is a lot of extraneous information in the question. This is a short put. The owner of the put (a long put) will make money when market prices decline since they can sell at a higher price (it is profitable to buy low and sell high). A short put has exactly the opposite payout— the seller of a put makes money when prices rise. As a result, this option has a positive delta. Since it is at-the-money, the magnitude of the delta is approximately 0.5.

4. Barbara, a litigant in a lawsuit, was recently awarded a call option to get EFG stock for a $0 strike. There is no dividend. What is the approximate delta and gamma of the call option?

   **A.** delta = +0.5, significant positive gamma
   **B.** delta = +1.0, significant positive gamma
   **C.** delta = +0.5, gamma = 0
   **D.** delta = +1.0, gamma = 0

Correct Answer: D

**Explanation:** An option to acquire stock for nothing is always deep in-the-money. For every dollar that the stock price goes up, the option goes up an equal amount (and loses money when the price falls). As a result, the delta is positive. Gamma approaches zero for very far in- or out–of-the-money options. If there were any dividends paid by the stock, this would be a rare case where early exercise is profitable.

5. Richard, a risk manager at a bank, wants to estimate the loss caused by owning a long put option given a $2 per unit rise in price of the underlying. The option is for 100,000 units, the delta is −0.6, gamma is 0.1, and interest rates are zero. Using a second-order approximation (a delta/gamma approximation) what is the expected profit or loss?

   **A.** +$120,000 (profit)
   **B.** −$100,000 (loss)
   **C.** −$120,000 (loss)
   **D.** −$140,000 (loss)

Correct Answer: B

**Explanation:** Richard owns a put option. It is going to lose money if the price in the underlying rises. With a delta approximation, Richard's option will change in value (100,000 units) × (−0.6 delta) × (+$2/unit change in price) = a loss of $120,000. Since he is long the option, gamma will reduce the loss somewhat. Knowing the loss is slightly smaller than the delta approximation is probably enough to answer the problem if the gamma factor equation is not remembered. The gamma component of the approximation equals (100,000 units) × (1/2) × (.1 gamma) × ($2 per unit)$^2$ = +20,000. The total loss is expected to be around $100,000.

6. Angela, a trader at a bank, has a large option portfolio on crude oil. The portfolio has delta = 0 but a large negative gamma. To reduce the gamma exposure to zero, what does she need to do?

   **A.** Buy options.
   **B.** Sell options.
   **C.** Take a position in the underlying asset.

**D.** Insufficient information is provided to answer the question.

Correct Answer: A

Explanation: The only way to get gamma is to buy options. While there are a number of decisions that still might need to be made (like whether to buy call options or put options), eliminating a negative gamma exposure requires the purchase of options.

7. Jennifer, a private investor, wants to buy options because they have no risk. What should be one of her primary concerns when buying options?
   **A.** She will benefit from an increase in market volatility.
   **B.** She will have a positive gamma position.
   **C.** She will have a negative theta position.
   **D.** The cost of the option will outweigh any possible benefits.

Correct Answer: D

Explanation: All of these statements are true. However, as a buyer of options, Jennifer is at risk that the price of the option outweighs any possible benefit. There is little downside to owning options. As a result, the option's pricing formulas generally ensure that the seller gets paid a fair price for selling an option.

8. Sabina, a junior trader at a hedge fund, owns a portfolio of options. She wants to estimate how much the option value will change every day if prices, volatility, and interest rates stay constant. What calculation should she perform?
   **A.** Sum the delta for every option in the portfolio.
   **B.** Sum the gamma for every option in the portfolio.
   **C.** Sum the theta for every option in the portfolio.
   **D.** Sum the rho for every option in the portfolio.

Correct Answer: C

Explanation: Theta is the Greek that is used to estimate the change in value of a portfolio due to the passage of time. If Sabina is net long options, she will lose money every day. If she is net short options, she will gain money every day.

9. Roger, a risk manager at a hedge fund, is at a meeting with the firm's chief risk officer. He is asked whether a rise in volatility will help or hurt profitability of the option trading desk. Roger only has the following Greeks in front of him:

   Delta:        0

   Gamma:        +$1.5MM

What should he say?
A. A rise in volatility will help profits.
B. A rise in volatility will hurt profits.
C. The portfolio will not change in value.
D. Insufficient information is provided to make an estimate.

Correct Answer: A

Explanation: The portfolio is market neutral since the delta equals zero. However, the portfolio is long a large amount of options since gamma is positive. Rising volatility helps long option portfolios. As a result, a rise in volatility will make the option portfolio more profitable.

10. Jean, the head trader at a hedge fund, has a long call position that she would like to liquidate. What combination of trades would remove that exposure?
    A. Buy a put option.
    B. Sell a put option.
    C. Sell a put option and sell a forward.
    D. Buy a put option and buy a forward.

Correct Answer: C

Explanation: A call option can be replicated by a short put option and a short forward. Selling a put (option B) will modify a call position so that it looks like a long position in the underlying. Answer C is correct because this exposure will also need to be removed.

# CHAPTER 9

1. As used in credit risk calculation, what does PD mean?
   A. Probability Density
   B. Population Density
   C. Probability of Default
   D. Potential Difference

Correct Answer: C

Explanation: In credit risk, PD refers to the probability of default. Like many two-letter acronyms, it may have different meanings (like all the other answers) in other contexts.

2. What is wrong-way risk?
   A. Wrong-way risk is a term that means that default probabilities are highly correlated with exposure.

B. Wrong-way risk describes the fact that a debit value adjustment leads to increased profits when your own credit rating worsens.

C. Wrong-way risk uses a skewed payoff distribution rather than a normal distribution.

D. Wrong-way risk describes risk at settlement, when one party has delivered their final payment, but the other has not.

Correct Answer: A

Explanation: Wrong-way risk describes risks that get more likely at the same time their magnitude gets larger.

3. What is the credit adjusted fair value if the risk-free fair value is $100, PD is 2.0 percent, and LGD is 50 percent?
   A. $99
   B. $100
   C. $101
   D. Insufficient information is provided to answer the question.

Correct Answer: A

Explanation: The credit-adjusted fair value can be calculated by multiplying the risk-free fair value by $(1 - PD \times LGD)$. An alternate way to eliminate incorrect answers is to realize that the credit-adjusted fair value will always be lower than the risk-free fair value.

4. In a credit risk sense, why are master netting agreements important?
   A. Netting provides a way to trade out of a position without exposing oneself to a large amount of credit risk.
   B. Netting reduces the size of credit exposures.
   C. Netting can reduce the size, frequency, and need for collateral payments.
   D. All of the above.

Correct Answer: D

Explanation: All of the reasons are benefits of netting exposures.

5. What happens if a trading counterparty to which you owe $1.2MM goes bankrupt? Assume that netting applies and there is no collateral.
   A. You still owe $1.2MM.
   B. You will owe the bankrupt company $(1 - LGD) \times 1.2MM$.
   C. You will owe the bankrupt company $(1 - PD \times LGD) \times 1.2MM$.
   D. Insufficient information is provided to answer the question.

Correct Answer: A

**Explanation**: You will still owe the bankrupt company money. If you fail to meet that obligation, you will default and this may trigger bankruptcy proceedings for you.

6. What is a situation where settlement risk is important?
   A. Credit Default Swap settlement
   B. Financial trades that are net settled
   C. Payoff on options contracts
   D. Physical commodity swaps

Correct Answer: D

**Explanation**: With a physical commodity swap, a large quantity of physical product (maybe 1 million barrels of crude oil worth $110 million) is exchanged for a large amount of cash ($100 million). Because the total size of each obligation can be very large, settlement risk is important in these markets. In contrast, for instruments that settle in cash, it is typical to only exchange the net difference in obligations.

7. Benjamin, a credit analyst at a hedge fund, is trying to calculate the default probability of a company that doesn't have traded CDS spreads. The company issued bonds at 6 percent. At the time of issuance, risk-free rates were 3.5 percent and the spread for liquidity risk was 50 basis points. The estimated recovery rate in event of a default is 40 percent.
   A. 2.00 percent
   B. 3.33 percent
   C. 5.00 percent
   D. 6.25 percent

Correct Answer: B

**Explanation**: The formula to estimate probability of default is PD = credit spread/LGD. The credit spread = (Bond Rate − Risk Free Rate − Liquidity Spread). When simplified (6 percent − 3.5 percent − 0.5 percent) this is 2 percent. The LGD equals 1 − Recovery Rate or 60 percent. Dividing the credit spread (2 percent) by the LGD (60 percent) gives an answer of 3.33 percent

8. A large hedge fund has agreed to sell an asset worth $1MM to a company in exchange for a payment due in one year. An analyst at the hedge fund needs to calculate the size of the repayment to incorporate default risk. Ignoring liquidity risks, if continuously compounded risk-free rates are 4 percent, the probability of default is 5 percent, and the LGD is 60 percent, what should be the size of the final payment?
   A. $932,000
   B. $1,000,000

    **C.** $1,040,000
    **D.** $1,072,000

Correct Answer: D

**Explanation:** The closest answer is $1,072,000. This is similar to giving the counterparty a $1MM loan for one year. To compensate the hedge fund for the default risk, the credit-adjusted interest rate will be the risk-free rate + PD × LGD. As a result, the 1-year interest rate will be 7 percent. Continuously compounded, the payment will be approximately $1,072,000. This can be found by calculating the future value of a payment at a 7 percent interest rate $(FV = PV \times e^{.07})$.

9. What kinds of companies have published credit ratings?
    **A.** All companies will have credit ratings published by major ratings agencies.
    **B.** Only publicly owned corporations that have issued common stock have credit ratings.
    **C.** Only publicly owned companies that are listed on the New York Stock Exchange or Nasdaq have published credit ratings.
    **D.** Only companies that have issued publicly traded debt and requested that their bonds be rated by a rating agency have published credit ratings.

Correct Answer: D

**Explanation:** Credit ratings are paid for by companies that are issuing bonds as a good-faith demonstration to potential bond buyers.

10. When performing a credit value adjustment on a trade where you owe the counterparty money, what will happen?
    **A.** The size of the loss will be increased since risk adjustment will never decrease the size of losses.
    **B.** A debit value adjustment (DVA) will be performed on losing positions which will reduce the size of the loss.
    **C.** The counterparty will make an adjustment to their trading positions to estimate the decreased loss, but no adjustment will be made to your own books and records.
    **D.** Insufficient information is provided to answer the question.

Correct Answer: B

**Explanation:** Adjusting your own loss positions for your credit will decrease the size of the losses. This result is counter-intuitive to most risk managers where greater risk will only increase the potential exposures and never decrease them.

# About the Author

DAVIS W. EDWARDS, FRM, ERP, is a senior manager in Deloitte & Touche's National Securities Pricing Center managing energy derivatives valuation. Prior to joining Deloitte, he was division director of credit risk at Macquarie Bank and senior managing director on the statistical arbitrage trading desk at Bear Stearns. He is a regular speaker on the topic of financial modeling and mathematics applied to real world problems. He is the author of the books *Energy Trading and Investing* and *Energy Investing Demystified*. Davis is director of the Houston chapter of the Global Association of Risk Professionals.

# Index